Dwelling in Mobile Times

In an era of increasing mobilities, places of residence are still vital. Unlike commuting, migrating or travelling, dwelling usually evokes – at least in modern Western thought – the idea of an immobile, private place to rest. This book explores the places, spaces and practices of dwelling in mobile times, and considers dwelling under the umbrella of broader transformations in society. The manifestations of these transformations are carved out on the level of everyday practices and experiences.

Bringing together eight case studies from Europe, the USA and Asia on subjects such as gentrification, homelessness and displaced persons, multi-local and diasporic lifeworlds, professional elites, and tourism, the book explores various and complex entanglements of mobilities and dwelling in detail. In doing so, the contributors critically analyse who may be, or has to be, mobile under which circumstances at present. This book thus demonstrates that mobility is more than movement between localities, and that to dwell is more than to be at a locality. Instead, mobilities and dwelling are both shaped and challenged by strong but shifting power relations and are thus deeply contested.

This book was originally published as a special issue of *Cultural Studies*.

Sybille Frank, Prof Dr phil., is Professor for Urban Sociology and Sociology of Space at the Department of Sociology, Technische Universität Darmstadt, Germany. She has held positions as guest professor at the Goethe University Frankfurt, as junior professor at the Technische Universität Berlin, as Visiting Professor for Research Activities at La Sapienza University, Rome, and as City of Vienna Visiting Professor for Urban Culture and Public Space at the Technical University Vienna. In 2016 Frank was a visiting researcher at the Alfred Deakin Research Institute for Citizenship and Globalisation at Deakin University in Melbourne and at the African Studies Unit of the New School of African and Gender Studies, University of Cape Town. Her work focuses on urban studies, tourism and heritage studies, comparative city research, and on the sociology of space and place. Recent publications include: *Stadium Worlds: Football, Space and the Built Environment* (ed., with Silke Steets, Routledge 2010), *Heritage-Outside-In*, special issue of *International Journal of Heritage*

Studies, vol. 22 (7) (ed., with Susan Ashley), *Wall Memorials and Heritage: The Heritage Industry of Berlin's Checkpoint Charlie* (Routledge 2016).

Lars Meier, Dr. habil., is a Guest Professor for Sociology and Social Inequality at the Department of Sociology, University of Frankfurt. He was a Guest Professor for Urban and Regional Sociology at the Technische Universität Berlin. His work focuses on social inequality and diversity, social and spatial transformations, urban studies, sociology of migration and qualitative methods. He has published in journals such as *Sociological Review*, *Space and Culture*, *Cultural Studies* and *Identities*. Recent publications include an edited book on *Migrant Professionals in the City: Local Encounters, Identities, and Inequalitites* (Routledge 2015), special issues on Absence (*Cultural Geographies*, 2013) and on the the limits of resistance in public spaces (*Space and Culture*, 2017).

Dwelling in Mobile Times

Places, Practices and Contestations

Edited by
Sybille Frank and Lars Meier

LONDON AND NEW YORK

First published 2018
by Routledge

2 Park Square, Milton Park, Abingdon, Oxfordshire OX14 4RN
52 Vanderbilt Avenue, New York, NY 10017

Routledge is an imprint of the Taylor & Francis Group, an informa business

First issued in paperback 2019

British Library Cataloguing in Publication Data
A catalogue record for this book is available from the British Library

ISBN 13: 978-1-138-71759-6 (hbk)
ISBN 13: 978-0-367-23126-2 (pbk)

Typeset in Myriad Pro
by RefineCatch Limited, Bungay, Suffolk

Publisher's Note
The publisher accepts responsibility for any inconsistencies that may have
arisen during the conversion of this book from journal articles to book chapters,
namely the possible inclusion of journal terminology.

Disclaimer
Every effort has been made to contact copyright holders for their permission to
reprint material in this book. The publishers would be grateful to hear from any
copyright holder who is not here acknowledged and will undertake to rectify
any errors or omissions in future editions of this book.

Contents

Citation Information

The chapters in this book were originally published in *Cultural Studies*, volume 30, issue 3 (May 2016). When citing this material, please use the original page numbering for each article, as follows:

Chapter 1
Dwelling in mobile times: places, practices and contestations
Lars Meier and Sybille Frank
Cultural Studies, volume 30, issue 3 (May 2016), pp. 362–375

Chapter 2
Seeing residential (im)mobilities in New York City
Jerome Krase
Cultural Studies, volume 30, issue 3 (May 2016), pp. 376–400

Chapter 3
'Almost like I am in Jail': homelessness and the sense of immobility in Cleveland, Ohio
Daniel R. Kerr
Cultural Studies, volume 30, issue 3 (May 2016), pp. 401–420

Chapter 4
Dwelling in the Temporary: The involuntary mobility of displaced Georgians in rented accommodation
Cathrine Brun
Cultural Studies, volume 30, issue 3 (May 2016), pp. 421–440

Chapter 5
Ephemeral Urban Topographies of Swedish Roma: On dwelling at the mobile–immobile nexus
Ingrid Martins Holmberg and Erika Persson
Cultural Studies, volume 30, issue 3 (May 2016), pp. 441–466

For any permission-related enquiries please visit:
http://www.tandfonline.com/page/help/permissions

Notes on Contributors

Cathrine Brun is Professor at the Department of Geography, Norwegian University of Science and Technology. Her research currently concentrates on protracted displacement and humanitarian practices of relief and recovery after disasters with special emphasis on South Asia and the South Caucasus.

Sybille Frank is Professor for Urban Sociology and Sociology of Space in the Department of Sociology at the Technische Universität Darmstadt, Germany. Her work focuses on urban sociology, on the sociology of space and place, and on tourism and heritage studies.

Nicola Hilti studied Sociology and Communication Sciences in Vienna and holds an interdisciplinary PhD from the ETH Zurich. Her main research foci are multi-locality and mobility, housing and social aspects of building density.

Daniel R. Kerr, Professor in the History Department at American University (AU), is the Associate Director of the Public History Program at AU. His work focuses on the methods and ethics of doing research with those living in extreme poverty.

Youna Kim is Professor of Global Communications at the American University of Paris, France, joined from the London School of Economics and Political Science where she had taught since 2004, after completing her PhD at the University of London, Goldsmiths College.

Jerome Krase, Emeritus and Murray Koppelman Professor at Brooklyn College of The City University of New York, is an activist-scholar serving as consultant to public and private agencies regarding inter-group relations and other urban community issues.

Ingrid Martins Holmberg has been Senior Lecturer at the Department of Conservation, University of Gothenburg since 2007. Her research has concerned urban renewal and urban history; heritagization of built environments and in particular the knowledge claims; places of subaltern groups in heritage management; old buildings in the perspective of circulation of meanings and materiality.

Lars Meier is Guest Professor for Sociology and Social Inequality at the Department of Sociology, University of Frankfurt. His research focuses on social inequalities and diversities, urban studies, globalization theory and qualitative methods. At the moment he is working in a research project on poverty in times of crisis.

Erika Persson has written a BA thesis about Roma places in Gothenburg, Sweden. The thesis was written within the research project *Rörligare kulturarv* funded by The Swedish National Heritage Board 2012–2014, and is also part of the exhibition *Vi är romer* [We are Roma] at the Gothenburg City Museum, inaugurated in 2013.

Dwelling in mobile times: places, practices and contestations

Lars Meier[a] and Sybille Frank[b]

[a]Institute for Employment Research (IAB), Research Department: Joblessness and Social Inclusion, Nuremberg, Germany; [b]Department of Sociology, Technische Universität Berlin, Berlin, Germany

ABSTRACT
Mobile people dwell in local environments. The present special issue considers the relation between mobility and dwelling. This introduction to the special issue on '(Im)mobilities of dwelling: Places and practices' provides a general introduction to places and practices of dwelling of highly mobile people and discusses why it is a promising subject for both cultural and mobilities studies that still needs to be addressed in its full theoretical and empirical significance. We carve out the state-of-the-art of research regarding (im)mobilities of dwelling and argue that dwelling and mobility are also an issue of power relations and contestations. Against this backdrop we demonstrate that mobility and dwelling are embedded in broader transformations of society, social inequalities and home. Moreover, this introduction demonstrates how the subsequent papers contribute to this integrated perspective on the mobile–immobile nexus.

Mobilities such as commuting between places of work and places of residence, migrating, being a tourist or fleeing from bad circumstances to a new place are accompanied by reaching, living, creating, experiencing, leaving, maybe also by being caught in concrete places. As we move from place to place, mobilities are closely interrelated to immobilities. This interrelation, however, may take various forms if one looks at the everyday practices of dwelling in mobile times. People leave dwellings in order to go to work, visit friends or business partners, travel leisurely around the world or to take up a new residence either voluntarily or involuntarily. But people also stay in dwellings in order to receive guests, arrange objects and socialize in them. People also rest, sleep, grow lonely or die in dwellings. In recent times, practices of dwelling have been put more and more on the move, since they are being transferred to new dwellings time and again, for example in case of ultra-mobile people.

Following the 'mobilities turn' in the social and cultural sciences, various studies have analysed practices of mobilities as well as their relationship with broader developments of society (Cresswell and Merriman 2011). Even if these works shed light on spatial practices observed in airports (Gottdiener 2001, Adey 2010a), border spaces and roads (Featherstone *et al.* 2004, Merriman 2007), their focal point is not on modes of dwelling, but on the ways spatial infrastructures enable or disable the mobility of subjects/sensuous bodies as well as of objects, ideas and images (Frank and Steets 2010). The relationship between mobilities, immobilities and moorings has been widely discussed over the last years (Urry 2003, Adey 2006, Cresswell 2006, Hannam *et al.* 2006, Sheller 2011, Cresswell 2012, Söderström *et al.* 2013). Accordingly, moorings have been considered essential for mobile subjects. For Urry (2007) moorings accompany mobilities because mobilities require fixed and materialized facilities such as the infrastructures of servers, airports or highways (Graham and Marvin 2001, Cresswell and Merriman 2011). These can be exemplified also as nodes in global networks that are spanned by spaces of flows (Castells 1996) or as the new centres of a globalized world, the Global Cities (Sassen 2001). But besides those technologic and material spatially fixed recourses also the mobile individuals stand still, rest and are related to localities (Gustafson 2009). Even if this seems to be sometimes overlooked in the context of the mobility turn, localities and places of residence are still vital (Büscher *et al.* 2010). Correspondingly, our special issue adds to a strand of mobility research that has put its focus on the spatial contexts of (im)mobilities (Skelton 2013).

Also mobile people dwell, are immersed in a local environment and are in the perspective of Heidegger (1952) and in that of phenomenology (Tuan 1977, Relph 1985, Seamon and Mugerauer 1985, Ingold 2000, Cloke and Jones 2001, Frers 2013) inseparable from the world. This 'Dasein' as way of being embedded in the world is often exemplified by Heidegger through romanticized harmonious rural settings such as a farmhouse in the German Black Forest (Heidegger 1952). But dwelling is also an issue of power and contestations – as it is realized in processes such as segregation, gentrification or displacement and in socio-spatial forms such as gated communities or shanty towns – and this special issue considers it as such in different spatial settings. It explores the significance of dwelling as a social experience in mobile times and discovers how mobile people dwell in places with the aim to analyse such relations between mobility and dwelling.

Unlike commuting, migrating or travelling, dwelling usually evokes, at least in modern Western thought, the idea of an immobile place to rest. Dwelling is often considered to be solely local. This perspective is accompanied by an understanding of place as being rooted. We follow a critique on such a conception of place and understand place as being porous and 'open to the externally relational' (Massey 2005, p. 183). Such a conception allows considering mobility and dwelling as integrated. To dwell means also to dwell in a place that is open to an outer world and that is under influence by mobility practices of mobile persons, for example, who are not only crossing a place but are also leaving an impact. This special issue explicates this integrative perspective in the subsequent three dimensions: (1) Mobility, dwelling and broader trans-formations of society; (2) Social inequalities, power relations and contestations of (im)mobility and dwelling and (3) Dwelling and home.

Mobility, dwelling and broader transformations of society

This special issue considers dwelling and mobility under the umbrella of broader transformations in society and carves out the manifestations of these transformations on the level of everyday practices and experiences.

With reference to intensified movements such as that of goods, infor-mation, capital and people, a 'mobility turn' (Cresswell 2006, Urry 2007, Canzler *et al.* 2008, Adey *et al.* 2014) has taken place in the social sciences that led to a 'new mobilities paradigm' (Sheller and Urry 2006) and sparked a vast interdisciplinary academic debate that has lasted for over a decade. As a consequence mobility is being perceived 'as a key component of the world today' (Adey 2010b). The main aim was to challenge the ways in which much social science research has been 'a-mobile' (Sheller and Urry 2006, p. 208) and to work on a 'sociology beyond societies' in a world concep-tualized as borderless (Urry 2000). But obviously, mobility is not a new phenomenon in a new era, just think of the colonial period, travel or mass migrations in former times, for example, or everyday bodily practices and movements.

What is different are today's concrete everyday mobile practices such as air travel or video conferencing (Strengers 2014) that are no longer typical mainly for businesses but are today ubiquitous also in many people's leisure time activities. Smart phones and the use of the World Wide Web allow staying connected while being mobile. But also the spread of cell phones and the lower costs of telephoning in general allows frequent communication over distance (Goggin 2006, Horst 2006, Thompson 2009) that 'link migrants and homelands in ways that are deeply meaningful to people on both ends of the line' (Vertovec 2004, p. 13). This allows also the development of new social relations as is the case within transnational families (Meier 2016a) that span different countries. Personal mobilities (Freudendal-Pedersen, 2009) such as commuting between workplace and residence, but also seeing family members and friends elsewhere have increased in general with more accessible, much faster and much cheaper transport and communi-cation technologies.

Such changes are not only associated with the development of new tech-nologies of transport and communication, but are also related to economic and political restructuring efforts as discussed in globalization theories (Harvey 1989, Castells 1996). In the recent era of 'flexible accumulation' with its new sectors of production, finance services and markets David Harvey has demonstrated that labour processes and labour markets but also consumption have become more flexible. Labour markets have undergone heavy restructuring with more flexible work regimes (Benner 2002) and flexible project-based work (Boltanski and Chiapello 2005). Time horizons of private and public decisions have shrunk and the speed up of economic processes but also of social life can be described as a new round in 'time-space compression' (Harvey 1989). Those transformations have led to a new status of 'social acceleration' (Rosa 2013) with a pressing need of flexibility (Sennett 1998) in the so-called 'liquid modernity' (Bauman 2000), the era of 'flexible accumulation' (Harvey 1989) or in 'late modernity' (Giddens 1991, Hall 1992a).

Today it has become easier to be mobile also at long distances and across borders of districts or nation states. In some cases, this allows people to move away from bad circumstances. But it has also become a norm to be mobile with more business trips and holidays, and to visit some of the iconic places the images of which are incessantly circulated through global communications media (Frank 2016a). More generally it is common to leave a locality for better job possibilities, to earn sufficient money and to dwell somewhere else. This is not only true for professionals moving to urban centres (see Meier 2015, Hilti 2016, in this issue, Kim 2016, in this issue) with developed service sector workplaces, but also for migrants sending remittance from the country of destination back to the country of origin (Martonea *et al.* 2011, Singh *et al.* 2012). Mobility has become a dominant discourse as an ideal of qualification (Brodersen 2013). It is a demand that is creating pressure for individuals to accomplish (Lyons *et al.* 2011). This is not only true for external forces requiring people to become mobile, for example being relocated by the employer or having to take a job or dwell somewhere else as a consequence of a regional crisis. But mobility as a demand to fulfil can also be recognized by the voluntary will of the individual to dwell in a new locality such as that of lifestyle migration (Benson and Osbaldiston 2014) or of tourists in hotels or resorts (see Frank 2016b, in this issue). Because being mobile might allow climbing the social ladder or keeping a good social position and delivers a higher amount of cultural capital (Bourdieu 1984) and to improve the own curriculum vitae. This special issue concentrates on dwellings as places to negotiate such demands imposed by an increasingly mobile society.

Mobilities also appear involuntarily such as long-standing residents being pushed out of places due to economic or political reasons (see Krase 2016, in this issue), refugees from Southern Europe who decide to move to Northern countries (see Holmberg and Persson 2016, in this issue), internally displaced persons in Georgia (see Brun 2016, in this issue), or homeless persons who are chased out and walk around the city to find shelter (see Kerr 2016, in this issue).

Material, political, cultural and affective dimensions of social life and space are interrelated in both permanent and temporal engagements in dwelling. This special issue analyses how dwelling is practiced in transformed societies. The transformations that have led to more mobility are accompanied by transformations in the arrangements and forms of dwellings as well. This is not only true because dwelling has become in more cases a multi-sited issue that we will consider in greater detail below, but also with respect to the material forms of dwelling such as its architecture. So more mobile and temporary elements such as moveable walls and desks that allow reshaping rooms to suit different needs can be seen in residences and offices. But in mobile times also temporary forms of residence are important such as tents, mobile homes, refugee camps, shanty towns, container settlements, trailer parks, hotels or short-term rented service apartments. Those temporary forms of dwelling are not in every case explicitly planned and conceptualized on the drafting table following political decisions, such as for example refugee camps organized by the UN, or service apartments erected to serve those temporary work forces such as white-collar migrant professionals or blue-collar workers to be away on a job.

Social inequalities, power relations and contestations of (im)mobility and dwelling

Mobilities are more than the simple movement between two or more localities and to dwell is more than to be at a locality. Movements and dwellings are shaped and challenged by structures of power. Like dwellings mobilities, too, are 'designed and planned "from above"' and are 'acted out, performed and lived "from below"' (Frank 2011, Jensen 2013, p. 5). Mobilities are attributed with meanings and are therefore context-related (Cresswell 2006). Accordingly, Zygmunt Bauman has exemplified that 'immobility is not a realistic option in a world of permanent change' (Bauman 1998, p. 2). But he demonstrated that the conditions are unequal. On the one hand, he recognized those whose reach became global. This refers to such persons who decided to foster their career by going abroad for some time with a self-definition of being a cosmopolitan who has 'the willingness to become involved with the Other' (Hannerz 2000, p. 239f). Those people are considered as 'tourists' (Urry 1990, Bauman 1993), 'migrant professionals' (Meier 2015), the 'transnational capitalist class' (Sklair 2001) or as the 'global elite' (Elliott and Urry 2010). On the other hand are those who are located and to be local(ized) is considered as 'a sign of social deprivation and degradation' (Bauman 1998, p. 2, see also Krase 2016, in this issue) as not having the possibility to be mobile. But the situation seems to be not that easy if we think of those who are pushed out and who are forced to be mobile as discussed above.

The articles in this special issue look at mobility in more detail and analyse who can or has to be mobile under which circumstances. The original meaning of social mobility as that of upward or downward mobility in the position in the social structure remind us of the importance of social inequality also with respect to spatial mobility (Faist 2013) that is often overlooked. The concept of motility is helpful in this regard as it characterizes the potential a person has to be mobile (Kaufmann 2002). This refers to the individual's economic, social and cultural capital and therefore considers the social position of the individual. Social and spatial mobility are considered to be related within this concept (on social inequality and mobilities see Ohnmacht *et al.* 2009). The relevance of the social position is obviously true for dwelling as well. In this context it is relevant to consider who is able to be in a specific place or has to be under which circumstances. Both, the kinds of mobility and of dwelling are also two expressions of one's social position and are related. This is why (im)mobilities of dwelling vary among different social groups. Accordingly, the mobility of finance managers in the business class sector of planes, their dwelling in well-equipped offices, service apartment or luxury hotels is obviously different from the kind of mobility of underprivileged migrants who travel in boats, trucks or by foot as well as their dwelling in tents, trailers or in poor-quality buildings.

Mobility, immobility and dwelling are contested issues. This is not only true with regard to social inequalities and different interests of social groups. Concretely, contestations occur in political conflicts or grassroots activities, for example around the planning of the landscapes of mobility (Sen and Johung 2013) such as new airports or highways but also around landscapes of dwelling such as upmarket apartments (gentrification), hotels or office-skyscraper like those that might change the skyline of the City of London (McNeill 2002). But mobility, immobility and dwelling are contested on the discursive level of meanings as well. What are good and desirable forms of dwelling or of mobility relates to ascribed and contested meanings.

Dwelling and homes

Home is more than a shelter; it is also a set of feelings (e.g. a feeling of belonging or a sense of comfort) with particular localities. But we speak here quite deliberately of 'a' home and not of 'the' home. This is because home is dynamic and is 'a process of creating and understanding forms of dwelling and belonging' (Blunt and Dowling 2006, p. 23) that can be unstable and might refer to different localities. Home emerges from a 'nexus of doings and sayings' (Schatzki 1996) as well as from affections and from often ideal-ized and nostalgic memories. Home can be 'a phantasmagoric place, to the extent that electronic media of various kinds allow the radical intrusion of distant events into the space of domesticity' (Morley 2000, p. 9, see also Kim 2016, in this issue).

Dwelling and home are related and home can be conceptualized as dwelling with senses of belonging. While considering dwelling as being physically involved in a concrete locality such as a residence, it is that home is a sense of belonging attached to locality/localities. This special issue concentrates on routines, places, performances, rituals and embodi-ments that evolve through practices of dwelling and analyse home as a multi-sited affair due to mobilities. Dwellings can be intertwined with per-sonal biographies, as places where belongings are collected and a unique interior is arranged. It is through personal experiences and through the spatial organization of physical objects that dwellings become significant to people and that dwellings acquire a meaning that reaches beyond the personal level (Davidson 2009). In this context of dwelling also the past of the spatial setting, the local history, might get some live. This is true for personal memories relating to specific spaces that might haunt people (Meier 2013a) or let them fall in nostalgia (Watson 2006, Kirk 2007, Meier 2013b) by dwelling in a spatial setting. Dwelling is not limited to a house, apartment or hotel but also to other places such as work places that are often associated with intense emotional relations. A phenomenological con-ceptualization of dwelling emphasizes the actual physical experience and proximity to places of persons.

In mobile times, home might be different, as it can refer to senses of belonging to multiple places and localities. This becomes evident if we con-sider experiences, memories and social relations such as those to close rela-tives living abroad, childhood memories of a residence where one was raised, or of mobile houses such as the tents of herders or mobile trailers. Rather than considering home and culture as localized or as rooted, James Clifford claimed to consider culture as 'travelling cultures' of mobile people with home as 'routes' (Clifford 1997) with a necessity to conduct multi-sited ethnography in different spatial settings across national borders (Marcus 1995) or to apply mobile methods such as travelling, driving, cycling or walking with people (Büscher *et al.* 2010, Fincham *et al.* 2010). Others argue that by conducting life interviews with migrants (Kalir 2012) or by autobiographies from mobile people (Letherby 2010) mobility can be analysed in a longitudinal perspective as well and that such a method does not inevitably need to be applied in different local set-tings or by participating mobilities. As this special issue is both on mobilities and on dwelling in localities, the papers it comprises apply to the latter methodological perspective and analyse (im)mobilities through interviews with people narrating their own (im)mobile experiences (see in this issue Kerr 2016, Brun 2016, Hilti 2016, Meier 2016b, Kim 2016) or by observations of (im)mobile practices (see in this issue Krase 2016, Holmberg and Persson 2016, Frank 2016b).

The papers in this special issue

This introduction to the special issue is followed by Jerome Krase's paper titled 'Seeing residential (im)mobilities in New York City' in which he analyses the effects of socio-economic transformation in New York City resident neighbourhoods on inequalities. This found its expressions also in enhancing the mobility of some while detracting the ability of being mobile from others. Krase demonstrates that neighbourhoods have different access to transport networks and that immobility is enforced by inequality through arrests and a stop-and-frisk policy of the poor and with a racial bias.

In his article '"Almost like I am in jail": Homelessness and the sense of immobility in Cleveland, Ohio' Daniel R. Kerr takes a different perspective on mobility, immobility and social inequality as he demonstrates that a specific group of poor, the homeless, are forced to be mobile in their everyday life by being pushed out of places. His article is based on oral histories of homeless people in Cleveland and demonstrates that the homeless feel that they are immobile because of being unable to escape their predicament. The homeless' activities of dwelling are considered as acts of resistance against being unwanted in places.

Those who are forced to be mobile are also studied in Cathrine Brun's contribution 'Dwelling in the temporary: The involuntary mobility of displaced Georgians in rented accommodation.' Her paper emphasizes the importance of engaging with power relations to understand (im)mobilities. Based on an empirical case study of internally displaced persons in Georgia, their dwelling situation in rented accommodation is debated and the experience of 'recognition' – conceptualized as a matter of social status (Fraser 2001) – through dwelling is discussed and employed for a better understanding of (im) mobilities.

Ingrid Martins Holmberg and Erika Persson introduce in their paper 'Ephemeral urban topographies of Swedish Roma: On dwelling at the mobile-immobile nexus' a transnationally displaced group: they examine traces of the multifaceted places of Roma dwellings in urban settings of Sweden until the 1950s, when the Roma were allowed to settle permanently within Swedish municipalities. While recent research has shown how government control and surveillance of the Roma led to their expulsion from urban spaces, Homberg and Persson uncover a long history of urban co-habitation. The moorings of Roman dwellings through corporality and materiality are analysed against the backdrop of being related to connections between 'here' and 'elsewhere'.

In her paper 'Multi-local lifeworlds: Between movement and mooring' Nicola Hilti provides a contemporary typology of the life worlds and practices of people who dwell in two or more living locations, for example because of work or for vacation. Based on qualitative research conducted in Switzerland, Hilti's study allows deeper insights into the diversity and the multi-layering of multi-local living. Uncovering the specific relationalities of the respective living locations and accompanying dwelling practices, Hilti argues that multi-local dwelling may be regarded as a distinctive socio-spatial strategy in our times.

Lars Meier's article 'Dwelling in different localities: Identity performances of a white transnational professional elite in the City of London and the Central Business District of Singapore' deals with the mobility of finance managers as a professional elite that has agreed to be sent to other countries time and again for a few months as part of their professional career. On the basis of identity 'performances' (Butler 1993) of being white and being part of a trans-national elite, the article demonstrates that the local context where the mobile finance managers dwell temporarily is of eminent importance for the performance of those dominant identities against the backdrop of con-tested images with roots in the colonial period.

In her paper 'Dwelling-in-motion: Indian Bollywood tourists and their hosts in the Swiss Alps' Sybille Frank examines the impact of the mobility of specific place images like that of Swiss towns and mountains transferred in Bollywood movies on the (im)mobilities of people, objects and ideas between India and Switzerland. Frank examines the transitory mode of dwelling of Indian Bolly-wood tourists in Switzerland, hosts' performances and local contestations around the Indian tourists' practices of dwelling-in-motion, using the example of a Swiss hotel in small municipality in the Swiss Alps. Frank's paper uncovers that colonial power relations rooted in ideas of 'the West and the rest' (Hall 1992b) are still very much apparent in local tourist space.

With her chapter on '"Willing to go anywhere for a while": Diasporic daugh-ters and digital media' Youna Kim covers the paradox of lived and mediated experiences with digital media on the example of educated and highly mobile generations of Korean, Japanese and Chinese women in London. The article demonstrates that for dwelling in a local context the electronic mediation of the World Wide Web plays a significant role in constituting and changing the way in which diasporic lives and subject positions are experienced that are relevant for identity formation.

This special issue considers the nexus of mobilities and immobilities through places and practices of dwelling in mobile times empirically in differ-ent local case studies with different mobile social groups. It formulates a twofold critique of mobilities studies from a cultural studies perspective:

firstly, as focusing too much on practices of mobilities while inevitably under-valuing the relevance of immobilities and dwelling in concrete localities and local contexts; secondly, to be somewhat blind in many cases to the relevance of power relations, social inequalities and contestations that are taking place in transformed and socially unequal societies and are important not only for the kinds of mobility but also for that of dwelling. Against this backdrop, this special issue hopefully can contribute to new perspectives in both cultural and mobility studies.

Disclosure statement

No potential conflict of interest was reported by the authors.

References

Adey, P. (2006) 'If mobility is everything then it is nothing: towards a relational politics of (im)mobilities', *Mobilities*, vol. 1, no. 1, pp. 75–94.

Adey, P. (2010a) *Aerial Life: Spaces, Mobilities, Affects*, Malden, MA, Wiley-Blackwell.

Adey, P. (2010b) *Mobility*, London, Routledge.

Adey, P., *et al.* (eds) (2014) *The Routledge Handbook of Mobilities*, London, Routledge.

Bauman, Z. (1993) *Life in Fragments. Essays in Postmodern Morality*, Cambridge, MA, Basil Blackwell.

Bauman, Z. (1998) *Globalization. The Human Consequences*, Cambridge, Polity Press.

Bauman, Z. (2000) *Liquid Modernity*, Cambridge, Polity Press.

Benner, C. (2002) *Work in the New Economy*, Malden, MA, Blackwell.

Benson, M. & Osbaldiston, N. (eds) (2014) *Understanding Lifestyle Migration. Theoretical Approaches to Migration and the Quest for a Better Way of Life*, Houdsmill & Basingstoke, Palgrave Macmillan.

Blunt, A. & Dowling, R. (2006) *Home*, London & New York, Routledge.

Boltanski, L. & Chiapello, E. (2005) *The New Spirit of Capitalism*, London, Verso.

Bourdieu, P. (1984) *Distinction. A Social Critique of the Judgment of Taste*, Boston, MA, Harvard University Press.

Brodersen, M. (2013) 'Mobility. Ideological discourse and individual narratives', in *Globalisierung, Bildung und grenzüberschreitende Mobilität*, eds J. Gerhards, S. Hans & S. Carlson, Wiesbaden, Springer VS, pp. 93–108.

Brun, C. (2016) 'Dwelling in the temporary: The involuntary mobility of displaced Georgians in rented accommodation', *Cultural Studies*, vol. 30, no. 2. (forthcoming)

Büscher, M., Urry, J. & Witchger, K. (eds) (2010) *Mobile Methods*, London & New York, Routledge.

Butler, J. (1993) *Bodies that Matter*, London, Routledge.

Canzler, W., Kaufmann, V. & Kesselring, S. (eds) (2008) *Tracing Mobilities. Towards a Cosmopolitan Perspective*, Aldershot, Ashgate.

Castells, M. (1996) *The Information Age. Economy, Society and Culture. The Rise of the Network Society,* vol. 1, Oxford, Blackwell.

Clifford, J. (1997) *Routes. Travel and Translation in the Late Twentieth Century*, Cambridge, Harvard University Press.

Cloke, P. & Jones, O. (2001) 'Dwelling, place and landscape. An orchard in Somerset', *Environment and Planning A*, vol. 33, no. 4, pp. 649–666.

Cresswell, T. (2006) *On the Move*, London & New York, Routledge.

Cresswell, T. (2012) 'Mobilities II. Still', *Progress in Human Geography*, vol. 36, no. 5, pp. 645–653.

Cresswell, T. & Merriman, P. (2011) *Geographies of Mobilities. Practices, Spaces, Subjects*, Aldershot, Ashgate.

Davidson, T. (2009) 'The role of domestic architecture in the structuring of memory', *Space and Culture*, vol. 12, no. 3, pp. 332–342.

Elliott, A. & Urry, J. (2010) *Mobile Lives*, London, Routledge.

Faist, T. (2013) 'The mobility turn: A new paradigm for the social sciences?', *Ethnic and Racial Studies*, vol. 36, no. 11, pp. 1637–1646.

Featherstone, M. (2004) 'Automobilities: An Introduction', *Theory, Culture & Society*, vol. 21, no. 4–5, pp. 1–24.

Fincham, B., McGuiness, M. & Murray, L. (eds) (2010) *Mobile Methodologies*, Basingstoke, Palgrave Macmillan.

Frank, S. (2011) 'From England to the world: ethnic, national and gender-based stereotyping in professional football', *Journal for the Study of British Cultures*, vol. 18, no. 1, pp. 69–81.

Frank, S. (2016a) *Wall Memorials and Heritage. The Heritage Industry of Berlin's Checkpoint Charlie*, London & New York, Routledge.

Frank, S. (2016b) 'Dwelling-in-motion. Indian Bollywood tourists and their hosts in the Swiss Alps', *Cultural Studies*, vol. 30, no. 2. (forthcoming)

Frank, S. & Steets, S. (eds) (2010) *Stadium Worlds: Football, Space and the Built Environment*, London & New York, Routledge.

Fraser, N. (2001) 'Recognition without ethics', *Theory, Culture & Society*, vol. 18, nos. 2–3, pp. 21–42.

Frers, L. (2013) 'The matter of absence', *Cultural Geographies*, vol. 20, no. 4, pp. 431–445.

Freudendal-Pedersen, M. (2009) *Mobility in Daily Life. Between Freedom and Unfreedom*, Aldershot, Ashgate.

Giddens, A. (1991) *Modernity and Self-identity: Self and Society in the Late Modern Age*, London, Polity Press.

Goggin, G. (2006) *Cell Phone Culture: Mobile Technology in Everyday Life*, London, Routledge.

Gottdiener, M. (2001) *Life in the Air: Surviving the New Culture of Air Travel*, Boston, MA, Rowman & Littlefield.

Graham, S. & Marvin, S. (2001) *Splintering Urbanism. Networked Infrastructures, Technological Mobilities and the Urban Condition*, London, Routledge.

Gustafson, P. (2009) 'Mobility and territorial belonging', *Environment and Behavior*, vol. 41, no. 4, pp. 490–508.

Hall, S. (1992a) 'The question of cultural identity', *Modernity and its Futures*, eds S. Hall, D. Held & T. McGrew, Cambridge, Polity Press, pp. 274–291.

Hall, S. (1992b) 'The west and the rest. Discourse and power', *Formations of Modernity*, eds S. Hall & B. Gieben, Cambridge, Polity Press, pp. 275–320.

Hannam, K., Sheller, M. & Urry, J., (2006) 'Mobilities, immobilities and moorings', *Mobilities*, vol. 1, no. 1, pp. 1–22.

Hannerz, U. (2000) 'Cosmopolitans and locals in world culture', *Theory, Culture & Society*, vol. 7, no. 2, pp. 237–251.

Harvey, D. (1989) *The Condition of Postmodernity*, Oxford, Blackwell.

Heidegger, M. (1952) 'Bauen Wohnen Denken', in *Darmstädter Gespräch. Mensch und Raum*, ed. O. Bartning, Darmstadt, Neue Darmstädter Verlagsanstalt, pp. 72–84.

Hilti, N. (2016) 'Multi-local lifeworlds. Between movement and mooring', *Cultural Studies*, vol. 30, no. 2. (forthcoming)

Holmberg, I.M. & Persson, E. (2016) 'Ephemeral urban topographies of Swedish Roma. On dwelling at the mobile-immobile Nexus', *Cultural Studies*, vol. 30, no. 2. (forthcoming)

Horst, H.A. (2006) 'The blessings and burdens of communication. The cell phone in Jamaican transnational social fields', *Global Networks*, vol. 6, no. 2, pp. 143–159.

Ingold, T. (2000) *Perception of the Environment. Essays in Livelihood, Dwelling and Skill*, London, Routledge.

Jensen, O.B. (2013) *Staging Mobilities*, London, Routledge.

Kalir, B. (2012) 'Moving subjects, stagnant paradigms. Can the "mobilities paradigm" transcend methodological nationalism?', *Journal of Ethnic and Migration Studies*, vol. 39, no. 2, pp. 311–327.

Kaufmann, V. (2002) *Rethinking Mobility*, Aldershot, Ashgate.

Kerr, D.K. (2016) '"Almost Like I am in Jail" Homelessness and the Sense of Immobility in Cleveland, Ohio', *Cultural Studies*, vol. 30, no. 2. (forthcoming)

Kim, Y. (2016) 'Diasporic daughters and digital media: 'willing to go anywhere for a while', *Cultural Studies*, vol. 30, no. 2. (forthcoming)

Kirk, J. (2007) *Class, Culture and Social Change. On the Trail of the Working Class*, Basingstoke, Palgrave Macmillan.

Krase, J. (2016) 'Seeing residential (Im)mobilities in New York City', *Cultural Studies*, vol. 30, no. 2. (forthcoming)

Letherby, G. (2010) 'Have backpack will travel. Auto/biography as a mobile methodology', in *Mobile Methodologies*, eds, M. McGuiness & L. Murray, Basingstoke, Palgrave Macmillan, pp. 152–168.

Lyons, K., & Hanley, J. (2011) 'Gap year volunteer tourism. Myths of global citizenship?', *Annals of Tourism Research*, vol. 30, no. 1, pp. 361–378.

Marcus, G.E. (1995) 'Ethnography in/of the world system. The emergence of multi-sited ethnography', *Annual Review of Anthropology*, vol. 24, no. 1, pp. 95–117.

Martonea, J., *et al.*, (2011) 'The impact of remittances on transnational families', *Journal of Poverty*, vol. 15, no. 4, pp. 444–464.

Massey, D. (2005) *For Space*, London, Sage.

McNeill, D. (2002) 'The mayor and the world city skyline. London's tall buildings debate', *International Planning Studies*, vol. 7, no. 4, pp. 325–334.

Meier, L. (2013a) 'Encounters with haunted industrial workplaces and emotions of loss. Class related senses of place within the memories of metalworkers', *Cultural Geographies*, vol. 20, no. 4, pp. 467–483.

Meier, L. (2013b) 'Everyone knew everyone. Diversity, community memory and a new established outsider figuration', *Identities – Global Studies in Culture and Power*, vol. 20, no. 4, pp. 455–470.

Meier, L. (2015) *Migrant Professionals in the City. Local Encounters, Identities and Inequalities*, London & New York, Routledge.

Meier, L. (2016a), '"I am now a nobody." Transformations of home and senses of belonging in the life narrative of a migrant worker in the industrial sector in Nuremberg', in *Transnational Migration and Home in Older Age*, eds K. Walsh & L. Näre, London & New York, Routledge, pp. 165–175.

Meier, L. (2016b) 'Dwelling in different localities: Identity Performances of a White Transnational Elite in the City of London and the Central Business District of Singapore', *Cultural Studies*, vol. 30, no. 2. (forthcoming)

Merriman, P. (2007) *Driving Spaces. A Cultural Historical Geography of England's M1 Motorway*, Malden, MA, Wiley-Blackwell.

Morley, D. (2000) *Home Territories. Media, Mobility and Identity*, London, Routledge.

Ohnmacht, T., Maksim, H. & Bergman, M.M. (2009) *Mobilities and Inequality. Making Connection, in Mobilities and Inequality*, eds T. Ohnmacht, H. Maksim, & M.M. Bergman, Aldershot, Ashgate, pp. 7–25.

Relph, E. (1985) 'Geographical Experiences and Being-in-the-World: The Phenomenological Origins of Geography', in *Dewlling, Place and Environment. Towards a Phenomenology of Person and World*, eds. D. Seamon & R. Mugerauer, Dordrecht, Springer, pp. 15–31.

Rosa, H. (2013) *Social Acceleration. A New Theory of Modernity*, New York, Columbia University Press.

Sassen, S. (2001) *The Global City*, Princeton, Princeton University Press.

Schatzki, T. (1996) *Social Practices. A Wittgensteinian Approach to Human Activity and the Social*, Cambridge & New York, Cambridge University Press.

Seamon, D. & Mugerauer, R. (1985) *Dwelling, Place, and Environment. Towards a Phenomenology of Person and World*, New Haven, CT, Yale University Press.

Sen, A. & Johung, J. (eds) (2013) *Landscapes of Mobility. Culture, Politics and Placemaking*, Aldershot, Ashgate.

Sennett, R. (1998) *The Corrosion of Character. The Personal Consequences of Work in the New Capitalism*, New York, Norton.

Sheller, M. (2011) *Mobility*, [online] Available at: http://www.sagepub.net/isa/resources/pdf/Mobility.pdf (accessed 18 August 2014).

Sheller, M. & Urry, J. (2006) 'The new mobilities paradigm', *Environment and Planning A*, vol. 38, no. 2, pp. 207–226.

Singh, S., Robertson, S. & Cabraal, A. (2012) 'Transnational family money. Remittances, gifts and inheritance', *Journal of Intercultural Studies*, vol. 33, no. 5, pp. 475–492.

Skelton, T. (2013) 'Young people's urban im/mobilities. Relationality and identity formation', *Urban Studies*, vol. 50, no. 3, pp. 467–483.

Sklair, L. (2001) *The Transnational Capitalist Class*, Oxford, Blackwell.

Söderström, O., *et al.* (2013) 'Of mobilities and moorings. Critical perspectives', in *Critical Mobilities*, eds O. Söderström, *et al.*, London & New York, Routledge, pp. 1–21.

Strengers, Y. (2014) 'Meeting in the global workplace. Air travel, telepresence and the body', *Mobilities*, [online], Available at: http://dx.doi.org/10.1080/17450101.2014.902655 (accessed 1 December 2014).

Thompson, E. (2009) 'Mobile phones, communities and social networks among foreign workers in Singapore', *Global Networks*, vol. 9, no. 3, pp. 359–380.

Tuan, Y.-F. (1977) *Space and Place. The Perspective of Experience*, Minneapolis, University of Minnesota Press.

Urry, J. (1990) *The Tourist Gaze: Leisure and Travel in Contemporary Societies*, London, Sage.

Urry, J. (2000) *Sociology Beyond Societies. Mobilities for the 21st Century*, London & New York, Routledge.

Urry, J. (2003) *Global Complexities*, Cambridge, Polity.

Urry, J. (2007) *Mobilities*, Cambridge, Polity.

Vertovec, S. (2004) 'Trends and Impacts of Migrant Transnationalism', Centre on Migration, Policy and Society Working Paper, vol. 3, University of Oxford.

Watson, S. (2006) *City Publics. The (Dis)Enchantments of Urban Encounters*, London, Routledge.

Seeing residential (im)mobilities in New York City

Jerome Krase

Brooklyn College, The City University of New York, New York, NY, USA

ABSTRACT
This chapter discusses and visually demonstrates how ethnicity and class affect residential (im)mobility and how that in turn affects the lives of local residents. It draws on decades long study of New York City's neighbourhoods focused on inter-class and inter-ethnic conflict and competition visible in vernacular landscapes [Krase, J. (2012) *Seeing Cities Change: Local Culture and Class*, Aldershot, UK, Ashgate; Krase, J. & Shortell, T. (2012) 'On the visual semiotics of collective identity in urban vernacular spaces', in *Sociology of the Visual Sphere*, ed. D. Zuev & R. Nathansohn, London, Routledge, pp. 108–128]. The mass movement of global capital into New York City has enhanced 'the potential mobility of some, while detracting from the mobility potential of others' [Sheller, M. (2011) 'Mobilities (Review Article)', *Sociopedia.isa*, [online] Available at: http://mcenterdrexel.wordpress.com/ (accessed 3 August 2013)]. Here, the rich get not only richer, but more mobile as the poor get poorer and less so. Burgess's classic study of the spatial distribution of human activity [1925. 'The growth of the city', in *The City*, ed. R. E. Park & E. W. Burgess, Chicago, University of Chicago Press, pp. 114–123] has been reinvigorated by the Mobility 'Turn' or 'Paradigm' [Urry, J. (2000) *Sociology Beyond Societies: Mobilities for the Twenty-First Century*, London, Routledge], which reiterates that spatial and other movements are critical elements of contemporary society.

Introduction

According to Sheller and Urry, although the significance of mobility in analyses of spatiality and spatial restructuring has been recognized by many social scientists, they continue not to fully ' … recognize how the spatialities of social life presuppose, and frequently involve conflict over, both the actual and the imagined movement of people from place to place, event to event' (Sheller and Urry 2006, p. 6). Also, their problematization of 'sedentarist' approaches that treats dwellings as deterritorialized natural steady-states is especially meaningful, as will be shown here residential neighbourhoods are more than 'terrains' serving as 'spatially fixed geographical containers for social processes' (Sheller and Urry 2006, p. 6).

For Sassen the contradictions of the global capital concentrate the more and less disadvantaged in cities where the marginalized can claim 'contested terrain' (2001). Hannam *et al.* recognize the contested nature of mobilities globally, but call for global studies to be connected to 'local' concerns about quotidian transportation, material cultures, and spatial relations (2006, p. 12). As Skeggs points out, 'Mobility is a resource to which not everyone has an equal relationship' (2004, p. 49). Informed by these concerns, this chapter looks at the local consequences of relative mobilities, such how the motility of one residentially immobile group affects another, as well as the unanticipated consequences of being less able to move. There are many ways by which residential mobility are represented in New York's neoliberal geography. From rapid to stagnant, various practices of movement (such as from-to, and in and around residence) are equally observable. Even though it has been argued that most quotidian mobilities have been increasing (Urry 2000, 2007, Cresswell 2006, Sheller and Urry 2006), relatively immobile, and in some cases fixed, residences of urban dwellers remain critical. This visually enhanced essay hopes to contribute to the broad spectrum of methods already employed in mobilities research that is breaking down disciplinary barriers and perhaps bridging 'the quantitative-qualitative divide' (Goetz *et al.* 2009).

The lingering effects of the global recession has added a new visual dimension to (im)mobility in the urban landscape via the abandonment, and destruction, of homes and businesses as well as increasing numbers of the homeless (Krase and Shortell 2013). Whether luxurious or humble, dwellings serve important symbolic and practical functions for residents of all social classes and cultural backgrounds. Some homes are merely places to rest away from work while others also serve as workplaces. For successful New Yorkers, residences are status symbols of upward socioeconomic movement such as movement from a modest to a luxury apartment. They also are embarrassing signs of failure and downward mobility best recognized as moving temporarily into public shelters, more permanent low-income housing, or taking up residence 'on the street' (Figure 1).

Individual and group attachment to places range from the psychological to the sociological. As to the former, Proshansky offered a notion of 'place-identity' – 'those dimensions of self that define the individual's personal-identity in relation to the physical environment by means of a complex pattern of conscious and unconscious ideas, beliefs, preferences, feelings, values, goals and behavioral tendencies relevant to this environment' (Proshansky 1978, p. 155). Sociologically, Lofland outlined how mobile and immobile groups colonized urban spaces ranging from residents of immobile 'urban villages' to ultra-mobile 'travelling packs' (Lofland 1985, p. 119). As a result of relative mobilities, city residents compete in ways that are often reported in local media but seldom in sociological literature, such as protests against parking

Figure 1. Homeless on Prospect Park West. Source: © [Jerome Krase].

regulations, and public school zones. Special issues often emerge in ethnically homogeneous areas where residents seek to restrict the movement of people through, as well as into their closed 'private spheres' (Lofland 1998).

Diverse, economically based, mobility potentials also produce contrasts between older and newer residents in local vernacular landscapes. For example, lower status 'invaders' can trigger 'fight, or flight' responses of older, more sedentary, groups as expressed in 'white flight' (Denton 2006, Massey *et al.* 2009). Some ethnic or religious groups are tied tightly to specific locales making them more reluctant to change their residences even when pressured to do so by outside forces (Wirth 1928, Suttles 1968, Krase 1982, Desena 1990). While increasingly diverse collections of migrants move into the city, economic factors also shape mobilities, such as in the gentrification of otherwise contested neighbourhoods. Gentrification, the process by which higher status residents displace those of lower status, is a major contributor to visibly contested neighbourhoods in New York's neo-liberal landscape (Zukin 1987, DeSena 2006, 2012, Osman 2012). Patch saw 'how gentrification is conditioned by and dependent upon older ethnic and industrial landscapes'. As opposed to 'the outcome of strictly rational economic behavior or the profit seeking motives of real estate capitalists … ' (2004, p. 173). Higher-class privileges also limit the motility of the less affluent. For example, newer, upscale housing in marginal districts often restrict access to people via doormen, private police, and security access codes.

Gentrification is only one way that everyday practices of dwelling, such as the appearance of dwellings and emotional landscapes, make residents feel at home. Bourdieu's distinctions between the tastes of 'necessity' and 'luxury' help us to understand both gentrified and ungentrified spaces.

> Taste is thus the source of the system of distinctive features which cannot fail to be perceived as a systematic expression of a particular class of conditions of existence, i.e., as a distinctive lifestyle, by anyone who possesses practical knowledge of the relationships between distinctive signs and positions in the distributions. (Bourdieu 1977, pp. 174–175)

The social alteration of spaces changes their meanings and may mean different things to different classes and ethnic groups. For example, the commercial streets once filled with shops catering to poor and working-class ethnics in Williamsburg, Brooklyn are now replaced with upscale boutiques, cafes, and organic food stores and vacant industrial spaces filled with hip restaurants, dance clubs, and art galleries (Waickman 2014). Ironically, ethnic or lower class vernaculars can be tamed and sold as 'ambiance'. Real estate ads often promote the pleasantly rough character 'frontier' neighbourhoods of working-class people and places. Just as shop windows or signs attract some inside they can repel others. The simplest analogy for this might be reading the menu posted outside the restaurant before deciding to enter.

For the less privileged, altering and maintaining urban spaces to feel at home is challenging. As Harvey noted:

> For those lacking power (especially 'low-income populations') the main way to dominate space is through continuous appropriation. Exchange values are scarce, and so the pursuit of use values for daily survival is central to social action. This means frequent material and interpersonal transactions and the formation of very small-scale communities. Within the community space, use values get shared through some mix of mutual aid and mutual predation, creating tight but often highly conflictual interpersonal social bonding in both private and public spaces. (1989, pp. 265–266)

Mobility and motility

'Mobility' speaks to the capability of moving or being moved. A related concept, that of 'motility' drawn from biology, concerns the capacity of spontaneous movement. According to Sheller, 'Mobilities research in its broadest sense concerns not only physical movement, but also potential movement, blocked movement, immobilization and forms of dwelling and place-making' (2011, p. 6). Other crucial ethical and justice issues concern uneven motility and mobility rights, especially for subaltern groups. In regard to both class as well as culture (ethnicity), Kellerman's model for potential mobilities is especially useful here. The model focuses on the accumulation of mobility needs, access, and competences, all of which lead to an appropriation process

(Kellerman 2012, pp. 174–175). 'Access' refers to the availability of mobility possibilities. 'Competence' refers to physical, acquired, and organizational mobility skills and abilities, at both the individual and societal levels. 'Appropriation' refers to the ways in which mobility agents evaluate mobility options in light of their personal levels of access and competences, weighed by aspirations, motives, and needs. It includes an element of 'choice of motility' and compromising, not just existing or imposed access and competences. Motility also depends on the social and cultural contexts within which people live such as religious and cultural norms (Kellerman 2012, p. 175).

New as well as 'renewed' leisure and entertainment spaces restrict access via entry or use fees as well as membership dues, thus decreasing the mobility rights of the poor. Sorkin (1992) and Davis (1998) especially have criticized privatization of spaces once accessible to the general public. Yet, despite restrictions, even poor people are mobile; for example, the homeless move through the city in search of shelter. Some are transported by city agencies to and from overnight shelters, especially in the winter months. Residents of low-income housing projects also move within and without of their residential domains. Whether rich or poor, movement is also influenced by a person's attitudes towards spaces and places. In Los Angeles, Boucher looked at the homeless in regard to public parks and argued that their immobility corresponds to what Rémy calls a 'non-urbanized situation' (1972); urbanity is essentially the ability to move. By close observation, Boucher (2012) demonstrated that even the homeless make choices within a limited range of possible moves. On the other hand, Lindsay (2012) looked at the mobility choices of more affluent residents in a gentrified East London neighbourhood where they feared predominantly black, local youths and 'the poor' as producers of disorder. As a result, for them the neighbourhood was temporary home, and they retreated from community involvement. Lindsay explained this by 'residential choice theory', in which those with the ability to choose rate prospective locales according to key criteria, such as value for money and local amenities, and expectations for social life.

As with the poor, there are also different types of gentrifiers with respect to their everyday practices of mobility. Rérat et al. (2009) differentiate gentrifiers broadly by lifestyle such as the 'new middle class', 'nonfamily households', 'dual career households', and 'transnational elites'. Lees et al. (2008, pp. 173–178) use a stage model of gentrification which refers to 'waves'. During the first wave, the activities of pioneer gentrifiers (including 'do it yourselfers') were critical in attracting investment. The second wave ('new build') anchored and stabilized the gentrification process. According to Lees et al., the third wave is characterized by public–private collaborations to facilitate ('super') gentrification. The observations in this chapter broadly concern 'nonfamily' and 'dual career' households (including 'hipsters') in second- and third-wave Williamsburg and Park Slope, Brooklyn.

These neighbourhoods have easy access by public transportation to the gentry's primary places of work in Manhattan. Exceptions to this rule are the artists and other pioneers who found low-cost workspaces in vacant industrial buildings in Williamsburg. First wave, gentrifiers are less dependent on local facilities for their needs and meet them by travelling outside the immediate area. As the area develops through the second and third stage, there is less need to go elsewhere as class and lifestyle specific shopping, restaurants, and recreation increase in the immediate area. Another interesting motility effect is the 'super gentry' whose children travel out of their new home territories until local schools are created for them (DeSena 2006). As will be discussed later in this chapter, bicycling seems to be a favoured means of personal transportation for many gentrifiers.

Globally, the poor have been allowed to occupy undesirable residential areas until they become attractive for investment and they are ejected. For example, Tait (2008) reported on how gentrification is forcing Roma to vacate their 550-year-old community of Sulukule, Istanbul, and Green reported on the 'pacification' of *favelas* in Rio Janeiro, Brazil in anticipation of the 2014 World Cup Soccer Tournament and the 2016 Olympics (Figure 2):

> … the country's poorest say they are being swept aside in a tidal wave of forced evictions and human rights abuses … On the roadside wall of Favela Metro in Rio de Janeiro, a colourful mural shows a weeping boy in Brazilian national kit

Figure 2. Pacified Favela in Rio de Janeiro. Source: © [Jerome Krase].

and a football containing the image of a skull. 'Destroying our community for the World Cup', is written in Portuguese. Red lines also cross through mock road signs portraying homes and families, with 'Thank you FIFA' painted above them. (Green 2012)

Residential mobility and motility in Brooklyn, New York

We turn now to examples of relative residential immobility as critical factors in contested vernacular landscapes of New York's largest borough, Brooklyn. Jackson tells us that vernacular landscapes are part of the life of communities, governed by custom and held together by personal relationship. In these 'everyday worlds of ordinary people' commercial vernacular landscapes especially play major roles in the establishment of the ethnic as well as social class character of city neighbourhoods (Jackson 1984, p. 6, Krase 2004). According to the 2010 United States Census, the population of Brooklyn was: 42.8 per cent White (35.7 per cent non-Hispanic White); 34.3 per cent Black; 19.8 per cent Latino (of any race); 10.5 per cent Asian; 8.9 per cent other races; 3.0 per cent Two or more Races; and 0.5 per cent Native American, Hawaiian, or Pacific Islander (Census 2010). New York has long provided both tourists and social scientists with a complex mosaic of social worlds. Globalization has also attenuated the historical disparities and residential class divisions, but its diversity can serve as a model for analysing mobility. The neoliberal critiques of Harvey (2007), and Brenner et al. (2010) show that the organization of spaces and their embedded social practices in, as well as its image, are dominated by those who control social and economic capital. As to making the city more competitive in the global economy Harvey asked:

> But, competitive for what? One of the first things Michael Bloomberg did was to say ' … We only want corporations that can afford to be here'. He didn't say that about people, but, in fact, that policy carries over to people. There is an out migration from New York City of low-income people, particularly Hispanics. They're moving to small towns in Pennsylvania and upper New York State because they can't afford to live in New York City anymore. (2007, p. 10)

According to Greenberg, the Bloomberg administration sought to 'brand' New York as a 'Luxury City' by attracting finance, information technologies, biotechnology, and media industries (Greenberg 2010, pp. 29–30). The goal was to ' … build a physical city that appealed to these global elites, by attracting high-end retailers, hotels, stadiums, and residential towers … ' (Greenberg 2010, p. 31). Instead of a dream neo-liberal city:

> The scale and pace of market- rate, 'luxury' real estate development under Bloomberg, alongside regressive tax policies that favor businesses and 'workers that can move', … Successive waves of gentrification and increases in the cost of living have pushed out mixed use, working class districts – from Harlem to Willets Point to downtown Brooklyn. (Greenberg 2010, p. 139)

Greenberg noted that at the same time ordinary people still struggled to keep their homes, the homeless and 'Occupy' protesters made counter claims about whose city is it is. In this way, quotidian streetscapes offer the viewer a layered record of both dominance and deprivation in what Mollenkopf and Castells (1991) called the 'Dual City' (Figure 3).

In this chapter, we consider a wide range of class and ethnic groups in Brooklyn. Each has more and less limited power to optimize their home territories to suit their desires and needs. Occasionally, they clash with each other within their shared spaces (Krase 2012, Krase and Shortell 2012). For Puerto Ricans, Sciorra framed the vernacular of *casitas*.

> It is within this imposed economic, political and social marginality that poor people of color struggle to change the existing conditions in with they live by creating spaces of their own design that serve as locations of resistance to a system of inequity and domination. by clearing … the detritus of urban decay to cultivate bountiful gardens and construct wood-frame structures typical of the Caribbean. These transformed sites serve as shelter for the homeless, social clubs, block associations, cultural centers, summer retreats and entrepreneurial ventures … (1996, pp. 61–62, see also Krase 2004)

There are several *casitas* in Williamsburg and other examples of the ways that Latinos try to optimize their environments. One of the most common fair weather sights are men expropriating sidewalks for games of dominoes on improvised tables while sitting on milk crates. Latino-owned grocery

Figure 3. Occupy Wall Street encampment. Source: © [Jerome Krase].

stores, or *bodegas* sell culturally appropriate foodstuffs, as well as serving as community centres, and for immigrants, as informal labour exchanges. This is also common in Afro-Caribbean neighbourhoods such as Crown Heights where busy commercial thoroughfares also offer international shipping and telephone services. The display of Puerto Rican, Dominican, Mexican, Jamaican, Barbadian, Haitian, Italian, and Israeli flags also claim dominion of local territory and are often incorporated in commercial signage as well as residential spaces. Other common features of Latino and Afro-Caribbean areas are storefront, mostly evangelical, Christian churches and local streets are also venues for religious and cultural parades or festivals.

Orthodox Jews ethnically optimize their home territories in the same general ways as others but require greater insulation from outsiders. They also require concentration; being unable, for example, to use motorized transport on the Sabbath their synagogues must be within walking distance. Their fear of outsiders is evidences by bars on windows, and other security measures such as private security patrols. Observing strict sex segregation is also necessary for them to feel at home. Almost all needs are met following strict religious guidelines for dress, food (Kosher), education, and health. Since it is a high-birthing population there are many childcare facilities and stores selling children's clothing, furniture, and baby carriages. As is true in Latino and Italian settlements, foreign language (Hebrew lettering) signs mark many establishments, and foreign languages (Hebrew and Yiddish) spoken on the street add more to the zone of comfort. Castells might refer to this as the 'symbolic marking of places' (Castells 1989, p. 350).

Many of the Afro-Americans, and many Latinos, discussed in this chapter are residents of low-income public housing, which offers them little opportunity for significantly changing the external appearance and use of structures and spaces. Therefore, they rely on the continuous appropriation of space, such as regularly congregating at specific locations, to assert their hegemony. On occasion, however, one can see officially sanctioned public art displays and, more often, unsanctioned graffiti. This includes, for example, youth gangs taking over playgrounds and 'tagging' spaces so that other gangs can see their boundaries.

Ethnic population maps of Brooklyn since the 1920s show the remarkable immobility of Black, Jewish, and Italian enclaves. Today most of New York's Ultra-Orthodox, Jews ironically, reside in Wirth's (1928) 'voluntary' ghettos of various degrees, whereas most Blacks occupy rather 'involuntary' ones. The immobility of Orthodox Jews is primarily due to regulations that tie them to local religious leaders and institutions. For Blacks limited residential mobility is due in large part to discrimination. Brooklyn's dwindling Italian American population remains tied to historically important immigrant enclaves, and is therefore voluntary. Beyond race and ethnicity, poverty increases the immobility of these already immobile racial and ethnic groups.

As Hetherington (1997) might note, their places are indeed dynamic – 'places of movement'.

> Places are like ships, moving around and not necessarily staying in one location. In the emerging mobilities paradigm places themselves can be seen as becoming or traveling, slowly or quickly, through greater or shorter distances and within networks of both human and non-human agents (Hannam et al 2006, p. 13).

Some of the Orthodox Jewish enclaves in Brooklyn, for example, have been relocated from Hungary, and Italian American and other ethnic enclaves, can also be seen as having moved their social relationships and practices from one place to another. As summarized by Hannam *et al.*:

> Places are about relationships, about the placing of peoples, materials, images and the systems of difference that they perform. We understand 'where' we are through 'vision in motion' practiced through the alignment of material objects, maps, images and a moving gaze. And at the same time as places are dynamic, they are also about proximities, about the bodily co-presence of people who happen to be in that place at that time, doing activities together, moments of physical proximity between people that make travel desirable or even obligatory for some. (2006, p. 13)

The Community Service Society mapped poverty in New York City and found that poverty and low incomes, unemployment, subsidized housing, emergency rent assistance, Housing Court actions, emergency feeding sites, disconnected youth, and low educational attainment were all highly concentrated in Upper Manhattan, the South Bronx, and Central Brooklyn. They concluded:

> New Yorkers are living with the effects of poverty in every part of New York City, but the experience of poverty remains closely tied to place. Half of the city's 1.4 million poor people live in neighborhoods where the poverty rate is at least 24.8 percent (compared to a citywide rate of 19.2 percent), and one-quarter live in neighborhoods where the rate is at least 34.1 percent. (Community Service Society and United Way 2008, p. 2)

Not unsurprisingly, Bloch and Roberts (2010) reported mortgage foreclosure rates were highest in areas with high minority populations. Figure 4 shows the spatial distribution of foreclosures in 2005, which covaries with poverty and race as well as the other factors cited by the Community Service Society study. In Brooklyn, the Community Districts hit hardest are Bedford-Stuyvesant (12 per cent White), Bushwick (24 per cent White), and East New York (18 per cent White). Mortgage foreclosures add to neighbourhood stress because abandoned and boarded up buildings become signifiers of poverty, which stigmatizes the surrounding area.

Although sharp distinctions are often made between them (Hannam *et al.* 2006), travellers and activities are not separate from destinations. Destinations partially depend

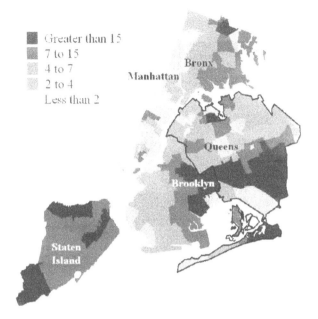

Figure 4. Mortgage Foreclosures in New York City. Source: Thomas P. DiNapoli, New York State Comptroller, Foreclosures in New York City, March 2011.

upon what is practiced within them … travel is not just a question of getting to the destination. Places are thus not so much fixed but are implicated within complex networks by which 'hosts, guests, buildings, objects and machines' are contingently brought together to produce certain performances in certain places at certain times. (Hannam *et al.* 2006, p. 13)

We can think of bicycles for gentrifiers as performative expressions of taste and status and not merely conveyances. Where one is going, or doing while moving or even standing still can also be seen as something about race, ethnicity, class, and gender. The special ways that Brooklyn's Ultra-Orthodox Jews travel shows how their insular ethnic neighbourhood changes its location. They convey themselves between home territories and through more or less hostile territory on their own, marginally 'public' transportation systems. For example, there is the B110 bus that connects the Ultra-Orthodox neighbourhoods of Williamsburg and Borough Park. Women are encouraged to sit in the rear section, as it would be illegal to require them to do so (Haughney 2011; Figure 5).

Similarly, there are car services, or 'gypsy cabs', catering only to Black Brooklynites that visibly dominate certain routes. Before the city cracked down on discrimination by regulated taxicabs, one Black-owned car service's

Figure 5. Orthodox Jewish bus. Source: © [Jerome Krase].

('Black Pearl') motto was 'We're not yellow. We go everywhere.' The Black community is also served by a legion of semi-regulated 'dollar vans' adapted from the Caribbean. The dollar vans and car services shadow official public bus routes connecting Black neighbourhoods to each other as well as popular shopping areas (Margonelli 2011).

Bike lanes – relative mobilities

A controversial project of the Bloomberg administration were bike lanes that were a part of citywide traffic calming efforts. In more affluent neighbourhoods, the plan set off protests by car owners who saw it as attacking their mobility because the lanes reduced parking spaces. More unexpected conflicts emerged as the network connected gentrifying areas such as Williamsburg and Park Slope via routes through an Orthodox Jewish enclave as well as predominantly Black and Latino low-income housing projects. In the process, they increased the motility of the gentry at the expense of the immobile (Figure 6).

> In response to last week's removal of bike lanes in the traditionally Hasidic neighborhood in Brooklyn, a group of local bike riders took it upon themselves to repaint the lane lines running down Bedford Avenue. The Hasids had asked the city to remove the bike lanes from the neighborhood, claiming the influx of bikers posed a 'safety and religious hazard'. … Last year the religious group

Figure 6. Bike Lane Map. Source: Bicycle Maps. New York City Bike Map. http://www.nyc.gov/html/dot/downloads/pdf/2015-nyc-bike-map.pdf

complained to the community board that many of the young, female cyclists who rode through the neighborhood were 'hotties', who 'ride in shorts and skirts', both of which are against their dress code. (Huffington Post 2010)

More tragically, the city installed fencing on a footbridge connecting sections of a Fort Greene housing project to keep vandals from throwing things off it. The addition reflected deeper social class issues of relative mobility as luxury apartment towers had risen nearby (Figure 7).

Last August, Stephen Arthur was riding home to North Park Slope on his bicycle when he was struck in the head by a brick thrown from one of the two ramps onto the footbridge. Though he was wearing a helmet, he crashed, tearing a ligament in his wrist and cutting his face.

Figure 7. Biker Through projects. Source: © [Jerome Krase].

Mr. Arthur, a 44-year-old computer programmer, was not the first cyclist on the eight-year-old Navy Street bike path to be hit by objects that youths – for years, residents say – have been throwing from the ramps ... Ed Brown, 47, the president of the Ingersoll Houses tenants' association, said the fence was a sign of a deeper issue: 'The disconnect between newer residents and longtime residents and people coming in the area via the bike lanes'. (Robbin 2012)

Conflict and competition also occurs between immobile groups when they are confined in the same residential spaces. McLaughlin reported that opponents to a housing plan at Williamsburg's Broadway Triangle say it favours Hasidic Jews by including too many three- and four-bedroom apartments to 'disproportionately accommodate the Hasidic community's large families' (Figure 8).

The plan also caps building heights at eight stories – which opponents charged is a nod to Orthodox Jews who cannot take an elevator on the Sabbath. They further contended that Orthodox Jews' attraction to the shorter buildings would create fewer housing opportunities ... for Williamsburg's Hispanic population and African-Americans from nearby Bedford-Stuyvesant. (McLaughlin 2009)

Figure 8. Puerto Rican flag in project window. Source: © [Jerome Krase].

Immobility and inter-ethnic violence

There is a long history of inter-ethnic conflict in New York City between store-owners, landlords, and local residents in minority communities (Osofsky 1966). The most recent ethnic entrepreneurs have been Korean immigrants who replaced Jews and Italians in crime-ridden, predominantly Black, areas in the 1970s and 1980s because of minimal investment requirements and fast cash. As Vanderkam wrote:

> Starting in the early 1980s, longstanding mutual distrust between Koreans and blacks, coupled with campaigns that encouraged blacks to shop at black-owned businesses, culminated in a series of black boycotts. Notorious activist Sonny Carson sent demonstrators out with signs reading, 'Don't shop with people who don't look like us'. But the Korean community rallied, and the Korean Produce Association provided cash assistance, saving at least some of the stores. (2011)

This was only one version of many inter-ethnic 'border crossing' incidents that resulted in violence in the 1980s and 1990. Two of the most infamous were the 1989 murder of Yusuf Hawkins in Bensonhurst, Brooklyn and the 'Crown Heights Riots'.

Bensonhurst

The immobility of Italian enclaves is based on ethnic culture as opposed to the religious requirement for Orthodox Jews, or discrimination and poverty for Blacks and Latinos. Miranda saw such insularity positively as:

> The tenacity in clinging to the old neighborhoods, partly sentimental, but also derivative from the extended family pattern, can act as a glue to hold the cities from becoming racial ghettos. The Italians have shown a readiness to live in neighborhoods adjacent to those of blacks and Puerto Ricans and fight it out for the turf. (1974, p. 447)

In Greenpoint, Brooklyn, DeSena (1990) documented defensive practices by working-class residents to restrict the influx of outsiders, especially blacks and Latinos, by an informal housing referral system (see also Rieder 1985). Alba *et al.* (1997) found that in contrast to other 'white ethnics' who left as minorities invaded, Italian settlements persisted. Because of their locations, and lower rents, Italian areas became magnets for immigrants as well as gentrifiers (Napoli 2004). Immobility also made inter-group conflict more likely.

The most highly publicized violent consequence was the 1989 murder of Yusuf Hawkins, an African-American youth, in Bensonhurst when he walked across an invisible boundary (Stone 1989, Krase 1994). The vernacular landscape colourfully introduced Kifner's 'Bensonhurst: a tough code in defense of a closed world':

> Banners and lights of red, white and green – the colors of the Italian flag -hang along 18th Avenue in Bensonhurst for the Feast of Santa Rosalia. Normally the neighborhood's biggest event of the year, the feast is overshadowed now by the murder of Yusuf K. Hawkins, a black youth who had ventured into the neighborhood to look at a used car and was surrounded by a crowd of white youths and gunned down. (1989)

Crown Heights riots

Like Orthodox Jews in Williamsburg, those in Crown Heights compete for space. In 1991, the death of Gavin Cato, a seven-year-old Black child from Guyana caused a riot in the ethnically mixed, and frequently racially tense, neighbourhood. As a consequence an Orthodox Jewish student, Yankel Rosenbaum, was murdered by a group of Black men within his own home territory. Gavin was struck by a car in the motorcade of a Hassidic Jewish leader.

When both a City and Hassidic ambulance came on the scene to administer to the driver an angry crowd gathered and attacked.

> … on Monday night, hundreds of black youths began running through the streets, smashing windows, turning over at least one car, shouting 'Jew! Jew!' Racing along President Street, a group of black youths surrounded Mr. Rosenbaum, a visiting rabbinical students and stabbed him at about 11:25 P.M., the police said. He died about an hour and a half later at Kings County Hospital. (Kifner 1991)

Although this was the nadir for relations between Blacks and Jews, the downward direction was set earlier. Over the course of a century, Crown Heights became home to a wide variety of middle-class Caribbean immigrants. In the 1950s it was the hub for the Jewish Lubavitcher Hasidic community. In the late 1960s and early 1970s, the peaceful coexistence between the groups was tested by community space and public resource issues that found expression in, sometimes heated, local political campaigns (Krase and LaCerra 1992, Henke and George 2004).

Race, poverty, and immobility: stop and frisk

According to Tesfahuney, 'Differential mobility empowerments reflect structures and hierarchies of power and position by race, gender, age, and class, ranging from the local to the global' (1998, p. 501, see also Massey 1994). Places and technologies that enhance the mobility of some can do so while at the same time they decrease the mobility of others, especially as they try to cross borders (Timothy 2001). Therefore, it is not surprising to discover that race and poverty-induced immobility produce other patterns and concentrations such as for crime and arrests. If authorities wish to make arrests, the geography of race and class is metaphorically like shooting fish in barrel. Gelman, Fagan and Kiss (2007) looked at claims of racial bias against the New York City Police Department's 'Stop-and-Frisk' Policy. Blacks and Hispanics represented 51 per cent and 33 per cent of the stops but were only 26 per cent and 24 per cent of the New York City population. Most important for mobility issues, they found evidence of stops (Figure 9):

> … that are best explained as 'racial incongruity' stops: high rates of minority stops in predominantly white precincts. Indeed, being 'out of place' is often a trigger for suspicion … Racial incongruity stops are most prominent in racially homogeneous areas. For example, we observed high stop rates of African-Americans in the predominantly white 19th Precinct, a sign of race-based selection of citizens for police interdiction. We also observed high stop rates for whites in several precincts in the Bronx, especially for drug crimes, most likely evidence that white drug buyers were entering predominantly minority neighborhoods where street drug markets are common. (Gelman *et al.*, p. 816)

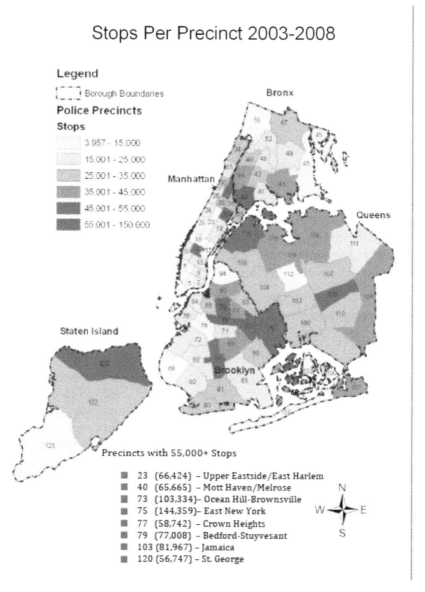

Figure 9. Stop-and-Frisk Map. Note: The Stop-and-Frisk Map mimics the Maps of Race, Poverty, Foreclosures, Bike Routes, et al. Source: Stop, Question & Frisk Policing Practices in New York City: A Primer. Center on Race, Crime and Justice, John Jay College of Criminal Justice, City University of New York. Page 9. March 2010. Published with permission.

Methods

Many of the photographs for this study were taken while I was in motion. Hannam *et al.* suggest that research on mobility could benefit from sensitive methods such as 'mobile ethnography' that involve participation by the researcher in the patterns of movement of the subjects under study (2006, p. 15). Ways and means of travel concern more than moving between points on paper and mental maps, but also experiences and performances. One gets to see and feel what happens in the course of travel such as the actions of fellow passengers and the goings on outside the windows. For example, maps showed locations of high incidence of mortgage foreclosures in Brooklyn where I travelled by car with a colleague to conduct a mobile photo survey (windshield survey). To observe and photograph in the Orthodox Jewish and contiguous low-income Black and Latino areas, I travelled by subway and photographed while walking on the street. In addition, on the return trip I photographed out of the window of a public bus as it travelled from there to downtown Brooklyn passing though several other low-income housing developments. One of these was where the bicyclist had been attacked, and the bus travelled through the pedestrian bridge from which the brick had been tossed. Along the route, Orthodox Jews were seen hitching rides at what appeared to be specific pick-up locations on the periphery of their neighbourhoods. There are three distinct Orthodox areas between which many travel by public and private motorized transportation. However, on the Sabbath and religious holidays they can be seen walking, sometimes several miles, between Orthodox neighbourhoods to attend special religious events and services.

My pedestrian and vehicular movements also made it possible to identify 'ethnically sensitive' transportation modes. For Orthodox Jews the most common are the 'yeshiva buses' that carry their children to religious schools outside the immediate area. Ethnically and economically sensitive means of transportation for school children are not the sole domain of Orthodox Jews. In other ethnic, as well as gentrified areas, private and parochial school buses, vans, livery cars, and, of course, parent-drivers can be seen ferrying children to schools in conveyances that reflect their class status. Close attention to the local landscape will occasionally include gentry on bikes taking their children to school.

The family service and other social service centres as well as homeless and women's shelters discussed in this chapter were also located from maps provided by city agencies or reported in newspapers. Finding the improvised shelters of homeless people was more serendipitous. However, based on many observations, they are found most frequently in areas that are vacant at night such as parks, industrial and commercial areas, and abandoned structures. Since my interest here was to observe generally accessible public spaces, I was not led to pursue the homeless to where they might have encampments or 'hidden' locations such as subway tunnels.

This work can be classified as what Pauwels calls 'researcher-initiated production of visual data and meanings' in which phenomena to be visually recorded are selected and processed as a 'proper scientific end product'

(2010, p. 551). Researcher-generated images offer more control over collection and greater ability to reflexively contextualize them. There is some gain from recognizing the value for ethnographers of their voluntary motion. However, it must be emphasized that my movement was not a *derive* or unplanned movement through a landscape as suggested by Debord (1955). Although the creative insightful aims might be similar, my visual excursions, are purposive methods for documentation for comparative analysis. (Shortell and Krase 2011) The research discussed in this essay might be classified as visual analytic 'autoethnography' (Chaplin 2011). Autoethnography is often criticized as less than rigorous. To ground it more solidly in social science methods, Anderson (2006) proposed an 'analytic' version of the research practice in which the researcher is a full member in the research group or setting, visible as such a member in published texts, and committed to developing theoretical understandings of broader social phenomena.

Conclusion

This chapter has looked at the local consequences of relative movement to show how the motility of residentially immobile groups affect each other. Examples have been given of high profile conflicts as well as other negative consequences for the poor and minority groups of their confinement. Ethical and justice issues of uneven motility and mobility rights as well as the agency of subaltern groups to move despite restrictions emanating from external as well as internal sources have also been addressed (Sheller 2011). We have also discussed a few of the ways that everyday practices of dwelling, such as the appearance of dwellings and emotional landscapes, make residents feel at home. In a related way, ethnic and class enclaves were shown to be dynamic 'places of movement' or 'movable relationships practiced in particular places' (Hetherington 1997).

Old and new ways of looking at residential immobility were synthesized to demonstrate how culture and class have increased 'the potential mobility' of some while decreasing it for others (Sheller 2011, Kellerman 2012). At the turn of the last-century residential mobility and immobility were spatially and visually represented in many different ways in the neo-liberal geography of New York (Harvey 2007, Brenner et al. 2010, Greenberg 2010). To partially demonstrate how the inflow of global capital into the 'Big Apple' made the rich more mobile, as the poor became less so, the classic ecological paradigm of intra-urban mobility (Burgess 1925) has been grafted to the mobility 'paradigm' (Urry 2000). Rather than treating local travel as a 'black box', global and local concerns about everyday transportation, material cultures, and spatial relations in New York City have been connected to show that residential neighbourhoods are more than 'terrains' serving as fixed 'containers for social processes' (Hannam *et al.* 2006).

Hannam *et al.* also suggest that research on mobility could benefit from sensitive methods such as 'mobile ethnography' that involve participation by the researcher in the patterns of movement of the subjects under study (2006, p. 15). Towards that end the author integrated fixed notions of neighbourhoods expressed in visual data mapping with analytic auto-ethnographic methods (Anderson 2006) and mobile photographic mobile techniques (Krase 2012, Krase and Shortell 2012, 2013).

Finally, this chapter problematized the simple notion of place, replacing the ontology of distinct 'places' and 'people' with one that recognizes places as complex relations with persons, and performances (Hannam *et al.* 2006, p. 13, Kellerman 2012).

Disclosure statement

No potential conflict of interest was reported by the author.

References

Alba, R. D., Crowder, K. & Logan, J. R. (1997) 'White ethnic neighborhoods and assimilation: the Greater New York region, 1980–1990', *Social Forces*, vol. 75, no. 3, pp. 883–912.

Anderson, L. (2006) 'Analytic autoethnography', *Journal of Contemporary Ethnography*, vol. 35, no. 4, pp. 373–395.

Bloch, M. & Roberts, J. (2010) 'Mapping foreclosures in the New York region', *The New York Times*, 30 May, [online] Available at: http://www.nytimes.com/interactive/2009/05/15/nyregion/0515-foreclose.html (accessed 30 November 2010).

Brenner, N., Peck, J. & Theodore, N. (2010) 'After neoliberalization?', *Globalizations*, vol. 7, no. 3, pp. 327–345.

Boucher, N. (2012) 'Going down to the place of three shadows, journeys to and from downtown Los Angeles public spaces', *Urbanities*, vol. 2, no. 2, pp. 45–61.

Bourdieu, P. (1977) *Outline of a Theory of Practice*, New York, Cambridge University Press.

Burgess, E. (1925) 'The growth of the city', in *The City*, ed. R. E. Park & E. W. Burgess, Chicago, University of Chicago Press, pp. 114–123.

Castells, M. (1989) *The Informational City: Information Technology, Economic Restructuring, and the Urban-Regional Process*, Oxford, Blackwell.

Census (2010) *Kings County, New York. Profile of General Population and Housing Characteristics*, [online] Available at: http://factfinder2.census.gov/faces/tableservices/jsf/pages/productview.xhtml?pid=DEC_10_DP_DPDP1 (accessed 3 August 2013).

Chaplin, E. (2011) 'The photo diary as an autoethnographic method', In: *The SAGE Handbook of Visual Research Methods*, eds. E. Margolis & L. Pauwels, Cornwall, SAGE Publications, pp. 241–262.

Community Service Society and United Way (2008) *Mapping Poverty in New York City, 2007-2008*, [online] Available at: http://www.cssny.org/publications/entry/mapping-poverty-in-new-york-city-pinpointing-the-impact-of-poverty-community (accessed 22 July 2013).

Cresswell, T. (2006) *On the Move; Mobility in the Modern Western World*, New York, Routledge.

Davis, M. (1998) *City of Quartz*, London, Pimlico.

Debord, G. (1955) Introduction to a critique of urban geography. Les Lèvres Nues 6. Available at: http://library.nothingness.org/articles/SI/en/display/2 (accessed 1 August 2014)

Denton, N. A. (2006) 'Segregation and discrimination in housing', in *A Right to Housing: Foundation for a New Social Agenda*, ed. R. G. Bratt, M. E. Stone & C. Hartman, Philadelphia, Temple University Press, pp. 61–81.

DeSena, J. N. (1990) *Protecting One's Turf: Social Strategies for Maintaining Urban Neighborhoods*, Lanham, MD, University Press of America.

DeSena, J. N. (2006) '"What's a mother to do?": gentrification, school selection, and the consequences for community cohesion', *American Behavioral Scientist*, vol. 50, no. 2, pp. 241–257.

DeSena, J. N. (2012) 'Segregation begins at home: gentrification and the accomplishment of boundary-work', *Urbanities*, vol. 2, no. 2, pp. 4–24.

Gelman, A., Fagan, J. & Kiss, A. (2007) 'An analysis of the New York City Police Department's "stop-and-frisk" policy in the context of claims of racial bias', *Journal of the American Statistical Association*, vol. 102, pp. 813, [online] Available at: http://www.stat.columbia.edu/~gelman/research/published/frisk9.pdf (accessed 17 December 2012).

Goetz, A., Vowles, T. & Tierney, S. (2009) 'Bridging the qualitative-quantitative divide in transport geography', *The Professional Geographer*, vol. 61, no. 3, pp. 323–335.

Green, G. (2012) 'How the build-up to the World Cup and Olympics is affecting Rio's favelas', *Metro*, 23 [online] Available at: http://metro.co.uk/2012/04/23/how-the-build-up-to-the-world-cup-and-olympics-is-affecting-rios-favelas-406668/ (accessed 30 July 2013).

Greenberg, M. (2010) 'Branding, crisis, and utopia: representing New York in the age of Bloomberg', in *Blowing Up the Brand: Critical Perspectives on Promotional Culture*, ed. M. Aronczyk & D. Powers, New York, Peter Lang, pp. 115–143.

Hannam, K., Sheller, M. & Urry, J. (2006) 'Editorial: mobilities, immobilities and moorings', *Mobilities*, vol. 1, no. 1, pp. 1–22.

Harvey, D. (1989) *The Urban Experience*, Baltimore, John Hopkins University Press.

Harvey, D. (2007) 'Neoliberalism and the City', *Studies in Social Justice*, vol. 1, no. 1, pp. 2–13.

Haughney, C. (2011) 'At front of Brooklyn bus, a clash of religious and women's rights', *New York Times*, 19 October, [online] Available at: http://www.nytimes.com/2011/10/20/nyregion/bus-segregation-of-jewish-women-prompts-review.html?_r=0 (accessed 2 January 2013).

Henke, H. & George, J. A. (2004) 'Relations between the Jewish and Caribbean American communities in New York City', in *Race and Ethnicity in New York City*, ed. J. Krase & R. Hutchison, Amsterdam, Elsevier, JAI Press, pp. 193–220.

Hetherington, K. (1997) 'In place of geometry: the materiality of place', in *Ideas of Difference*, eds. K. Hetherington & R. Munro, Oxford, Blackwell, pp. 183–199.

Huffington Post (2010) 'Hipsters, Hasidic Jews fight over bike lanes in Williamsburg', *Huffington Post*, [online] Available at: http://www.huffingtonpost.com/2009/12/08/hipsters-hasidic-jews-fig_n_384579.html (accessed 19 July 2011).

Jackson, J. B. (1984) *Discovering the Vernacular Landscape*, New Haven, CT, Yale University Press.

Kellerman, A. (2012) 'Potential mobilities', *Mobilities*, vol. 7, no. 1, pp. 171–183.

Kifner, J. (1989) 'Bensonhurst: a tough code in defense of a closed world', *New York Times*, 1 September, [online] Available at: http://www.nytimes.com/1989/09/01/nyregion/bensonhurst-a-tough-code-in-defense-of-a-closed-world.html?src=pm (accessed 19 February 2011).

Kifner, J. (1991) 'A boy's death ignites clashes in Crown Heights', *New York Times*, [online] Available at: http://www.nytimes.com/1991/08/21/nyregion/a-boy-s-death-ignites-clashes-in-crown-heights.html?scp=3&sq=yankel+rosenbaum&st=nyt (accessed 19 February 2011).

Krase, J. (1982) *Self and Community in the City*, Washington, DC, University Press of America.

Krase, J. (1994) 'Bensonhurst, Brooklyn: Italian American victimizers and victims', *Voices in Italian Americana*, vol. 5, no. 2, pp. 43–53.

Krase, J. (2004) 'Visualizing ethnic vernacular landscapes', in *Race and Ethnicity in New York City*, ed. J. Krase & R. Hutchison, Elsevier, Amsterdam, JAI Press, pp. 1–24.

Krase, J. (2012) *Seeing Cities Change: Local Culture and Class*, Aldershot, UK, Ashgate.

Krase, J. & LaCerra, C. (1992) *Ethnicity and Machine Politics: The Madison Club of Brooklyn*, Washington, DC, University Press of America.

Krase, J. & Shortell, T. (2012) 'On the visual semiotics of collective identity in urban vernacular spaces', in *Sociology of the Visual Sphere*, ed. D. Zuev & R. Nathansohn, London, Routledge, pp. 108–128.

Krase, J. & Shortell, T. (2013) 'Seeing New York City's financial crisis in the vernacular landscape', in *Cities and Crisis: New Critical Urban Theory*, ed. F. Kuniko, pp. 188–217.

Lees, L., *et al.* (2008) *Gentrification*, New York, Routledge.

Lindsay, I. (2012) 'Social mixing: a life of fear', *Urbanities*, vol. 2, no. 2, pp. 25–44.

Lofland, L. H. (1985) *A World of Strangers: Order and Action in Urban Public Spaces*, Prospect Heights, IL, Waveland Press.

Lofland, L. H. (1998) *The Public Realm: Exploring the City's Quintessential Social Territory*, New York, Aldine Gruyter.

Margonelli, L. (2011) 'The (illegal) private bus system that works', *The Atlantic.com*, [online] Available at: http://www.theatlantic.com/national/archive/2011/10/the-illegal-private-bus-system-that-works/246166/ (accessed 31 December 2012).

Massey, D. S. (1994) *Space, Place, and Gender*, Minneapolis, University of Minnesota Press.

Massey, D. S., *et al.* (2009) 'The Changing Bases of Segregation in the United States', *The Annals of the American Academy of Political and Social Science*, vol. 626, pp. 74–90.

McLaughlin, M. (2009) 'Racial and religious discrimination alleged in Triangle homes plan lawsuit', *New York Daily News*, [online] Available at: http://articles.nydailynews.com/2009-09-10/local/17934118_1_hasidic-jews-racial-bias-housing-preservation-and-development (accessed 22 September 2011).

Miranda, G. E. (1974) 'Ozone Park revisited', in *The Ordeal of Assimilation*, ed. S. Feldstein & L. Costello, Garden City, NY, Anchor Books, pp. 443–449.

Mollenkopf, J. H. & Castells, M. (1991) *Dual City*, New York, Russell Sage.

Napoli, P. F. (2004) 'Little Italy: resisting the Asian invasion, 1965-1995', in *Race and Ethnicity in New York City*, ed. J. Krase & R. Hutchinson, London, Elsevier/JAI Press, pp. 245–263.

Osman, S. (2012) *The Invention of Brownstone Brooklyn: Gentrification and the Search for Authenticity in Postwar New York*, New York, Oxford University Press.

Osofsky, G. (1966) *Harlem: The Making of a Ghetto: Negro New York 1890-1930*, New York, Harper and Row.

Patch, J. (2004) 'The embedded landscape of gentrification', *Visual Studies*, vol. 19, no. 2, pp. 169–187.

Pauwels, L. (2010) 'Visual sociology reframed: An analytical synthesis and discussion of visual methods in social and cultural research', *Sociological Methods Research*, vol. 38, pp. 545–581.

Proshansky, H. M. (1978) 'The city and self identity', *Environment and Behavior*, vol. 10, no. 2, pp. 147–169.

Rémy, J. (1972) 'Urbanisation de la ville et production d'un régime d'échanges', *Sociologie et sociétés*, vol. 4, no. 1, pp. 101–120.

Rérat, P., *et al.* (2009) 'From urban wastelands to new-build gentrification: the case of Swiss cities', *Population, Space and Place*, [online] Published online in Wiley InterScience (www.interscience.wiley.com), doi:10.1002/psp.595.

Rieder, J. (1985) *Canarsie: The Jews and Italians of Brooklyn Against Liberalism*, Cambridge, MA, Harvard University Press.

Robbin, L. (2012) 'Bridge's partial fencing points to a bigger divide', *New York Times*, 29 January, [online] Available at: http://www.nytimes.com/2012/01/30/nyregion/fencing-of-brooklyn-footbridge-irks-some-residents.html?ref=nyregion (accessed 13 January 2012).

Sassen, S. (2001) 'The global city: strategic site/new frontier', [online] Available at: http://www.india-seminar.com/2001/503/503%20saskia%20sassen.htm (accessed 3 August 2013).

Sciorra, J. (1996) 'Return to the future; Puerto Rican vernacular architecture in New York City', in *Re-presenting the City: Ethnicity, Capital and Culture in the Twenty-First Century Metropolis*, ed. A. D. King, London, Macmillan, pp. 60–92.

Sheller, M. (2011) 'Mobilities (Review Article)', *Sociopedia.isa*, [online] Available at: http://mcenterdrexel.wordpress.com/ (accessed 3 August 2013).

Sheller, M. & Urry, J. (2006) 'The new mobilities paradigm', *Environment and Planning*, vol. 38, no. 2, pp. 207–226.

Shortell, T. & Krase, J. (2011) 'Seeing difference: spatial semiotics of ethnic and class identity in global cities', *Visual Communication*, vol. 10, no. 3, pp. 367–400.

Skeggs, B. (2004) Class, Self, Culture. London: Routledge.

Sorkin, M. (1992) *Variations on a Theme Park*, New York, Hill and Wang.

Stone, M. (1989) 'What really happened in Bensonhurst?', *New York Magazine*, 6 November, pp. 46–56.

Suttles, G. D. (1968) *The Social Order of the Slum*, Chicago, University of Chicago Press.

Tait, R. (2008) 'Forced gentrification plan spells end for old Roma district in Istanbul', *The Guardian*, 22 July, [online] Available at: http://www.guardian.co.uk/world/2008/jul/22/roma.turkey (accessed 18 June 2011).

Tesfahuney, M. (1998) 'Mobility, racism and geopolitics', *Political Geography*, vol. 17, no. 5, pp. 499–515.

Timothy, D. J. (2001) *Tourism and Political Boundaries*, London, Routledge.

Urry, J. (2000) *Sociology Beyond Societies: Mobilities for the Twenty-First Century*, London, Routledge.

Urry, J. (2007) *Mobilities*, London, Polity.

Vanderkam, L. (2011) 'The Korean grocer disappears, the American dream lives on', *New York Daily News*, [online] Available at: http://www.nydailynews.com/opinions/2011/01/13/2011-01-13_the_korean_grocer_disappears_the_american_dream_lives_on.html (accessed 13 January 2011).

Waickman, C. (2014) 'Whose Williamsburg?', [online] Available at: http://thesixthborough.weebly.com/whose-williamsburg.html (accessed 7 March 2014).

Wirth, L. (1928) *The Ghetto*, Chicago, University of Chicago Press.

Zukin, S. (1987) 'Gentrification: culture and capital in the urban core', *Annual Review of Sociology*, vol. 13, pp. 129–147.

'Almost like I am in Jail': homelessness and the sense of immobility in Cleveland, Ohio

Daniel R. Kerr

History Department, American University, Washington, DC, USA

ABSTRACT
Drawing on oral histories conducted with the Cleveland Homeless Oral History project between 1999 and 2005, the article addresses the unhoused interviewees' overwhelming sense of being immobile. This understanding spoke both to the reality of being restricted to shelters, but it also spoke to the larger feeling of being stuck and unable to escape their predicament. This subjective sense was belied by their everyday reality of constant movement. The article explores the disjuncture between the rhetoric and the embodied practice of movement and stillness. While the rhetoric of immobility spoke to their understanding of oppression, and served as a 'mobilizing' language, their resistance frequently involved establishing dwelling spaces in places where they were unwanted. In the context of homelessness in the twenty-first century, the very practice of dwelling can be a radical act through which the unhoused build power by laying claim to home.

As Ralph Pack and I settled into our seats in the public library in downtown Cleveland, I had barely turned the recorder on when he started telling me a story about a trip he took in the late 1960s:

> I remember one of my friends wanted to go to Mexico, and he wanted me to go with him for company and all that. And we stopped in El Paso Texas – never been there before. It is a fair sized city. So I said to him, 'Frank, where are we going to stay?' He said, 'On the outskirts of every big city, there's always a cheap hotel.' And there was; we got a room there for two dollars. You could take off at any time, and you didn't have to give it a second thought. You could hit the road at anytime and every town – every town had several cheap hotels you could go to. I didn't really appreciate it at the time. (Pack 2000a)

Like most of his stories, this one had a point. He wanted me to know that the demolition of cheap hotels or flophouses across the country had restricted poor folks' ability to travel. He reemphasized his argument in a subsequent interview:

At one time guys from Cleveland that were broke would say, 'Hey I'm on a Chicago detour to somewhere.' Today a guy in Cleveland, their mobility and their freedom's been destroyed because they know that if they get to Chicago or Detroit, there isn't going to be any cheap housing. You're almost immobilized, and tied down to one spot. (Pack 2000b)

As the proponents of 'nomadic theory' (Deleuze and Guattari 1983, Virilio 1997) have been critiqued for their romanticized view of mobility (Sheller 2011), Pack himself could be charged with the same failing. However, the fact that his critique of immobility is shared by so many of the narrators I have interviewed suggests the analysis cannot be easily discounted solely as misguided romanticism. In over a hundred oral history interviews I conducted with unhoused people in Cleveland, Ohio between 1999 and 2005, my narrator's subjective sense of their own immobility became a central theme to their stories as they reflected on the changing city around them. This sense of immobility spoke both to the reality of being restricted to physical structures such as shelters, and to the larger sense of being stuck and unable to escape their predicament. This subjective sense was to some extent belied by their everyday reality, as the condition of homelessness in the early twenty-first century in Cleveland, Ohio was hardly one of physical stasis. Rather the unhoused were often on the move to access the essentials for their everyday survival such as food, showers, clothing, health care, and shelter. Furthermore, the large majority travelled extensively through the metropolitan region as they sought access to work as day labourers. Going to the same job site on a daily basis and sleeping in the same bed each night were privileges few of my narrators had. They created temporary dwellings in shelters and public spaces on a nightly basis. Recent work in the field of critical mobilities offers a lens to better understand the disjuncture between the rhetoric and the embodied practice of movement and stillness (Creswell 2006, Adey 2010, Sheller 2011). While the rhetoric of immobility spoke to their sense of oppression, and served as a 'mobilizing' language – a call to action, their resistance on the other hand frequently involved establishing dwelling spaces in places where they were unwanted. An analysis of the dynamic of power behind their mobility and immobility opened up possibilities for them to intervene with counter movements and perhaps more importantly practices of dwelling that became a source of their power from below.

Dramatic changes restructured the experience of impoverished people in Cleveland, Ohio in the second half of the twentieth century. In the late 1950s, industrialists began relocating manufacturing out of the city. Over the next two decades they built an industrial ring on the outskirts of the Greater Cleveland Metropolitan region. This shift facilitated the rise of the day labour industry in the late 1960s, which specialized in supplying workers for these plants on a day-to-day basis. The new labour agencies offered a solution to absenteeism by taking over responsibility for transporting the workers. This emerging labour market expanded dramatically in the 1980s as the day labour agencies took over most of the risks of employment by assuming the responsibility for paying unemployment insurance and workers compensation. By offering workers for lease, the agencies offered manufacturing companies an interchangeable and flexible labour force that they could draw upon as needed. Urban renewal projects, the construction and expansion of Cleveland State University, and the development of a new baseball stadium and basketball arena destroyed the cheap rooming houses and flophouses that bordered the central business district. During the 1970s and 1980s the demolition and destruction of tens of thousands of affordable housing units in the city's residential neighbourhoods further accelerated what would become a housing crisis. By the mid-1980s, public officials and business leaders struggled to address the emerging spectacle of people living in extreme poverty on the city's downtown sidewalks. Seeking to contain the unhoused and push them out of the central retail and commercial areas, they established a system of emergency shelters in a warehouse district that stood a 20-minute walk east of Public Square – the centre of the city (Kerr 2011).

The city's emergency shelter system was still fairly new and not fully solidified when I made the first steps to begin what would become the Cleveland Homeless Oral History Project. In January 1996, I co-established a weekly free picnic on Sunday afternoons in Public Square. Our group, called Food Not Bombs, originally tried to share our meals in other spaces in the city without much luck. With the help of an unhoused guide, we learned that every Sunday afternoon a large number of people walked across the downtown park to get to the Tower City shopping mall after the public library closed. In order to stay out of the elements, they would spend their early evenings pretending to be shoppers in the mall while they waited for the shelters to open for the night. We set up buckets, coolers, and boxes filled with food we prepared throughout the morning and afternoon and made it clear anyone could stop by and help his or her self. Our picnic, which continued every week for a decade, ended up forming an eddy or a momentary place of dwelling in this micro-migratory flow as people gathered around the food to hang out and talk and make this space on Public Square their own.

The early conversations centred on the food we were eating, local and national politics, and sports. The unhoused, living most of their lives in public spaces, remained very protective of their privacy and were reticent to talk about their lives. Nonetheless these routine conversations and our habitual weekly return to the same space established this location as a place to gather and dwell. It was not until three years of hanging out and relationship building that I brought video recording equipment to the meals.

Rather than ask people about their life histories, I asked them to explain why they thought homelessness had become such an entrenched part of the city. This line of questioning offered them greater say into how much of their personal lives they wanted to bring into their analysis. Most turned to their life experiences as a way to strengthen the legitimacy of their arguments. I played their videos on a television at the picnic – they knew during their interviews that their audience included other unhoused people. The presence of the television helped turn the park into our living room as people gathered around the TV to watch the interviews. The method created a dialogue as the interviews began to reference one another. As narrators sought to expand the audience, I established a radio show in 2000 where I interviewed them live on-air. Picking up the narrators, interviewing them in the tight confines of the basement studio, and driving them to their next destination helped establish close bonds with the narrators. I frequently supported their calls to action, participated in their protests, brought supplies to their camps, and did my best to aid their efforts to make a place for themselves in the city. Between 1999 and 2004 I conducted over one hundred recorded interviews (Kerr 2003, 2008).[1]

In the early winter of 2000 I began holding formal workshops at a drop in centre that was centrally located and served both men and women who lived in the emergency shelters that were located within a short walking distance. The centre offered food, respite from the weather, and showers but little programming. The director of the agency that operated the centre agreed to let me use a room separate from the main gathering area to conduct meetings. I advertised the workshops with flyers and verbal announcements and made it clear that we would be exploring the causes of homelessness. The workshops consisted of a series four weekly meetings that included close to 10 participants in each meeting. During the workshops we watched the videos and the participants identified six themes that they saw as central to the rise of homelessness in the city: (1) the transformation of the downtown business district into an entertainment centre and the consequent elimination of the rooming house hotels, (2) the loss of affordable housing and the subsequent gentrification of the near west and eastside neighbourhoods, (3) the emergence of the day labour industry, (4) the expansion of the criminal justice system and the increasing criminalization of poverty, (5) the elimination of welfare benefits, and (6) the institutionalization of a system of privatized shelters and homeless social services. In the last of these workshops the participants concluded that it would be most productive to focus organizing efforts on the miserable conditions of the shelters and the exploitative conditions within the day labour industry. Intriguingly, these areas of focus (their homes and their work) most directly shaped the everyday lives of unhoused Clevelanders (Kerr 2003, 2008, 2011).

Subsequent workshops conducted in the men's and women's emergency shelters and other drop in centres confirmed these themes and led to the formation of the Day Laborers' Organizing Committee. They also led to several separate protests designed to improve shelter conditions and sustain the right to sleep outside of the shelters on the city sidewalks, abandoned buildings, and other encampments. The interviews themselves coupled with the discussions they spurred in the workshops became an active part of a larger process of political mobilization. My active support of the decisions the workshop participants arrived at strengthened the rapport I had within the community and opened up new opportunities for interviews. As it became clear the research would facilitate their own ends, as they defined them, the participants became more actively engaged with the collaborative project.

From skid row to homeless shelter

Ralph Pack was one of the more popular narrators when I showed the interviews on Public Square and in the subsequent workshops in the shelters and drop in centres. In each of his interviews he artfully interwove his life story with a trenchant critique of present day inequality. With his father he migrated to the city in 1945 from West Virginia when he was 14 years old. Perhaps the early move, one he had little choice in and resented as a child, made him especially attentive to the dynamics of power that shaped his own ability to come and go as he pleased. When they arrived to the city they moved to a rooming house district just east of the central business district, an area with flexible and affordable housing that facilitated the large migration of workers to this burgeoning industrial region in the post-Second World War period. His father found work at Monarch Aluminum making pots and pans, a job Pack tried when he turned 17, hated, and soon quit. In the early days, Pack frequently wondered why he had ever left West Virginia. From his dad's point of view, things looked different: 'Those were the days of big wages. He'd been working in the mines. This looked like a real good deal to him' (Pack 2000a). Tens of thousands of other industrial workers made that same decision as they came to the city from Appalachia and the South and filled the manufacturing jobs at the peak of the Fordist era of production.

Over the course of his life Pack grew to love his new city. Throughout his adult life, he moved from menial job to menial job and from cheap hotels to cheap rooming houses, but he managed to make a home for himself in downtown Cleveland. Nostalgically, Pack (1999) recalls,

> At one time downtown Cleveland was a haven, almost a utopia, for lower income people. There were a thousand cheap hotels and cheap rooming houses. Even dishwashers at one time had their own apartment, room, or whatever. What a deal those hotels were. The area had all kinds of cheap restaurants. Downtown was a great place for the poor man.

The city had three rooming house districts that had served as the entrance point to the city for most of the industrial migrants in the post-Second World War era: downtown, the Hough neighbourhood on the city's eastside, and the

Ohio City neighbourhood on the city's westside. For those who came downtown, 50 cents a night would get them a cubicle at places like the Arch Hotel on Eagle Avenue or the L&K Hotel on Bolivar Road. The cubicle was not fancy – the walls stopped short of the ceiling and were topped with chicken wire to prevent a neighbour from climbing over and stealing one's things. Rooms with solid walls and shared bathrooms, available at places like the Lake Hotel and the Gilsy on East 9th Street, could be obtained from 85 cents up to 3 dollars a night. Apartments could be rented for $30 a month in the rooming house district just east of downtown (Kerr 2011). Pack (2000a) remembers: 'You always had a little room or apartment and you could drink some and you could live a fair life on just a few bucks'. And no doubt the bars were an important space for building community in this relatively transient neighbourhood.

During the depression, relief policy sought to discourage migration by restricting access to benefits to those who had claims to residency in the city. Reformers sought to close the cheap hotels as they struggled to discourage panhandling downtown. This hostility to 'transients', however, dramatically changed in the Second World War when federal policy sought to encourage and rationalize migration – even promoting the carving up of properties into smaller units to address the war-housing crisis. This permissive attitude towards rooming house districts continued for nearly two decades until a recession in 1958 left many workers unemployed, drastically slowed the migration to the city, and severely impacted the real estate market in the areas that catered to recent migrants. With property values plummeting, in the early 1960s sociologists began producing studies that focused on and ultimately devalued the residents of downtown 'skid row' districts. For Donald Bogue (1963) and Howard Bahr (1973), the residents of 'skid row' were merely alcoholics and 'disaffiliated' homeless men.

Over the next three decades, nearly all the cheap hotels, rooming houses, restaurants, and clothing stores in downtown Cleveland had been demolished or closed down. With the benefit of hindsight, Pack differentiates his living situation in the 1960s from those who live in the downtown shelters today. For him the difference does not lie in the intrinsic qualities of the people. In Pack's version the hotels offered far greater autonomy; one could come or go as he or she pleased without bringing your belongings with you. And it was extraordinarily rare that someone slept outside. Pack (2000a) vividly recalls when a friend told him that he crashed in Erieview Cemetery to sleep off an alcohol binge in 1970: 'And I just looked at him and I wondered why, because you could always get enough money from your friends or bum enough to get a room for a night'.[2]

By the 1990s Pack moved from downtown to the Near West Side, a formerly working-class neighbourhood undergoing gentrification, where he lived in a small room leased to him by an old friend. To supplement his social security check, he started working for the temporary agencies. After a long day racking and plating automobile parts, Pack (2000b) for the first time realized how extensive the housing crisis had become:

> The van from AmeriTemp took us out, and on the way back after the day's work the driver was asking these guys – and these were men who had been working all day and they had been working regularly there – where they wanted to be dropped off. And I thought at first it would be their homes and buildings where they stayed, but they all selected their own [camp] site or own sleeping bag under the different bridges that we passed.

Over the course of his life, Pack witnessed dramatic changes in the city – participating himself in the second great migration north, living at the margins during the peak of the United States reign as the manufacturing centre of the world, and watching the urban and industrial landscape radically transform around him in the post-Fordist era. During the bulk of his adult life, Pack prized the fact that he could quit his job when he was bored or had a grievance and could leave his dwelling place when he felt mistreated by his landlord. For him, the changes taking place in the city are anything but a sign of progress. He argues that they have led to new limitations on mobility and that they have turned the balance of power in favour of landlords and employers. Back in the 1960s,

> you could leave one place in the morning and you could find another that night. There were so many that the tenant was the boss. Today, the landlords have restrictions. You got to have references; you got to have security deposits. They have character checks; earning minimum wage, it is nearly impossible to find any affordable housing. (Pack 2000c)

The capital that flowed into downtown, building new hotels, sports facilities, office buildings, and shopping centres, and flowed out to the new industrial belt on the outskirts of the metropolitan region, dramatically reshaped and constrained the movements of an increasing number of impoverished people in the city (Skeggs 2004). Contingent workers who travelled daily throughout the metropolitan region to work did not make enough to access traditional forms of housing. In addition to their daily travels for work, they needed to traverse the inner ring neighbourhoods of the city to access food, clothing, showers, and refuge. To rest, many turned to the emergency shelters that the city and county established in the 1990s east of the central business district. Seeking to avoid these warehouses, others built encampments on the city sidewalks and in the marginal public spaces they made their own.

The shelter as jail

As the early interviews emphasized and the workshops confirmed, for unhoused Clevelanders the shelter itself most clearly represented the culmination of institutionalized homelessness. I asked my narrators to describe how homelessness had become so entrenched in the city, nearly all responded in part by addressing the role shelters played in their everyday lives. Like Pack, they framed their condition as one marked by restricted movement. Rather than seeing shelters as humanitarian spaces or even as a refuge from the elements, they perceived shelters as sites that were designed to contain them. My archival research in the city's mayoral papers emphasized that this perception was not ill-founded (Kerr 2011).

Shepard (2001), who first went to the emergency men's shelter at the age of 14, explains: 'Basically the shelters are horrible. It's like prison basically. They tell you when to sleep, when to eat'. Johnson (2001) agrees:

> A lot of the shelter programs, the way the people in charge, the staff treats you, is reminiscent of how they were treated while they were behind lock up. To be treated as though we are inmates I think is sort of counterproductive.

On the emergency women's shelter, Crosby (2001) states: 'It's almost like I'm in jail'. An ex-felon himself, Molchan (2001) draws the same conclusion: 'Actually you are in a penitentiary more or less'. (Wells and Germany, 2000) offers a poignant description of his shelter:

> To me it is an open penitentiary. It's not a penitentiary where you got shotguns and towers looking at you, guard dogs or they call the goon squad in your cell to pull you out if you don't come out. Other than that, you know yeah, it's like an open penitentiary.

The emergency shelters have literal parallels to jails – they close their doors at night – no one gets in or out until the morning. The men have a fenced in yard where they can go out to sit and smoke. At the women's shelter, resident Pamela Wagner explains:

> [The staff] know us women, some of us do smoke, so they're decent about that. They're like, 'We go out to have this cigarette, you can come out and have a cigarette too. If we don't go out, nobody goes out. Period.' So that's it. There ain't no playing around. The doors get shut. (O'Dell and Wagner 2000)

Over and over again my narrators expressed a sense of being trapped, caged, and immobile while in the shelter. Comparing the shelter to a jail points to the subjective experience of being oppressed. Feminist theorist Marilyn Frye writes:

> The experience of oppressed people is that the living of one's life is confined and shaped by forces and barriers which are not accidental or occasional and hence avoidable, but are systematically related to each other in such a way as to catch one between and among them and restrict or penalize motion in any direction. It is the experience of being caged in: all avenues, in every direction, are blocked or booby trapped. (1983, p. 4)

This sense of claustrophobia pervades the interviews.

The shelters had originally been built as warehouses in an area just east of the downtown business district. The outmigration of manufacturing, retail, and residents rendered the original uses of the warehouses obsolete. Because the area lacked any residents or merchants that could generate political opposition to a shelter, it became the most politically suitable and practical place to contain unhoused people. Police could push people sleeping on the downtown sidewalks towards the shelter without too much difficulty while nearby labour agencies could recruit from these large pools of labour. Many of these vacant buildings in the 1990s took on a new use – literally warehousing the impoverished. With that said, the shelters also served as homes for many of my narrators (others refused to sleep in the shelters and stayed in camps and abandoned buildings). Getting in the shelter each night required standing in a long line and once inside the shelter residents stood in line a second time to access food. These lines, or liminal spaces (Mountz 2010), became important sites for organizing as residents shared news, flyers, and petitions. They also served as an unintentional space for community building as residents became familiar with people they did not know through the ordeal standing in line next to them. These conversations became an important part of creating a dwelling within this institutional space. Residents had more choice who to sit next to, sleep alongside, and hangout with in the other spaces of the shelter. They turned loading docks into porches as they sat down in circles in the early evening hanging out and politicking. While residents did not have any formal claims to bunks within the facility, they did recognize one another's claims to areas within the shelter – creating a socially recognized division of space within a large undifferentiated room full of bunk beds. Each of these spaces, the lines, the loading docks, and the bunks became important sites for organizing and mobilizing against the shelters and day labour agencies. While residents used the language of immobility to define the shelter, through their everyday practice and micro movements they created dwelling spaces within this hostile institution (Schatzski 1996, Blunt and Dowling 2006, Davidson 2009). These spaces became pivotal to their political efforts that sought to transform the shelter as an institution.

The walking city

Edward Wells uses the term 'open penitentiary', and the word open is significant. Everyday in the morning the shelter residents are kicked out of the men and women's facility by 6:00 a.m. And that begins a day of walking – the twenty-first century city is a walking city for the homeless. Sheptock (2012) argues,

> Homeless people do a lot of traveling. The average person would get out your bed walk a few feet into the kitchen and cook a meal. Homeless people they get out of their bed in shelter or on the street and they have to go a mile, three miles to get their breakfast. And that becomes very time consuming.

Everyday survival requires daily migrations by foot to meal sites, drop-in centres that have showers and clothing, and warm spaces to stay out of the elements during the day. When folks are not heading towards the day labour agencies to get sent out on a shift, they are walking to nearby churches, to social service agencies, to the library, across the river to meals at churches on the Near West Side – all to take care of everyday needs. Appling (1999) argues,

> After you have eaten your meal at St Augustine Church, after you have taken your bath at Cosgrove, you understand this here, you are still back out on the street, with a clean butt and a clean pair of drawers on. But the next day what is it? It is the same thing all around again.

From the shelter, the bath and meal he reference require a seven-mile walk. This daily criss-crossing over the landscape of the city helped to establish an intimate understanding with the city's landscape and played a role in my narrator's claim to the city. Walking facilitated their practices of dwelling as it gave them a clear sense of how spaces changed throughout the day, week, and across seasons. They used this knowledge to establish camps in spaces that remained hidden to housed residents. Sometimes these spaces were in the open in the most public spaces, but they were hidden because no one who mattered to downtown businessmen came to those spaces at night. They knew where the public parks were where they could sit and meet others – the spaces that served as gathering nodes in the many paths across the centre of the city. They knew where and when meal trucks from various churches stopped, and had a clear sense of how urban space was policed. This keen sense of where they were allowed to go and not go helped them navigate through the streets and private spaces downtown in spite of active efforts keep them out of well-trafficked areas. This knowledge also opened up the possibility for them to choose to go to places that were forbidden to them as a form of resistance. Most importantly, it strengthened my narrators' physical claim to the city. As Wagner (2000) argued, 'I have seen so much happen in *my city*'. Addressing ongoing gentrification, Jimenez (1999) argues, 'They are building all these 1, 2, 300,000 dollar homes in *my city*'. The city belonged to my narrators because they walked across it everyday.

Day labour and the van ride

A primary destination for many of these daily walks was one of the city's day labour agencies. Each of the agencies maintained an office within walking distance of the emergency shelters and many of them actively recruited workers within the shelters. Eighty percent of the men and 70 percent of the women who lived in the emergency shelters regularly worked for one of these agencies. My narrators reported that they would arrive at an agency between five and six in the morning, and they would then wait hoping their name would be called. Being in extreme poverty, without access to transportation, and oftentimes with a criminal record hanging over their head many of the unhoused are unable to find work except through these agencies. Johnson (2001) argues getting paid daily is a necessity,

> I know lots of fellows who've missed job opportunities because they weren't going to be paid for the first two, three weeks. And when you're homeless and you have zero dollars in your pocket, or in a bank, that's what you're up against. The temp agencies know that that daily check is what keeps the men and women coming back over and over and over again.

This dependency on day labour agencies is new. Clarence Dailey remembers,

> Back in the '60s and '70s, you could basically walk off one job or get fired from one job and be back on another job within an hour or two. Now, that the temp agencies have taken over control, the companies don't really want to hire anyone because they don't want to pay the benefits, the vacation, the sick pay. (Dailey and Molchan 2001)

As he sees it, the balance of employment risk has shifted increasingly onto the shoulders of the worker. Furthermore, one can no longer walk to most of the jobs that are available.

When arriving at the agency in the morning, day labourers have little idea where they will be sent to work or what kind of job they will do. A study conducted in the summer of 2001 found that the most common job performed by both homeless men (65.3%) and women (66.7%) day labourers was punch press operator. Day labourers also reported working as machine operators, assemblers, operatives in plastics and plating factories, janitors and housekeepers, launderers, gravediggers, welders, painters, tow motor operators, grinders, truck drivers, etc. Homeless men and women were sent out to labour at factories, warehouses, restaurants, hotels, stadiums, city maintenance and landscaping crews, universities, and cemeteries. These workers were assigned the hottest, dirtiest, most back-breaking, and dangerous labour in northeast Ohio (Kerr and Dole 2005).

Hennigan (2001) explains how the dependency on the labour agency for transportation impacts the workers' ability to negotiate the conditions under which they will work:

> You know what benefits a lot of these companies is a lot of these guys are coming in and don't have transportation because they can't afford it. And then they drive you out to some job that's way out in the middle of nowhere.

You're coming from like downtown Cleveland or the inner city somewhere, and you're wanted out in like Saybrook [one hour's drive] or, Twinsburg [45 minute drive], or, God knows where, with no way to get back. So you have the option of working that job, or sitting there and waiting for a ride back. There's no really way you can leave, you can't get out.

It is a mobility the workers have little control over. Even when day labourers do have access to a car, the agencies require them to take the company van to ensure greater oversight into the time workers arrive. While the companies are diligent about delivering workers to the client company on time, interviewees frequently reported that drivers were late picking them up – sometimes four to five hours late after completing their day's work. In other cases, workers reported that the van ride home never materialized, leaving them stranded in a far off suburban location. In neither case were the workers compensated either for their time travelling or for their time waiting for the vans to pick them up. The agencies charge workers for the van rides. Several narrators reported being sent out to a work site where they were not hired and were nevertheless charged for transportation fees. One day labourer found herself in debt to the temporary labour agency after being stranded at a work site for eight hours where she was not needed (Kerr and Dole 2005).

Day labourers typically arrive at the agency around 6:00 a.m. and if they are fortunate, they are sent out on first shift. With an hour-long van ride, workers begin getting paid (almost always the minimum wage) when they check in at the client company's plant. If they work a full day, they will finish their assignment at 5:30 p.m. (a half-hour meal break is unpaid), wait another half hour for the van to come pick them up, arrive back at the agency at 7:00 p.m., and wait an additional hour to receive their check and have it cashed. For a 14-hour day from the time they arrive at the agency to the time they leave, the check includes 8 hours of pay. In addition to deductions for taxes, the day labourer is charged approximately six dollars for the van ride, a dollar for cashing the check, and frequently additional money for safety equipment such as gloves, goggles, or disposable respirators. During the course of this study, minimum wage stood at $5.15 an hour. Workers typically saw less than $30 in their pocket and had actual earnings less than $2.15 an hour. With the present minimum wage ($7.25 an hour) the earnings work out to less than $3.30 an hour (Kerr and Dole 2005).

Robert Molchan addresses the dilemma this puts workers in:
The average guy that works for a temporary service brings home – he may gross forty to fifty-five dollars, all right? But his bring-home after he pays for his ride to and from work, to the job and back from the job, pay his taxes, the taxes that come out of there, Social Security, Medicare, City Tax and Federal Tax, he may bring home thirty dollars, thirty-five dollars – after grossing fifty-five dollars. So out of that thirty, thirty-five dollars, he might have went to the restaurant next door, as which is my case because there is a restaurant next door that

gives us credit so that we can get coffee in the morning, cigarettes in the morning, something for lunch in the morning for when we go to work. By the time you come in and cash your check, you've got thirty-five dollars, you go in, you pay your bill, now you've got twenty-five dollars. You can't get a room for twenty-five dollars. (Dailey and Molchan 2001)

Unlike the shelters, the gathering spaces within the agencies, vans, and work sites offer limited opportunity to critique the agencies themselves. Employees of the labour agencies and sites of employment monitor speech in these spaces and in some companies they prohibit any speech whatsoever on site. The waiting rooms within the agencies proved to be the areas where grievances were most likely aired. Nonetheless, many narrators reported instances of retaliation against those who publicly complained. The fear of not getting sent out to work as a form of punishment loomed large (Kerr and Dole 2005).

While few liked the lack of stable employment, and almost all expressed a desire to have a permanent job, my narrators did argue that their ability to do a wide range of jobs was a testament to their skill as workers. They used their working experience as a means to counter the language that devalued them as 'unskilled' workers. Robert Molchan emphasizes his expertise as a machinist while highlighting the exploitation of the agencies:

Three and a half years ago I was making the main part that stands up in a nuclear reactor as a temp. I was making six bucks an hour. The man that was on the payroll was making eighteen bucks an hour. No difference in what we were doing, except I was a temp and he was on payroll. I still had to mic it, I still had to use the verniers, I still had to go by the blueprints. (Dailey and Molchan 2001)

Untangling the web

In reflecting on the condition of being homeless, Gill (2001) argues, 'It's a system. They set up for you to fail if you're caught in this web'. While assessing the difficulty of finding housing while working day labour, Deuce (1996) concludes, 'We're out here stuck'. In spite of the daily mobility of the unhoused population, by foot and van, this pervasive sense of being stuck speaks to their subjective experience of oppression. As addressed here, there are real limits and real constraints on mobility. The policies of the shelters, the lack of access to transportation, and the loss of cheap hotels across the country all restrict movement. These constraints, however, exist alongside required daily migrations that are an essential part of the survival and labour routines of the unhoused. Given the limited access to jobs, the elimination of general assistance benefits, the federal cuts to welfare, and the organized campaigns to police public space, there is limited choice in these movements. More than the lack of movement, it is the decreased autonomy in controlling one's movements that distinguishes the post-Fordist era from the Fordist one. It is this perceived lack of control that shapes the unhoused narrators' perception of being trapped, stuck, and caged. While my narrators express a sense of being stuck, they demonstrate a sophisticated understanding of the power dynamics that shape their daily movements, including a recognition of the limitations of the efforts to control their bodies. While my narrators intimately understood the reality of their extensive movements, intriguingly they turned to a language of immobility as a means to mobilize resistance. The anxiety of being 'stuck', of claustrophobia, spurred a metaphoric 'movement'. And 'movement' more often then not meant engaging in the practice of dwelling in institutional and public spaces.

The shelter as an institution was nearly universally hated – both by the narrators who lived within them and those who avoided the facilities at all costs. Unhoused people's rejection of the constraints of the shelter led to the emergence of several organized encampments across downtown in the mid-1990s. People turned public sidewalks and parks into dwelling spaces of their own. By the late 1990s, large numbers of people took to sleeping on steam grates across downtown. The most organized camp on the city sidewalks formed outside of the county welfare building. One of my narrators, Calvin Thomas, reflected on how he ended up sleeping there after leaving an extremely overcrowded living condition with his family. He made his way to the welfare building seeking housing assistance, but when none was forthcoming he joined the camp outside. He reflected: 'It was nice because there was a lot of people. They were homeless like I was … We stood out through the winter … we slept outside in the snow.' Thomas (2000) recalls that for the most part everyone worked together: 'It was like a home away from home.' When churches brought food to the camp, the residents organized to ensure it was distributed fairly. When a few newcomers began hassling the church groups, the others formed a group called Rosewater 2000 to ensure that the area in front of the welfare building would remain 'a charitable zone'. They helped create a space where people could sleep safely and network with supporters on the city sidewalks (Kerr 2011).

By 1999, this camp and others had created significant tensions with downtown business leaders. During the Christmas holiday season, Cleveland Mayor Mike White responded to their concerns and commenced a campaign to arrest people sleeping on the downtown sidewalks and parks. He turned to a 70-year-old ordinance that prohibited leaving trash on the sidewalk – arguing the bedding, the belongings, and the sleeping people themselves were subject to this law. He reasoned the arrests would have the humanitarian result of forcing the homeless to move to the emergency shelters. But he made no effort hide his primary motivation. In a press release, he justified the campaign as a necessary tactic to 'attract holiday shoppers downtown and revelers to the Flats' (Kerr 2011, p. 233).

To counter the mayor's new policy, the unhoused used their intricate understanding of the city's downtown landscape to settle in the place where they were most explicitly unwanted. On an evening three days before Christmas, as thousands of city residents came down to Public Square to see the yearly display of Christmas lights, several hundred unhoused people and their supporters gathered on Public Square and erected a colourful shantytown in front of the mall at Tower City. On the very site where I had conducted my video interviews, they constructed a large tent out of blue tarps – building their own nativity scene with themselves as the living characters to reference Mary and Joseph's inability to access housing. They hung banners saying, 'We're not Dreaming of a White Christmas!' and 'I'm Homeless, Arrest Me!' They passed out flyers to stunned onlookers and attracted a throng of reporters by the spectacle of defiance. At 3:00 a.m. the mayor came downtown to oversee the police raid of the encampment. As the police tore down the tents and arrested the protestors, television news cameras caught the mayor directing the operation from a large plate glass window across the street. While the camp came down and five people were arrested, the next morning the American Civil Liberties Union sought an injunction in federal court against the mayor's policy. City attorney Anthony Garafoli countered: 'We are not harassing them. We want them in shelters. We don't want them on the streets.' The federal judge issued an injunction to prevent the further removal of unhoused people from downtown sidewalks. In February 2000, the city formally agreed not to arrest or threaten to detain any individuals for 'performing innocent, harmless, inoffensive acts such as sleeping, eating, lying, or sitting in or on public property' (Kerr 2011, pp. 233–234). Through their protest, the protestors solidified their right to create dwelling spaces on public property.

That July the city sought to demolish a building that had been taken over and turned into an encampment by another group of unhoused people. The residents dubbed the former bakery building Camelot. Within the cavernous building they set up a basketball court, established their own bedrooms, and marked these spaces as their own with various creative flourishes (Campbell 2000a). The city sent a delegation of outreach workers with maps to show the residents of Camelot (Figure 1) where they could find the emergency shelters. One resident, Dave Campbell, responded to the city's proposal in a letter to the mayor: 'We wonder why you keep sending people out to ask us to sleep in a shelter when we have our own housing here at Camelot.' He invited the mayor to visit:

> We will have food and can provide you with a bunk if you want to sleep over. We would love to sit down and discuss the sad state of the shelters in Cleveland, the lack of affordable housing, or our fine house that we have constructed for ourselves here on E. 55th and Chester. (Campbell 2000b)

The mayor did not respond to the bold offer; rather he set a deadline for the residents to leave. The residents sent out a series of press releases declaring they would not move. The pledge brought flocks of reporters from the local press to the building the night before the city planned to demolish the building. Dozens of supporters of Camelot set up an encampment outside its entrance in an effort to shield those inside. The following morning top figures in the mayor's administration, including his Development Director, Chief of Police, Safety Department Director, and a handful of his assistants, stood outside the building bewildered by the occupants' militant refusal to leave their home. Throughout the day, the story became the biggest news event in the city, as reporters flocked to the residents seeking interviews (Kerr 2011). While the building was eventually cleared and torn down, a small handful of unhoused people ground the machinery of development to a halt for a day by refusing to move. In both this case and the protest on Public Square, the unhoused had created a dwelling space as a deliberate act of resistance.

While many resisted the shelters from outside the institutions, others did so from within. In the 1990s the city established a series of men's and women's 'emergency' shelters that were supposed to be temporary way stations towards transitional and then permanent housing. They were not meant to become a home. Within these spaces, residents had neither rights to a permanent bunk of their own nor a place to store their belongings. The Salvation Army and other non-profit groups that ran the shelters for the city and

Figure 1 Dave Campbell shows off his 'fine house' in Camelot. Note the hanging suit jacket, the family photo on the table, and the wig underneath.

county refused to allow the people who lived in these facilities to join a resident's council nor have a say in how the facility was run (Kerr 2008). Nonetheless, the residents redefined the meaning of the spaces within these adapted warehouses, turned lines into community gathering places and loading docks into porches, and used these spaces within the shelter to organize against both the day labour agencies and the shelter operators.

Meeting in a common area in the city's largest emergency shelter, which was run by the Salvation Army, residents formed the Low Wage Workers' Union (LWWU) in the fall of 2000. In early 2001 the group began collecting signatures in the long lines at the shelter and on the loading docks seeking to establish a strict code of conduct for all labour agents that recruited workers within the shelters. Seeking to protect their domestic space from the commercial world, they argued the shelter was their home and predatory agents should not be allowed in. Our studies had found that these agents were especially egregious in giving misinformation about wages, hours, and working conditions (Kerr and Dole 2005). The executives within the day labour companies, however, had close ties with the shelter operators, gave donations to the non-profits that ran the shelters, and even had representatives that sat on the advisory board of the Salvation Army. The LWWU collected over two hundred signatures from the three hundred residents in the men's shelter. Ultimately the Salvation Army acquiesced to the residents' wishes and banned all labour agents from recruiting in its facilities. The women's shelter followed suit shortly thereafter (Kerr 2008).

The campaign to ban labour agents from the shelters led to an even more ambitious petition drive by the facility's residents. In 2002 they sought to ban the Salvation Army itself from operating the shelter. Raymond Robinson began organizing the petition drive after hearing the shelter staff refer to the residents as 'maggots'. He argued: 'This particular staff, they are disrespectful, they are uncaring, they are just plain downright full of malice and hatred against the residents that stay at Lakeside.' The staff had become outsiders in the residents' home. Not only had the Salvation Army failed to provide any of the services it promised before it opened the shelter in 2000, the organization demanded that the residents in Robinson's words 'completely turn over their lives to the organization' to gain access to minor privileges, including better food, a permanent bed, a locker and the ability to stay in the facility 24 hours a day. Over 350 men living in the shelter signed a petition calling for the city to remove the Salvation Army in order to 'rectify and otherwise change these inhumane and unjustified acts of degradation against us' (Robinson 2002).

Over the next several months an unauthorized residents' committee lobbied City Council to 'remove' the Salvation Army from the shelter and allow the men living in the facility to run the site. The Salvation Army refused to negotiate with the group or give into any of its demands. The organization, however, fired the director of the shelter, freshly painted the interior with pastel colours, and alleviated some of the most abusive practices of its staff. In spite of these reforms, in December 2004 the city and county ended its contract with the Salvation Army to run the shelter and turned the facility over to Lutheran Metropolitan Ministries. While the residents were unable to take over the shelter, they showed that by tapping into the power that arose out of the dwelling spaces they created and the practices of dwelling they engaged within the shelter, they would be able to reconfigure the policies that shaped their lives (Robinson 2002, Kerr 2011).

As Ralph Pack argues, taking a 'Chicago detour' today would be substantially more difficult than it was in the mid-twentieth century. Leaving an apartment in the morning and finding another that afternoon is unheard of for a growing percentage of people living in poverty. Whole districts of cheap hotels and rooming houses have been levelled while tens and thousands of other affordable units have been destroyed. The experience of being hired at the factory gate has become a distant memory. Day labour agencies have managed to become an integral part of the labour market over the past 40 years. As wages have decreased and access to affordable housing has been curtailed, homelessness has become an entrenched institution in the urban landscape. A growing number of people without housing find their lives and movements constrained by shelters, day labour agencies, and policing strategies that seek to regulate their movements.

The city's effort to create spaces for containing and confining the unhoused unintentionally led to the creation of spaces that cultivated unique forms of resistance. The unhoused are especially attuned to the structures of power that limit the autonomy they have over their own movements. Using this understanding, they have deliberately chosen to create dwelling spaces where they are unwanted or where they were never meant to make a claim of home. In the context of homelessness in the twenty-first century, the very practice of dwelling can be a radical act through which the unhoused build power by laying claim to home.

Notes

1. All interviews in the Cleveland Homeless Oral History Project have been donated to the Cleveland Public Library.
2. Rossi (1989) concludes from his research that skid row residents in the 1960s had incomes three times higher than the homeless of the late 1980s.

Disclosure statement

No potential conflict of interest was reported by the author.

References

Adey, P. (2010) *Aerial Life: Spaces, Mobilities, Affects*, Malden, MA, Wiley Blackwell.

Appling, J. (1999) Interview with author, September 5, 1999, Public Square, Cleveland, Ohio.

Bahr, H. (1973) *Skid Row: An Introduction to Disaffiliation*, New York, Oxford University Press.

Blunt, A. & Dowling, R. (2006) *Home*, London, Routledge.

Bogue, D. (1963) *Skid Row in American Cities*, Chicago, Community and Family Study Center.

Campbell, D. (2000a) Interview with author, July 17, 2000, Frost Radio, Cleveland, Ohio.

Campbell, D. (2000b) Open letter from Rosewater 2000 to Mayor Mike White, July 31, in author's possession.

Cresswell, T. (2006) *On the Move*, London, Routledge.

Crosby, B. (2001) Interview with author, May 8, 2001, Frost Radio, Cleveland, Ohio.

Dailey, C. & Molchan, R. (2001) Interview with author, March 20, 2001, Frost Radio, Cleveland, Ohio.

Davidson, T. (2009) 'The role of domestic architecture in the structuring of memory', *Space and Culture*, vol. 12, no. 3, pp. 332–342.

Deleuze, G. & Guattari, F. (1983) *Anti-Oedipus: Capitalism and Schizophrenia*, Minneapolis, University of Minnesota Press.

Deuce (1996) Interview with author, September 29, 1996, Public Square, Cleveland, Ohio.

Frye, M. (1983) *The Politics of Reality: Essays in Feminist Theory*, Freedom, CA, The Crossing Press.

Gill, D. (2001) Interview with author, October 23, 2001, Frost Radio, Cleveland, Ohio.

Hennigan, M. (2001) Interview with author, May 15, 2001, Frost Radio, Cleveland, Ohio.

Jimenez, J. (1999) Interview with author, September 5, 1999, Public Square, Cleveland, Ohio.

Johnson, J. J. (2001) Interview with author, June 5, Frost Radio, Cleveland, Ohio.

Kerr, D. (2003) '"We know what the problem is": using oral history to develop a collaborative analysis of homelessness from the bottom up', *Oral History Review*, vol. 30, no. 1, pp. 227–245.

Kerr, D. (2008) 'Countering corporate narratives from the streets: the Cleveland Homeless Oral History Project', in *Oral History and Public Memories*, eds. P. Hamilton & L. Shopes, Philadelphia, Temple University Press, pp. 231–251.

Kerr, D. (2011) *Derelict Paradise: Homelessness and Urban Development in Cleveland*, Amherst, University of Massachusetts Press.

Kerr, D. & Dole, C. (2005) 'Cracking the temp trap: day laborers' grievances and strategies for change in Cleveland, Ohio', *Labor Studies Journal*, vol. 29, pp. 87–108.

Molchan, R. (2001) Interview with author, March 20, 2001, Frost Radio, Cleveland, Ohio.

Mountz, A. (2010) *Seeking Asylum: Human Smuggling and Bureaucracy at the Border*, Minneapolis, University of Minnesota Press.

O'Dell, D. & Wagner, P. (2000) Interview with author, September 24, 2000, Public Square, Cleveland, Ohio.

Pack, R. (1999) Interview with author, September 12, 1999, Public Square, Cleveland, Ohio.

Pack, R. (2000a) Interview with author, January 19, 2000, Cleveland Public Library, Cleveland, Ohio.

Pack, R. (2000b) Interview with author, June 6, 2000, Frost Radio, Cleveland, Ohio.

Pack, R. (2000c) Interview with author, July 30, 2000, Frost Radio, Cleveland, Ohio.

Robinson, R. (2002) Interview with Chris Dole, June 18, 2002, Frost Radio, Cleveland, Ohio.

Rossi, P. (1989) *Down and Out in America*, Chicago, Chicago University Press.

Schatzki, T. (1996) *Social Practices: A Wittgensteinian Approach to Human Activity and the Social*, Cambridge, Cambridge University Press.

Sheller, M. (2011) 'Mobility', *Sociopedia.isa*. doi:10.1177/205684601163

Shepard, D. (2001) Interview with author, May 15, 2001, Frost Radio, Cleveland, Ohio.

Sheptock, E. (2012) Interview with Alison Kootstra, MLK branch of DCPL, Washington, DC

Skeggs, B. (2004). *Class, Self, Culture*, London: Routledge.

Thomas, C. (2000). Interview with author, November 14, 2000, Frost Radio, Cleveland, Ohio.

Virilio, P. (1997). *The Open Sky*, London: Verso.

Wagner, P. (2000). Interview with author, August 8, 2000, Frost Radio, Cleveland, Ohio.

Wells, E. & Germany, J. (2000). Interview with author, March 14, 2000, Bishop Cosgrove, Cleveland, Ohio.

DWELLING IN THE TEMPORARY
The involuntary mobility of displaced Georgians in rented accommodation

Cathrine Brun

Department of Geography, Norwegian University of Science and Technology (NTNU), Trondheim, Norway

ABSTRACT
This article responds to the call from forced migration studies for increased engagement with the mobilities paradigm, as well as to criticism of the mobilities paradigm for not engaging sufficiently with immobility and power relations. The article analyses the experiences and strategies of internally displaced persons (IDPs) in rented dwellings in Tbilisi, in the South Caucasus state of Georgia, who are among the most mobile groups of IDPs in that country. To understand the relationship between mobility and immobility, the article applies Heidegger's notion of 'dwelling' and more recent developments of that notion, together with the discussion between Honneth and Fraser on 'recognition'. First, the article introduces internal displacement in Georgia. Second, it discusses the housing situation for the IDPs. Third, the theoretical concepts of 'dwelling' and 'recognition' are developed to enable analysis of experiences and practices of mobility and immobility. Fourth, the various trajectories through which IDPs have come into their rented dwellings are discussed, and processes of deterritorialization and reterritorialization and the experience of recognition through the dwelling are analysed. The conclusion addresses the role of dwelling and recognition for efforts to understand the relationship between mobility and immobility.

Staying in one place makes you into someone .... I do not move homes, I just move houses. (Displaced 33-year-old Georgian man from Abkhazia, living in rented accommodation in Tbilisi with his mother)

Introduction

Since the early 1990s, approximately 250,000 Georgians who fled Abkhazia following its battle for independence from Georgia have lived as internally displaced persons (IDPs) at different locations in Georgia. The experiences of these IDPs parallel those of many people displaced by war across the globe: Displacement by war is more often than not protracted. The IDP status is a temporary one and is only intended as a short-term measure for when people need extra protection and assistance while a more permanent solution is sought. However, the temporary status of displaced persons and refugees often lasts for 5, 10, 20 or more years and is experienced by many as a permanent temporariness (see Brun 2008, Brun and Fàbos in press). There seems to be, however, a reluctance on the part of national and international actors to solve the various displacement crises that have become a symptom of our time: these are crises that are not inevitable, but result from political action and inaction (Loescher and Milner 2009). The image of the visible, encamped and passive displaced person often stands in contrast to the many self-settled IDPs and refugees in the world. Self-settled IDPs and refugees are people who live with family and friends or in rented dwellings, often in urban areas. Frequently less visible than people in organized settlements, often not living in the place where they first registered as displaced – if they registered at all – and having less access to assistance and protection, self-settled displaced people represent a heterogeneous group about whom we know much less than we do about the paradigmatic victim[1] of the encamped refugee.

In this article, I analyse the experience of self-settled IDPs residing in rented dwellings, who are among the most mobile of the displaced people in Georgia (DRC 2011). IDPs renting their residences move reluctantly but frequently from dwelling to dwelling – some as often as every year. They thus experience a double temporariness. First, their temporary status as IDPs is conditioned on a possible future return to where they were displaced from; they wait for return and in the meantime reside temporarily in their current dwellings. Second, people do not stay very long in one rented dwelling before moving on to the next; they live very temporary lives in the dwellings they occupy. The relationship of these individuals to their temporary dwellings is conditioned by their humanitarian status as IDPs, by their socio-economic status, and by the strong desire within Georgian society to keep people in the IDP status because the existence of these IDPs and their possible return to Abkhazia symbolize the hope of regaining control over Abkhazia.

The current globally accepted status of 'IDP' is a complex category that involves political, legal, humanitarian, social, cultural and economic dimensions. Despite the mobility of the internally displaced, people falling into this category have been fixed in significant ways to particular territories and particular locations. Understanding the mobility of the self-settled IDPs in Georgia may thus respond to the call from forced migration studies (Gill et al. 2011, Hyndman and Giles 2011) and carceral geographies (Moran et al. 2012) for a more sophisticated understanding of power relations in research on mobility (see also Faist 2013). Inherent in this call is a critique of the tendency of existing mobilities research to draw a connection between mobility, autonomy and freedom (Moran *et al.* 2012). The publications that introduced the mobilities paradigm opened up for research on the relationship between movement and moorings, and even mentioned forced migration (see Hannam *et al.* 2006, Urry 2007, Sheller 2011), but such perspectives have not been particularly prominent in mobilities research until recently. In addition, refugees and IDPs – once displaced – are often depicted as immobile and passive (see Malkki 1992, Hyndman and Giles 2011). There is scope for more discussion across the two fields of mobilities research and forced migration regarding the extent to which mobility indicates agency, and immobility the inability to move. Further problematization of the relationship between mobility and immobility – or what in this context would more appropriately be called 'stillness' (see Gill 2009, Cresswell 2012) – will improve the way in which we view society through the lens of mobility. In this context, it is particularly the ways in which people's mobilities are regulated, the ways in which people challenge the regimes set to control them, and the role of humanitarian categories or statuses that are most relevant. Inspired by the call from Hyndman and Giles (2011) to engage with the mobilities paradigm in forced migration studies, I seek to illustrate the tensions inherent in the experience of mobility and the role of the status of 'IDP' in this experience. I will examine the relationship between mobility, immobility and the role of the IDP status by applying Heidegger's notion of dwelling and Honneth and Fraser's discussion of 'recognition'.

I explore the relationship between mobility and immobility through an analysis of the experience and practices of dwelling in the temporary by examining, first, internal displacement in Georgia and, second, the housing situation for the internally displaced. Then, third, I engage theoretically with 'dwelling' and 'recognition' to develop an understanding of how to analyse the experience and practices of mobility and immobility. Fourth, I discuss the various trajectories IDPs have had into their rented dwellings before analysing processes of deterritorialization and reterritorialization and the experience of recognition through the dwelling.

I seek to apply the conceptual approaches mentioned above to material gathered as part of a larger project on homemaking in temporary dwellings during protracted displacement. In the larger project, I interviewed 39 IDPs in the urban centres of Tbilisi and Kutaisi during two periods of fieldwork in Georgia in 2010 and 2012 (Brun 2012, 2015a, b). Of those interviewed, nine were renting, while two interviewees had rented earlier. I also interviewed representatives from 15 UN and nongovernmental organizations and two government departments. As I discuss below, people in rented accommodation are difficult to find as they are relatively invisible. The networks I used to access interviewees in rented accommodation differed from those of my earlier research in the country in 2003, and I relied on organizations and research assistants for finding research participants. Since I do not speak Georgian, the research assistants also acted as interpreters. All quotations are thus the interpreters' translations from Georgian to English.

Internal displacement, territoriality and the governance of mobility in Georgia

As the new postcolonial nation-states emerged following the dissolution of the Soviet Union, nationalist movements led to the 'unmixing' (Brubaker 1995) of some ethnic groups and what could be termed a 'reclaiming of the past' (Kuzio 2002). In 1992, when Abkhazia declared independence from Georgia, 46 % of the population in Abkhazia was ethnic Georgians. The Georgian authorities refused to accept the secession claim, and Georgian forces entered Abkhazia to regain the disputed territory. During the fighting and after the defeat of the Georgian forces, the ethnic Georgian population, fled their homes in Abkhazia and the majority moved in to Western and central Georgia. The conflict left an estimated 10,000 people dead and some 250,000 displaced (Amnesty International 2010). In 2014, the conflict may be described as being frozen, with periodic outbursts of war – most recently the war between Russia and Georgia in August 2008. Since the 2008 war, many scholars believe that Georgia has de facto lost control over Abkhazia (Kabachnik 2012), but the nationalist discourse of a unified Georgia, including Abkhazia, remains strong, and the internally displaced play an important role in keeping alive Georgia's hopes of regaining control over Abkhazia.

Georgia's territorial claim on Abkhazia continues to influence policies towards the IDPs. Most of those displaced in the 1990s have retained their IDP status until now. The Georgian government readily accepted the individuals fleeing Abkhazia as IDPs and established a number of initiatives to assist them with housing and living costs. A law on IDPs was adopted in 1996, though a state strategy for IDPs was not put into place until 2007 (Government of Georgia 2007). This inertia in establishing a formal state strategy may be partly accounted for by the fact that return was strongly desired both by the IDPs themselves and by the Georgian government. Indeed, return is still believed by the government and most IDPs to represent the only valid solution to the displacement and the conflict between Georgia and Abkhazia. Kabachnik (2012) describes the discourse on return, and the accompanying uncertainty and fear surrounding questions related to Georgian nationality and territorial integrity, as 'Georgia's cartographic anxiety'. He likens the gaining of independence by a separatist region to an '"amputation", leaving "wounds" and "scars"' (Kabachnik 2012, p. 47). Accordingly, the return of the IDPs to Abkhazia is a concern not just for the IDPs themselves, but for the whole Georgian nation. The prolonged IDP status must be understood in the context of this need for a continued inclusion of Abkhazia in Georgia.

The ethnic Georgian IDPs that settled in Georgia after their displacement were often born in Abkhazia and, although ethnically Georgian, were more often fluent in Russian than in the Georgian language. Though well educated, they struggled after their displacement to find employment in the collapsing labour market of the newly independent state. Most IDPs settled and continue to live in Western Georgia and in and around the Georgian capital Tbilisi. The government of Georgia regulates their mobility in various ways, but a substantial number – perhaps as many as half – live in places other than where they are registered as IDPs (DRC 2011). Since 2008, it has become more difficult for IDPs to transfer their displacement status from one place to another, and it is no longer possible to transfer this displacement status from a place in 'the regions'[2] to Tbilisi. Before the new state strategy was put in place, the location of registration did not affect people's status or access to IDP benefits. However, as housing became a primary focus of assistance, the importance of the location of registration changed, as this location formed the basis for where housing assistance would be provided.[3]

The multiplicity of dwelling(s)

In the context of the new state strategy, people are categorized according to their dwellings. The main categories cover the collective centres, which are mainly provided by the government of Georgia, and accommodation in the private sector. Collective centres comprise a heterogeneous set of buildings, such as student dormitories, hotels, kindergartens, hospitals and accommodation built for factory workers but occupied by IDPs for the last 20 years. These centres are generally not designed for permanent occupation or for families.

The collective centres are the most visible form of dwellings for IDPs. There is a degree of social stigma attached to living in these centres, but at the same time they also represent an important social base for many of the residents and are considered a relatively stable form of housing.

Private-sector accommodation is believed to have accounted for approximately half of the dwellings of IDPs when the state strategy was established in 2007. There is little available information about the 'privately accommodated IDPs', but it is common to distinguish between three types of dwellings: owned, borrowed and rented. According Georgia's Ministry of Refugees and Accommodation (MRA), there were 4,396 families who *owned* their dwellings in 2007 (MRA 2010). The second type of dwelling in the private sector is *borrowed dwellings* – that is, where people stay with family and friends or in an empty house without paying rent. The latter seems to be more common in rural areas and regional capitals than in Tbilisi, where housing is scarce. The third category, which will be the focus in the remainder of this article, covers *rented dwellings*. The second and third categories in the private sector are believed to encompass approximately 40,000 families (MRA 2010).

Through the government's 'durable housing solutions' from 2007,[4] housing assistance to the displaced has largely concerned transfer of ownership[5] of IDPs' existing living spaces in the collective centres (MRA 2010). So far, it is primarily the transfer of ownership of uncontested spaces in the collective centres that has been completed. Some people in collective centres that were privately owned have been asked to move and given compensation of USD 7,500, which the MRA considers a 'durable housing solution'. No new dwelling spaces are planned for IDPs living in Tbilisi under the national strategy, but there are plans to build new houses in the regions, and work on this has already begun in some places. IDPs who already own a house will be provided with a one-off monetary payment. The strategy states that it is not known how many in the private sector will need housing or monetary support, and no specific plans have been made for those in rented accommodation. The state strategy is vague on the issue of how assistance might be provided to IDPs not living where they are registered. To help people where they are currently living has been listed as one of the goals, but it seems that assistance is being offered to people on the basis of where they are registered, not where they dwell. People living in rented accommodation have seen the assistance that the more visible group of people in the collective centres has received and are waiting for the state to look in their direction and recognize their needs and dreams for more stable dwellings.

Dwelling in a temporary status

As both a noun and a verb, dwelling implies a particular place or locale and an activity; it gives no indication of time, nor that the place or locale in question is static, so one can dwell both temporarily and permanently, and one can dwell while in motion. (Long 2013, p. 332)

The expression 'a dwelling' refers to a residence, an abode, but 'dwelling' may also be a verb – it is a way of being, a way of doing and a way of relating. In this article, these two meanings of 'dwelling' – as a verb and as a noun – overlap. The notion of 'dwelling' has become inseparable from the (later) work of Martin Heidegger. In his famous essay 'Building Dwelling Thinking', dwelling is about being in the world; it is to live and to be at home in the world, rather than merely existing: 'The way in which you are and I am, the manner in which we humans *are* on the earth is *Buan*, dwelling' (Heidegger [1954] 1971, p.145). Being in the world is about being somewhere – a place where we make the world meaningful (Cresswell 2009, p. 171). Dwelling in Heideggerian terms may be described as a form of 'nest, where people open a space of being, and initiate and secure bordered place, sheltering themselves from the outside world' (Gielis and Van Houtum 2012, p. 800).

Heidegger's 'dwelling' – despite the implicit nationalism and authenticity embedded in the concept (Elden 2001, Harrison 2007) – has been interpreted in many different ways within the social sciences. It has come to dominate much of the writing on dwelling and home in the booming research trend on home that we have seen in recent years (see Mallett 2004, Blunt and Dowling 2006). Dwelling has been used in the humanist tradition of togetherness, belongingness and wholeness, as well as in the post-humanist/anti-humanist tradition, and could be seen as a precursor to actor-network theory and the latter's notion of the 'fourfold' (Harrison 2007). A common denominator for much work inspired by Heidegger is the emphasis on the relational nature of dwelling (Latimer and Munro 2009). Keeping things, enabling the caretaking of material and non-material relations of which we are a part, is essential for how dwelling will be understood in the remainder of this article. Through their dwelling people engage with their surroundings, and the dwelling is the starting point for how people become involved in society and how people can build social relations. The notion of dwelling has the potential to enable improved understanding of the relationship between the inside and the outside, the public and the private; dwelling is a space of both the self and the other (Varley 2008).

How, then, might Heidegger's notion of dwelling be a relevant starting point for studying the relationship between mobility and immobility? Two fundamental dimensions of 'dwelling' emerge from the interviews I have analysed. The first concerns the urge to find or establish a place in society, a struggle that corresponds with dwelling as being in the world. For IDPs in rented dwellings, the meaning of mobility in the process of dwelling becomes crucial, as I show below. The second dimension considers how dwelling is meaningful and influential for how the internally displaced are considered by society, how IDPs relate to others in that society, and how society relates to them.

A meeting point in these two understandings of dwelling is the seeking of recognition by the displaced. Though citizens of the country in which they reside as internally displaced, Georgian IDPs often express a feeling of not being recognized as members of that society, suggesting that their status as internally displaced excludes them from full membership because they are always only temporarily present: there is a societal expectation that they will return to Abkhazia. In order to frame the analysis of dwelling and include power relations, I introduce the process of 'recognition', which makes it possible to see how this involuntary mobile population can find its place and relate to others in the Georgian society. This process of recognition engages with a multiplicity of scales, and concerns people's identity and societal status. Discussions between Axel Honneth and Nancy Fraser on the meaning of recognition provide an important example of how recognition may be engaged with at different scales (Fraser and Honneth 2003). Though Honneth and Fraser see their models as irreconcilable,[6] I find it useful to consider the two models together. Inspired by Hegel, Honneth (1995, 2002) considers recognition as key to specifying the conditions under which human beings can form an identity, and thus focuses on three modes of recognition (Kofoed and Simonsen 2012): the private sphere, the legal sphere and a sphere of achievement. In his understanding, it is through these spheres that an individual's self-confidence and sense of membership in a community is established. In the private sphere, Honneth (1992, p. 193) describes recognition as the emotional ties that are developed in families and among friends, where 'people acknowledge each other with special feelings of appreciation'. In the legal sphere, it is the mutual recognition that persons have in identifying each other as persons who share equal rights and responsibilities. Recognition takes place, according to Honneth (1992), when individuals see themselves as sharing the same legal rights as all other members of their community. Finally, the sphere of achievement represents social acceptance – even acceptance of 'unconventional lifestyles'; it is a form of solidarity experienced between members of a society. These spheres of recognition set out a moral infrastructure that is a precondition for a social life-world able to protect its members.

Honneth emphasizes that the identity model of recognition does not outline an institutional framework in which these forms of recognition may be realized. Here, Nancy Fraser's status model of recognition[7] becomes useful for including the institutional mechanisms that contribute to realize people's social standing in the society. Her formulation of the status model of recognition is a response to Honneth's identity model, which she criticizes of simplifying group identity and hence obscure the complexity of people's lives (Fraser 2001). Fraser emphasizes an understanding of recognition that helps to reintroduce redistribution as an important dimension of the struggle for recognition. Redistribution is related to socio-economic injustices such as exploitation, economic marginalization and being deprived of an adequate material standard of living. According to Fraser, misrecognition takes place when institutions structure interaction according to cultural norms that impede parity of participation. Examples of such institutional practices might include the ways in which mobile populations are treated in a society, or property laws and social welfare policies that stigmatize certain groups in a society. The aim of the status model of recognition is to 'establish the subordinated party as a full partner in social life, able to interact with others as peers' (Fraser 2001, p. 25).

The status model of recognition has been accused of attempting to analytically separate redistribution and cultural identity (Young 1997), and of inconsistency (Armstrong 2008). Nevertheless, I find Fraser's work meaningful and an important contribution when used in combination with Honneth's spheres of recognition to analyse dwelling and status as a way of understanding (im) mobility and protracted displacement. For example, the IDP category changes content during protracted situations of displacement, as it shifts from a humanitarian category to a social category (Brun 2010). The IDP category becomes part of people's identities and shapes the experience of various social positions. There is a tendency to treat people only as displaced, whereby the humanitarian status becomes more prominent and visible than other statuses and categories. By introducing the status model of recognition, with its more direct emphasis on redistribution and recognition and misrecognition, we can better understand the relationship between dwelling (as a noun and a verb), the temporary status and mobility.

Trajectories towards the rented dwelling

There are two different renting systems in Georgia, both for IDPs and non-IDPs. The first is called *Kira* in the vernacular. In *Kira*, rent is paid on a monthly basis and the period for which the dwelling is rented is often not specified. The second system is called *Gira*, which means 'mortgaged apartment', under which a deposit is paid to the owner/landlord and property is rented for a specified number of years, normally two or three. A contract is made between the renter and the owner that states that when the contract period is over, the owner must give the deposit back. In the meantime, the owner has access to money that can be invested in other projects, and thus the deposit may be considered a type of loan. There are substantial risks involved in *Gira*. One problem is the possibility of a decrease in the value of the currency during the contract period. Those I interviewed paid between USD 10,000 and 15,000 for their *Gira*, which is less than the cost of buying a flat on the outskirts of Tbilisi. Of the interviewees in the material analysed here, three were renting under the *Gira* system.

Trajectories towards and into rented accommodation varied considerably among the people I interviewed, but some common paths may be identified among this most mobile group of IDPs (DRC 2011). Many interviewees moved from the regions and into Tbilisi quite early on in the history of their displacement, following the intensive urbanization that has taken place since independence. They managed to find vacant rooms in a collective centre and later had those rooms transferred to their ownership. However, people did not stop coming to Tbilisi after vacant rooms in collective centres became scarce; people's mobile lives towards rented dwellings are distinguished by the search for livelihoods and better life chances. Before arriving in Tbilisi, some people lived in collective centres in the regions, but others were renting. Those who were renting could often no longer pay the rent where they were living and had to move. Wages in Tbilisi are higher than in the regions, but living costs are also higher. Some people moved to Tbilisi from the regions, but were later provided with a dwelling in the region in which they originally registered; however, when they returned to occupy that dwelling, they were often unable to find employment and decided to move back to Tbilisi and rent a dwelling in the city.

> The first place we lived after displacement was Senaki [Western Georgia]. Our registration is in Senaki. We want to change our registration to Tbilisi, but we cannot do that. We were renting a house in Senaki. My father worked in the army. But later – when the economic conditions in the country deteriorated – we could not pay the rent. So we had to move from there. After I finished school, we moved from there and we rented a room in Tbilisi. Then for two years we lived in a collective centre, but we were kicked out from there when the collective centre was sold. My mother went to Russia, my father moved back and forth between Tbilisi and Senaki where he has started an agricultural business. We have lived in this place [a rented room in a collective centre], and we are waiting for the government to give us a room. (Young displaced man, just finished a degree at Tbilisi University)

Some buildings used as collective centres were handed over or sold to private owners, and their residents had to move and were given USD 7,500 in compensation. Many found, however, that the compensation was insufficient to buy a dwelling in the city. The money they received was used for rent and other outlays, such as medical expenses in the privatized healthcare system or the deposit in the *Gira* system.

One family I interviewed lived in a collective centre in a village close to Batumi (in Adjara, Western Georgia). When their collective centre was to be sold, the family was reluctant to move as they had employment and friends and relatives in the immediate vicinity. However, they were forced to do so and given the standard compensation of USD 7,500. One of the sons in the family worked in the military in Tbilisi, and the whole family (husband, wife, wife's father, two sons, a daughter, a daughter-in-law and a baby) decided to move to the city. Their *Gira*-rented flat in Tbilisi had one small bedroom, one living room, a kitchen and a bathroom.

Another category of internally displaced in rented dwellings are those who have been abroad for some period of time during their displacement. Many individuals and families went to Russia after their displacement from Abkhazia. There were already close links with Russia. Many people had studied in Russia or had family members there. Additionally, until the 2008 war, Russia was the main destination country for labour migration from Georgia. However, with the relationship between Russia and Georgia turning sour, many irregular and regular Georgian migrants in Russia returned to Georgia. Some were deported and others left because of the increasing difficulty of being Georgian in Russia. Georgians who had lived in Abkhazia were granted IDP status when they returned from Russia. Along with the IDP status, they were also provided with USD 2,000 to help them begin their new lives. Many people had lost their savings on the journey back to Georgia or were unable to access those savings. While some found a living space in a collective centre, mainly assisted by family and friends, others ended up in rented accommodation in Tbilisi.

Displacement has taken place over a period of 20 years, and the second generation of internally displaced is now gravitating towards the city. In Georgian society, many children continue to live with their parents after marriage, but some move out to find their own living spaces. The Georgian proposals for durable housing solutions, however, contain no measures for the second generation. Solutions are formulated on the basis of the original family that moved from Abkhazia 20 years earlier. The fact that those who were children during displacement have now grown up and started their own families has not been taken into account. Members of the second generation need to find their own places in society and may move from the regions towards the city for education and employment.

Deterritorialization/reterritorialization

> I do not remember how many places I have stayed for the last 10 years, maybe nine or ten? … Sometimes I was living there for a couple of years, sometimes for a couple of months. Often when you arrive at a new place, it is not in the condition that the house owner promised, so you immediately start looking for a new place. And then you move again. Another time we rented and didn't know the house was for sale, and then soon after we had moved in, the house was sold and we had to move. It is difficult to move houses all the time. (Displaced man, aged 33, living in rented accommodation with his mother)

There have been attempts to bring Heidegger's notion of dwelling into conversation with the work of other scholars in order to reorient 'dwelling' (Harrison 2007). Gielis and Van Houtum (2012) explore the relationship between Heidegger's *monadic* (being, permanence) and Deleuze and Guattari's *nomadic* (becoming, temporality) understanding of dwelling. They suggest a continuum in which monadic and nomadic form the outer extremes of dwelling which in many ways represents a classic tension in much of the literature on migration, diaspora and mobility, between roots and routes, between bounded place and free flow (Malkki 1992, Kaplan 1996, Brun 2001, Massey 2005, Sheller 2011). The disassociation of Deleuze and Guattari's understanding from Heidegger's *dwelling as being* is made clear in the authors' statement on 'becoming and heterogeneity, as opposed to the stable, the eternal, the identical, the constant' (Deleuze and Guattari [1980] 1987, p. 361). The relationship between being and becoming, between the monadic and nomadic, is clearly illustrated in their discussion of the migrant and the nomad – which is a symbolic way of distinguishing between being and becoming. While a migrant dwells by reterritorializing, a nomad dwells in deterritorialization – in an open space 'without borders or enclosure' (p. 380).

It is individuals' socio-economic status that determines what kinds of dwelling are possible to find where. It is also their socio-economic status that determines the continued mobility between rented dwellings. Most people I interviewed did not have a contract when they were renting in the *Kira* system. As mentioned above, among IDPs from Abkhazia, it is those in rented accommodation in Tbilisi that have the lowest levels of housing stability. According to a survey by the Norwegian Refugee Council (NRC 2013), IDPs living in rented dwellings in Tbilisi tend to expect to change accommodation within a year. The housing instability is often caused by circumstances outside their control, and renters in the *Kira* system describe considerable vulnerability and insecurity. They tend to live in fear of the owner increasing the rent, which would force them to find a cheaper dwelling. A young woman renting a flat in a suburb of Tbilisi with her parents and brothers stated that they were always looking for somewhere else to live so that they could move in a controlled fashion rather than being forced to leave at short notice. This volatility also affects individuals' social networks and social capital. Building and maintaining relations becomes difficult in the temporariness of the rented dwelling, as another young woman, Monica,[8] states:

> Everyone here knows that we are renting. They know that today or tomorrow we will be leaving. Neighbours are only considering us to be here for a short time. (Monica, came to Tbilisi to work in a factory when she was 17, and has lived in somewhere between 10 and 15 places in Tbilisi since she arrived in 1999)

Echoing Simmel's notion of the stranger, the internally displaced in Georgia often feel like the stranger who comes today and stays tomorrow (Brun 2015a). However, for IDPs in rented dwellings, they are the strangers who come today and *leave* tomorrow. They are the deterritorialized migrants who struggle to reterritorialize but have no power and resources to do so. Their deterritorialization does not necessarily lead to reterritorialization; rather, as Haesbaert (2013) notes, moving towards a new territory corresponds to a process of increasingly precarious territorial constructs. According to the NRC (2013), if given a choice, most people in private accommodation would prefer to stay in the place, city or village in which they are currently living. When considering the rented dwelling of IDPs, we need to understand the living space in the context of the more common rural-to-urban movements that are taking place. As Monica's husband (who is not an IDP but a migrant from the regions) said: 'it is easier for us non-IDPs because we have a place to return to if we cannot make it in the city. If you are an IDP, you do not have a home to return to'.

The deterritorialization that results from the unwilling movement involved in becoming an IDP, and later from the movements between rented dwellings, prevents IDPs from reterritorializing and find that new place, and consequantly limiting the possibility of a home. One can be mobile as a migrant as long as there is a particular centre of gravity – a location that may be termed home – or an opportunity to reterritorialize. When the possibility of home disappears, mobility becomes unbearable. This, I think, reflects many IDPs' experiences of the temporariness in their mobile lives. As Heidegger ([1954] 1971, pp. 143–144) suggests,

> The truck driver is at home on the highway, but he does not have his shelter there; the working woman is at home in the spinning mill, but does not have her dwelling place there; the chief engineer is at home in the power station, but he does not dwell there.

Mobile IDPs find it difficult to feel at home anywhere accessible to them:

> It is difficult to change places so often and adapt to new places. After living there for two or three years, I have become used to a place. But when I am just about to get used to a place I have to move again and have to re-establish again …. Since I left Abkhazia, I do not move homes, I just move houses.
> *Interviewer*: What is home to you?
> It is the place where there is a house that belongs to you, you decorate it as you want, you live there for as long as you can get adjusted to the environment and to that space. It is not just a house, it encompasses a neighbourhood, the people you learn to know and then you become familiar. It is the surroundings in general, a home is much more than a house in my view. (Displaced man, aged 33, living in rented accommodation with his mother)

Relational dwelling: mobility as misrecognition

Dwelling is relational, and the way in which dwelling forms a starting point for social relations, the keeping together of things and relations, was one of the main topics raised by interviewees. Being unable to improve one's living conditions, having no control over one's physical space, is experienced as a loss – a primary deprivation in terms of making a life and finding a place within the Georgian society.

> Now we have to start looking for a new place, our [*Gira*] contract expires in four months. I wish we could get our own house. As we are not in our own city, at least if we owned our house, it would feel more like home. I want to be able to improve my living space, to decorate and to invest in the space …. My daughter always says, we do not need new clothes, let us save for the fridge we can have in our new flat. (A woman, approximately 50 years old, who came from Russia in 2007)

Living spaces are often substandard, with plumbing frequently a problem, windows draughty, walls damp, and floors stripped of wood or other covering.

The flats I visited were sometimes furnished when rented out, but sometimes not. Common for all flats was that the families living there would have few of their own belongings – they were not investing in things before they knew they had a space they could control. Monica's family had bought one lamp and a baby cot for their newborn baby – otherwise they were reluctant to invest money or energy in the rented dwelling. The low material standards of the dwellings form a reminder of people's status. Lack of control is felt both in relation to the immediate physical space and in relation to the politics of mobility towards IDPs. People renting in Tbilisi are anxious that the only assistance they might be able to access is a government-provided residence outside Tbilisi, far away from their current livelihoods. This would be another form of forced movement. In addition to the lack of security in the material dwelling itself, the dwellings and the process of moving are also significant in the identity formation and notions of self developed by the internally displaced:

> I always have to reinvent myself when I move to a new place. (A woman in her 40s, living in rented accommodation since the family's return from Russia in 2008)

The two forms of recognition – identity and status – come together in the dwelling. The dwelling constitutes and symbolizes in this case Honneth's three dimensions of recognition: the personal, the legal and the social. Though a private space, the dwelling determines one's status both socially and legally.

> When renting you are no one in the society. You are not going to stay, so people cannot be bothered to be in touch. (Displaced man, aged 33, living in rented accommodation with his mother)
> We are IDPs and we are living in the private sector. No one knows about us. From the outside we are invisible. No one cares about people like us. There are so many people in the collective centres, and the government and organizations are only interested in them. (Woman, approximately 50 years old, who came from Russia in 2007)

In this case, misrecognition is experienced as a depreciation of one's identity and status by the surroundings (Fraser 2001, Honneth 2002). We need to understand how the movement of IDPs is normatively evaluated in the Georgian society. As noted earlier, there is an interest in keeping people in the IDP category and, consequently, IDPs are excluded from becoming full citizens. IDPs are wanted as long as they abide by their IDP status and the expectation that they will stay put. Exclusion takes place when people move away from where they were registered as IDPs, because that movement challenges the understanding of the place of IDPs within the Georgian society. How people make sense of the world is intimately related to how people are recognized in the society. In Georgia, the IDPs from Abkhazia are needed to help maintain the notion of a whole/unscarred Georgia. As a result, people are stuck in a humanitarian category that has been emptied of much its original content. At the same time, they are fixed to the places where they first registered as IDPs rather than where they dwell.

Recognition and misrecognition may be identified by identifying people's level of participation in society (Fraser 1995, 2001) and their experience of that level of participation. In the case of IDPs in rented accommodation, there is a lack of participation which is experienced through their invisibility. One example of invisibility is related to voting. People in rented dwellings can only register their names at the flat if the owner agrees. It was not common among the people I interviewed to register their names with the address of the flat, which meant that their invisibility was experienced at many levels. First, they were not known to the state: they were still considered as living at the location where they and their families first registered when they became IDPs in the 1990s. Second, they cannot vote where they reside because they are not registered. Third, there is no recognition in their neighbourhood. They are the strangers that come today and leave tomorrow. And, as Fraser (2001, p. 24) puts it, when some actors are regarded as 'inferior, excluded, wholly other or simply invisible, hence as less than full partners in social interaction, then we should speak of misrecognition and status subordination'.

Among the people interviewed, there is clearly a norm of ownership inherent in the discussion about rented dwellings. People long for the owned dwelling; they believe that ownership of a dwelling will change their status, give them recognition within society and make them feel at home. Ownership is believed to lead to the reterritorialization and the recognition they dream of. An owned property does not necessary solve all problems, but for the people interviewed dwelling is associated with being still, and with the possibility of keeping a place of their own, investing in that dwelling, being surrounded by things that provide comfort and nurturing relationships with neighbours. The mobile IDPs in rented dwellings longed for stillness, for the control over their lives that may mean voluntary immobility rather than forced mobility. For them, it is stillness and a permanent dwelling that may provide recognition.

When stillness becomes the aim

People in protracted displacement are generally thought of as relatively immobile – stuck in one location while waiting for a solution. In this article, however, I have shown that many IDPs remain on the move. Their situation is the result of an initial movement in search of a better life – a movement away from where they first registered and hence a movement that challenges how the internally displaced are governed. In the strategies of those dwelling in rented accommodation, however, mobility comes to represent a precarious status. The relationship between mobility and stillness for this group is fraught with tension. IDPs in rented dwellings are involuntarily mobile and long for stillness because 'staying in one place makes you into someone', as one inter-viewee commented. I have shed light on the relationship between mobility and immobility through notions of 'dwelling' and 'recognition'. Three main conclusions may be drawn from the analysis.

First, new discussions on Heidegger's notion of 'dwelling' have made it poss-ible to better understand dwelling-in-mobility and the extent to which mobility can be understood through the process of dwelling. Dwelling and mobility are not mutually exclusive, but the dwelling becomes an important starting point for how IDPs can control their mobility. Second, in discussions of forced migration, policy categories and the humanitarian status form a crucial starting point for understanding how people are being considered. A status makes it possible to understand people's position in society and is relevant for identities and a more general social standing. The concept of 'recognition' enables a more nuanced picture of how social status can be influential in efforts to under-stand the relationship between mobility and immobility, how certain groups in society – in this case IDPs in rented accommodation – are not accepted because of the nature of their mobility. Engaging with recognition enables an analysis of how power, status and inequality are produced through mobility and shape the experience of staying in a rented dwelling. Third, the rented dwelling comes to symbolize the migrants' precarious social and legal IDP status, as well as his or her identity as an IDP. Through the temporary dwelling, identities other than the temporary identity of the displaced disappear. People become invisible, faceless – they cannot be recognized.

If we integrate redistribution with recognition in Fraser's (2001) under-standing, redressing misrecognition would mean changing social institutions. Looking more generally at how displaced populations are understood and treated in the territorial politics and politics of mobility in Georgia may help to understand how political possibilities for making and accessing home are created, as well as the significance of mobility in that process. The governance of mobility promotes territorialized policies that seek to fix groups of people to particular territories (see Lash and Featherstone 2001). By studying mobility among IDPs in rented accommodation, we gain insight into what Sheller (2011, p. 2) refers to as 'the power of discourses, practices, infrastructures of mobility in creating the effects of both movement and stasis'. Displaced people in Georgia (and elsewhere) resist being fixed to one place, but their reterritorializations become precarious because institutions are established only to control their mobility, not to facilitate mobility and enable stillness in locations and dwellings of their own desire.

Acknowledgements

Thanks to the editors of the special issue, Sybille Frank and Lars Meier for inviting me to contribute and for their constructive comments during the process. I am grateful to all the research participants in Georgia and to Julia Kharasvili of the IDP Women's Association Consent in Georgia for her hospitality and generosity and for sharing ideas. Thanks to Mariam Naskidashvili and Khathia Kardeva for research assistance and to Nicholas Van Hear for valuable comments on an earlier draft.

Notes

1. I borrow the term 'paradigmatic victim' from Chua et al. (2000). It has also been used in the context of refugees by Lubkemann (2008).
2. The 'regions' is a term for most areas of Georgia outside Tbilisi and its surroundings.
3. Although it has been impossible to find an official statement declaring that assistance is provided on the basis of where one is registered, this seems to be the common practice.
4. 'Durable housing solutions' is a term that plays on the discourse of durable solutions in forced migration, where it refers to attempts to find solutions in which forced migrants cease to be forced migrants. A durable solution is believed to be achieved when internally displaced persons have been integrated into the local community in which they settled after displacement, when they have been resettled and live permanently in another location within their country as local citizens of that place, or when they return to the place from which they were displaced (see Brun 2008 for a discussion of these principles in the context of internal displacement).
5. I use 'transfer of ownership' here to distinguish this process from the general 'privatization' of property that took place in Georgia from 1992 (following independence). While collective centres were not privatized in the first wave of post-independence privatization, privatization of buildings that housed collective centres and had commercial value has gradually taken place, making IDPs living in such buildings vulnerable and forcing many to move, a subject to which I will return below. There is no information available on how many Georgians currently live in rented dwellings.
6. For example, Honneth's emphasis on authentic identities is problematic in this context. See Zurn (2003) and Bankovsky and Le Goff (2012) for further discussion of Honneth and Fraser's conversations on recognition.
7. Axel Honneth (2002, p. 505) discusses the variation in the meanings of 'recognition' between English, French and German. In German, the 'concept appears to denote essentially only that normative situation associated with awarding a social status, whereas in English and French it encompasses the additional epistemic sense of "identifying" or "knowing again"'.
8. Not her real name.

Disclosure statement

No potential conflict of interest was reported by the author.

References

Amnesty International (2010) *In the Waiting Room: Internally Displaced People in Georgia*, London, Amnesty International.

Armstrong, C. (2008) 'Collapsing categories: Fraser on economy, culture and justice', *Philosophy and Social Criticism*, vol. 34, no. 4, pp. 409–425.

Bankovsky, M. & Le Goff, A. (2012) 'Deepening critical theory: French contributions to theories of recognition', in *Recognition Theory and Contemporary French Moral and Political Philosphy: Reopening the Dialogue*, eds. M. Bankovsky & A. Le Goff, Manchester, Manchester University Press, pp. 3–22.

Blunt, A. & Dowling, R. (2006) *Home*, Abingdon, Routledge.

Brubaker, R. (1995) 'Aftermaths of empire and the unmixing of peoples: historical and comparative perspectives', *Ethnic and Racial Studies*, vol. 18, no. 2, pp. 189–218.

Brun, C. (2001) 'Reterritorialising the link between people and place in refugee studies', *Geografiska Annaler, Series B: Human Geography*, vol. 83B, no. 1, pp. 15–25.

Brun, C. (2008) *Finding a Place. Local Integration and Protracted Displacement in Sri Lanka*, Colombo, Social Scientists' Association.

Brun, C. (2010) 'Hospitality: becoming 'IDPs' and 'hosts' in protracted displacement', *Journal of Refugee Studies*, vol. 23, no. 3, pp. 337–355.

Brun, C. (2012) 'Home in temporary dwellings', in *International Encyclopedia of Housing and Home*, eds. S. J. Smith, M. Elsinga, L. Fox O'Mahony, O. S. Eng, S. Wachter & R. Dowling, Oxford, Elsevier, pp. 424–433.

Brun, C. (2015a) 'Active waiting and changing hopes: toward a time perspective on protracted displacement,' *Social Analysis*, vol. 59, no. 1, pp. 19–37. (Special issue on Conflict, mobility and uncertainty edited by C. Horst and K. Grabska.)

Brun, C. (2015b) 'Home as a critical value: From shelter to home in Georgia', *Refuge*, vol. 31, no.1, pp. 43–54. (Special issue on Making Home in Protracted Displacement, edited by C. Brun and A.H. Fàbos.)

Brun, C. & Fàbos, A.H. (in press) 'Homemaking in limbo.' *Refuge*, vol. 31, no.1, pp. 5–18. (Editorial for special issue on Making Home in Protracted Displacement.)

Chua, P., *et al.* (2000) 'Women, culture, development: a new paradigm for development studies?', *Ethnic and Racial Studies*, vol. 23, pp. 820–841.

Cresswell, T. (2009) 'Place', in *International Encyclopedia of Human Geography*, eds. N. Thrift & R. Kitchin, vol. 8, Oxford, Elsevier, pp. 169–177.

Cresswell, T. (2012) 'Mobilities II: still', *Progress in Human Geography*, vol. 36, no. 5, pp. 645–653.

Danish Refugee Council (DRC) (2011) *Survey Reports on Privately Accommodated IDPs in the Samegrelo Region and Tbilisi. An Analysis of Housing Situations and Conditions as well as Durable Housing Solutions in Private Accommodation*, Georgia, Swedish International Development Cooperation Agency/Danish Refugee Council.

Deleuze, G. & Guattari, F. (1987) *A Thousand Plateaus: Capitalism and Schizophrenia*, trans. and foreword by Brian Massumi, Minneapolis, MN, University of Minnesota Press. (Originally published 1980).

Elden, S. (2001) *Mapping the Present: Heidegger, Foucault and the Project of Spatial History*, London, Continuum.

Faist, T. (2013) 'The mobility turn: a new paradigm for the social sciences?', *Ethnic and Racial Studies*, vol. 36, no. 11, pp. 1637–1646.

Fraser, N. (1995) 'From redistribution to recognition? Dilemmas of justice in a 'post-socialist' age', *New Left Review*, vol. I/212, July–August, pp. 68–93.

Fraser, N. (2001) 'Recognition without ethics', *Theory, Culture & Society*, vol. 18, no. 2–3, pp. 21–42.

Fraser, N. & Honneth, A. (2003) *Redistribution or Recognition? A Political-Philosophical Exchange*, London, Verso.

Gielis, R. & Van Houtum, H. (2012). 'Sloterdijk in the house! Dwelling in the borderscape of Germany and the Netherlands', *Geopolitics*, vol. 17, pp. 797–817.

Gill, N. (2009) 'Longing for stillness: the forced movement of asylum seekers', *M/C Journal*, vol. 12, no. 1.

Gill, N., *et al.* (2011) 'Introduction: mobilities and forced migration', *Mobilities*, vol. 6, no. 3, pp. 301–316.

Government of Georgia (2007) *State Strategy for Internally Displaced Persons Persecuted*, Tbilisi, Government of Georgia.

Haesbaert, R. (2013) 'A global sense of place and multi-territoriality: Notes for a dialogue from a 'peripheral' point of view', in *Spatial Politics: Essays for Doreen Massey*, eds. D. Featherstone & J. Painter, Chichester, Wiley-Blackwell, pp. 146–157.

Hannam, K., *et al.* (2006) 'Editorial: mobilities, immobilities and moorings', *Mobilities*, vol. 1, no. 1, pp. 1–22.

Harrison, P. (2007) 'The space between us: opening remarks on the concept of dwelling', *Environment and Planning D: Society and Space*, vol. 25, pp. 625–647.

Heidegger, M. (1971) 'Building dwelling thinking'. in *Poetry, Language, Thought*. Trans. and introduction by Albert Hofstadter, New York, Harper & Row, pp. 145–161. (Originally published 1954).

Honneth, A. (1992) 'Integrity and disrespect: principles of a conception of morality based on the theory of recognition', *Political Theory*, vol. 20, no. 2, pp. 187–201.

Honneth, A. (1995) *The Struggle for Recognition: The Moral Grammar of Social Conflicts*. Trans. Joel Anderson, Cambridge, Polity.

Honneth, A. (2002) 'Grounding recognition: a rejoinder to critical questions', *Inquiry: An Interdisciplinary Journal of Philosophy*, vol. 45, no. 4, pp. 499–519.

Hyndman, J. & Giles, W. (2011) 'Waiting for what? The feminization of asylum in protracted situations', *Gender, Place and Culture*, vol. 18, no. 3, pp. 361–379.

Kabachnik, P. (2012) 'Wounds that won't heal: cartographic anxieties and the quest for territorial integrity in Georgia', *Central Asian Survey*, vol. 31, no. 1, pp. 45–60.

Kaplan, C. (1996) *Questions of Travel: Postmodern Discourses of Displacement*, Durham, NC, Duke University Press.

Kofoed, L. & Simonsen, K. (2012) 'Re(scaling) identities: embodied others and alternative spaces of identification', *Ethnicities*, vol. 12, no. 5, pp. 623–642.

Kuzio, T. (2002) 'History, memory and nation building in the post-Soviet colonial space', *Nationality Papers: The Journal of Nationalism and Ethnicity*, vol. 30, no. 2, pp. 241–264.

Lash, S. & Featherstone, M. (2001) 'Recognition and difference: politics, identity, multiculture', *Theory Culture & Society*, vol. 18, no. 2–3, pp. 1–19.

Latimer, J. & Munro, R. (2009) 'Keeping and dwelling: relational extension, the idea of home, and otherness', *Space and Culture*, vol. 12, no. 3, pp. 317–331.

Loescher, G. & Milner, J. (2009) 'Understanding the challenge', *Forced Migration Review*, vol. 33, pp. 9–11.

Long, J. C. (2013) 'Diasporic dwelling: the poetics of domestic space', *Gender, Place & Culture*, vol. 20, no. 3, pp. 329–345.

Lubkemann, S. C. (2008) *Culture in Chaos: An Anthropology of the Social Condition in War*, Chicago, IL, University of Chicago Press.

Malkki, L. H. (1992) 'National geographic: the rooting of peoples and the territorialization of national identity among scholars and refugees', *Cultural Anthropology*, vol. 7, no. 1, pp. 24–44.

Mallett, S. (2004) 'Understanding home: a critical review of the literature', *The Sociological Review*, vol. 52, no. 1, pp. 62–89.

Massey, D. (2005) *For Space*, London, Sage.

Ministry of Refugees and Accommodation (MRA) (2010) *IDP Housing Strategy and Working Plan*, Tbilisi, Government of Georgia.

Moran, D., *et al.* (2012) 'Disciplined mobility and carceral geography: prisoner transport in Russia', *Transactions of the Institute of British Geographers*, vol. 37, pp. 446–460.

Norwegian Refugee Council (NRC) (2013) *Privately Accommodated IDPs in Georgia. Needs Assessment*, Tbilisi, NRC.

Sheller, M. (2011) *Mobility*, Sociopedia.isa.

Urry, J. (2007) *Mobilities*, Cambridge, Polity.

Varley, A. (2008) 'A place like this? Stories of dementia, home, and the self', *Environment and Planning D: Society and Space*, vol. 26, no. 1, pp. 47–67.

Young, I. M. (1997) 'Unruly categories: a critique of Nancy Fraser's dual systems theory', *New Left Review*, vol. 222 (1997), pp. 147–160.

Zurn, C. F. (2003) 'Identity or status? Struggles over recognition in Fraser, Honneth, and Taylor', *Constellations*, vol. 10, no. 4, pp. 519–537.

EPHEMERAL URBAN TOPOGRAPHIES OF SWEDISH ROMA
On dwelling at the mobile–immobile nexus

Ingrid Martins Holmberg and Erika Persson

Department of Conservation, University of Gothenburg, Gothenburg, Sweden

ABSTRACT
Although celebrating five hundred years in Sweden in 2012, only little attention has been given to the Roma's long-term presence in the Swedish landscape, and even lesser to their historical presence in urban contexts. Bearing in mind the Roma's twentieth-century European history and knowing of their contemporary situation, this knowledge gap is no surprise. This paper will present a study that has assembled various traces of Roma dwelling in a Swedish urban setting from the late nineteenth century until the 1950s. The study enables a pinning down of the mobile–immobile nexus around which the Swedish Roma everyday cultural practices of dwelling evolved during the particular period before citizenship and subsequent settlement: regulation, seasonality, income opportunities and material devices. Hereby it hopes to contribute to an understanding of Roma urban dwelling as moored in history by corporeality and materiality, and as related both with locality and with 'elsewhere'. The following questions are posed: Which were these urban places of dwelling and what characteristics do they have; what kinds of social connections and interactions were established at these places (co-habitation); in what sense can these places reveal a differentiated Roma history of dwelling? Besides uncovering a particular ephemeral 'multi-sitedness', the study also reveals Roma urban dwelling as related to broader spectrum of tenure than hitherto recognized.

Introduction

Although celebrating five hundred years in Sweden in 2012[1] only little attention has been given to the Roma's long-term presence in the Swedish landscape, and even lesser to their historical presence in urban contexts. Bearing in mind the Roma's twentieth-century European history and knowing of their contemporary situation (Hancock 2002, 2010, SOU 2010:55, Selling 2013), this knowledge gap is no surprise. This paper will present a study that has assembled various traces of Roma dwelling in a

Swedish urban setting from the late nineteenth century until the 1950s. The study enables a pinning down of the mobile–immobile nexus around which the Swedish Roma everyday cultural practices of dwelling evolved during the particular period before citizenship and subsequent settlement. Hereby it hopes to contribute to an understanding of Roma urban dwelling as moored in history by material forms, as related with locality and with 'else-where' (Söderström 2014, p. 3), and as a spatio-temporal co-presence of het-erogeneous components. The following questions are posed: Which were these urban places of dwelling and what characteristics do they have; what kinds of cross-cultural connections and interactions were established in these places; in what sense can these places reveal a Roma history of dwelling more differentiated than hitherto recognized?

For many reasons a focus on historical Roma dwelling and presence in an urban context brings forth vulnerable exposure. But in parallel it can bring forth a history of interaction and connectedness: with other people, with different services, with the physical materiality of landscape, with routes of escape, routes of connectivity and with 'elsewhere'. There are however many and severe difficulties in tracking these local places and sites. This is related to several things. Mayall (2004, p. 26) notes that historical research has come 'rather late to Gypsy studies and to a large extent the study […] has been undertaken outside the world of mainstream academic history', focusing instead on 'language, folklore and customs'. A decade later Roma his-toriography has itself become an issue of serious concern (cf. Marsh 2008, Palosuo 2009, Reading 2012). As previously stated by Lucassen (1998) with regard to historical studies of migratory and travelling groups, by Dimitrios (2011) with regard to historical studies of sedentary Roma, and also apparent in the current study of Roma urban sites, the scarcity of empirical sources of Roma dwelling is an initial and very critical threshold for any study within this field.

As often put forth from a postcolonial studies perspective, history and memory of subaltern groups is a tricky field of research: the strands of thought and knowledge of their history are established by the socio-cultural majority in power; very few contributions stem from the community of concern; the existing representations are loaded with stereotypes and depre-ciation; their known history is beside one of atrocity, largely made up of silence and lacunae; but moreover, also the fact that many groups define themselves by inventing origins (not to be conflated with 'then') as a contem-porary identity politics. This is a foregrounding of roots and rootedness that obscures the fact of the world as 'always and already mixed' (cf. Said [1979] 2003, Spivak 1988, Lundahl 2013). The recent works of Reading (2012, 2013) push the particularities of Roma memory and history one step further in point-ing out how the hegemonic discursive figures are made up by conflations of historical facts with populist disparagement, why mediations of the atrocious memory of slavery of East European Roma resembles a Sisyphus's work. There are thus many constraints to be tackled when searching for traces of Roma historical dwelling.

We have used the concept of 'assemblage', mostly connected with the works of Deleuze or De Landa, as a departure for tracing and reconnecting the heterogeneous and sometimes disparate components that have entered into relation with one another within the phenomenon of concern: 'Roma urban places before settlement in Gothenburg, Sweden'. The onto-epistemology of the assemblage opens up for a study of the various connections and interconnections between materiality, subjects, events, signs or linguistic utterances, etc., and their multi-scale appearance, that is, beyond singular social, spatial or cultural 'levels'. The assemblage of concern here is made up by components of varying character, stability and duration. What we are discerning are contours of a kind of dwelling that, on the one hand, shows many similarities with conventional (majority's) tenure spectrum in that it has some stability over time and also that it, surprisingly, seems to have taken place within the spectrum of the conventional housing market, but that, on the other hand, shows some particularities related to duration, position, design and kinds of interaction. This observation points at a need to insert sensitivity to power relations into the assemblage perspective.

From here, the issue of mobility in historical urban dwelling becomes a particularly crucial but only recently discussed matter: 'Histories of urban settlement typically focus on conditions of stasis, when continuous habitation in a particular location enabled the accumulation of physical evidence' (Pieris 2013, p. 185). As discussed in Holmberg (forthcoming), 'physical evidence', understood as materiality (buildings, fundaments etc.) or written sources (traces of regulation), have had the most exhaustive influence on place narratives and place identity over time. Returning to the issue of traces and information further down, we will here only point out that the mobility perspective enables for identifying dwelling of a kind that has left very scarce material evidence; that needs to be conceived of as in terms of 'multi-sited', that is, as being made up by many different sites used recurrently on periodic basis (here primarily termed seasonality); which needs to be conceived of within the frameworks of regulation (but also beyond); which consists of a plethora of encounter and co-existence (here referred to as co-habitation).

The ways in which Roma urban dwelling evolved during the decades of concern is considered as an outcome of housing strategy but also, and which will be extended upon in the following, of the period's nationally implemented regulation of mobility among the inhabitants within the nation. Accordingly, the Roma dwellings found in this study relate very differently to a mobility–immobility axis, some occur several times over many years while other display singular appearance. Focusing on the nodes and sites that were used for dwelling – thus only occasionally touching upon the trajec-tories, routes and connections over and between these sites – the issue of mobility in this case becomes concentrated to the question of how Roma urban dwelling has evolved and how it has created shifting and changing topographical patterns of over time. A mobility perspective, challenging social science 'to change both the objects of inquiry and the methodologies for research' and problematizing any 'sedentarist' approaches […] that treat place, stability and dwelling as a natural steady-state' (Hannam et al. 2006, p. 5), is here used to enable for a relational understanding of urban sites. Drawing on Arijit Sen and Jennifer Johung (2013, p. 207) our conception of 'mobility of dwelling' is one arranged within the dialectics of movement and stasis, but also related to various kinds of thresholds that direct mobility: 'Landscapes of mobility are not unmediated panoramas of free flows of people and moving objects. Rather they are tethered by instances of stability and stasis, borders and check-posts.'

Dwelling, and Roma multi-sited dwelling in particular, is a particular instan-tiation of mobility versus stasis. In mapping out topographical patterns of Roma urban dwelling in Gothenburg, Sweden, this paper intends to contrib-ute to an urban history of co-habitation and, in doing so, undermining a per-sistent imagery of the urban as mainly made up by socio-spatial and cultural divisions. We hereby intend to open up for a historical socio-cultural complex-ity that can be helpful both in questioning the contemporary understanding of European identities and in bringing forth a politics of radical inclusion beyond the territories of the nation-state (cf. Hannam et al. 2006, p. 10; Sheller 2011, p. 2, cf. Faist 2013).

Terminology and sources

It is impossible to avoid getting entangled in definition, classification, categ-orization and clarification of the conflict-loaded terminology that enfolds around the object of study. Some fixes in this ocean of definitions have to be pointed out, as well as some current scholarly positions. We will also clarify the terminology in use in this paper.

In the national context of Sweden where neither race nor ethnicity is offi-cially registered,[2] Roma spatial history is particularly difficult to trace. It thus needs to be stressed that the assemblage 'Roma urban places before settle-ment' presented here is fundamentally constrained by a particularly complex and difficult empirical situation. In tracing the assemblage, all kinds of source material have been heeded: notations and representations in Government Official Reports and newspapers (found in clippings at media archives and Folk Lore archives), topographic literature, contemporary oral accounts from the places of concern and other. The data are also derived from many different formats of representation (photographs, maps, articles, personal testimony, statistics, etc.). The entry was by looking for accounts of 'zigenare' and/or 'Roma' and connections to certain distinct topographic sites and place-names. To be noted is that, while these ethnifying terms entail specific historical connotations (see below) in this context they are here used as provisory devices helping to flesh out the assemblage.

Today the term 'Roma' is established on a pan-European political level as a uniting term for a broad spectrum of communities and groups who conceive of themselves as related in one sense or another Roma.[3] Although embraced by many, discussion and objection to this term has continued on many levels. In line with both endonym practice and research results revealing a more complex history than hitherto known, Ian Hancock, researcher and spokes-man of Roma groups, today recommends the use of the particular name of each Roma group. On a smaller spatial scale and within Swedish minority poli-tics of 2009, again a complex situation enfolds. The Swedish minority politics term is based on the principle of 'self-identification', and that is why the term Roma refers to several different communities that only partly identify with each other when it comes to historical, linguistic, religious and cultural belongings.[4] In daily speech and within current politics of identity, a dividing line is generally drawn between Resande [travellers] and Swedish Roma [Roma]. These terms have historical correspondents in the terms 'tattare' [tra-veller] and 'zigenare' [gypsy]. For the purpose of this paper our attention has been limited to the part of the Roma minority who refer to themselves as 'Swedish Roma' and who in the historical sources most frequently are referred to as 'zigenare'.[5] Since the historical term 'zigenare' generally is considered pejorative by Roma people[6] and also is an exonym, we consequently use the term 'Roma', only using the historical terminology when citing the sources.[7]

The historical situation of Roma groups, neither having an officially recog-nized 'homeland' (that could moor them into geo-history), nor an unques-tioned right to stay and dwell where desired (due to various regulations), brings the issue of mobility and migration into the scene. The spatial migration of Roma is however seldom related to upward or downward social mobility as in many other cases and has only little to do with own voli-tion, but should instead be understood in relation to a subaltern position (cf. Hannam et al. 2006, pp. 10–11, Sheller 2011, p. 6).

Legal formatting of Roma mobility and stasis

The Roma have throughout history constituted a very small part of the Swedish population.[8] Although an official register of race or ethnicity is lacking, there are some numbers in 'special registers': in the Government Offi-cial Report of 1923 the number of Roma was set at 250 individuals out of 6 million inhabitants within the nation (SOU 1923:2); thirty years later the number was tripled into 740 individuals (SOU 1956:43). The Swedish numbers are miniscule,[9] but in relation to the current ambiguity concerning the number of European Roma – estimated as 4 million in 2002, as 9.1 million in 2007, as 12 million in 2010, and by some Roma organizations estimated as 14 million (SOU 2010:55, Liégeois 2012, p. 19)[10] – it is necessary to understand all numbers as both deeply embedded in state politics as well as identity politics, and as an issue that will probably never settle completely.

Despite the small numbers of Swedish Roma, the amount of state measures aiming to control Roma groups as well as the perseverance of these measures has been strikingly disproportionate. Turning to the twentieth century it is well known that Roma mobility and dwelling was controlled and criminalized with particular frenzy through, first, restrictions of movement, immigration and trade; second, through culling; and also, third, through assimilation politics.

There are, according to Reading (2012, 2013) and based on studies of Romanian Roma, a handful of intense and violent discursive figures that obscure the facts of Roma historical persecution, and one of them concerns dwelling: the discourse of 'Roma nomadism'. This device transforms the Roma into 'the Other' (since they lead their lives in ways different from 'normal' people), but second and most important, it makes the Roma alone responsible for what in fact is legally embedded expulsion. Below, Roma mobility will be highlighted through the lens of how some different legal devices structured mobility within Europe and Sweden. As will be shown, these structures were partly directed towards Roma in particular, but partly also had more general aims. We here discern the particular modes of a 'differential mobilities', played out through regulation and with the effect of ordering different subjects over time–space along the axes of mobility–immobility, scape–mooring and movement–stillness (Sheller 2011, p. 5).

The issue of Roma dwelling needs to be put in the context of how regulatory devices have determined not only the very existence (or absence) of Roma dwelling, but also that it has determined the sources to knowledge about these places and dwellings (Holmberg, forthcoming). This need for acknowledging Roma historical subordination is one side of the coin.

The other side of the coin is about the very historicity of mobility and vagrancy. When looking at general European conditions, it is obvious that mobility was something very different within pre-modern times and prior to contemporary industrialized society. Then local and regional demands for services and labour made up a different scene, requiring an abundance of itinerant craftsmen, traders and workers. Also movement itself, over longer and shorter distances, made up a constituent everyday duty for most individuals, but especially for those having their provision within transport, public or clerical administration, craft and trade. Vagrancy, in and of itself, permeated and structured socio-spatial relations on every social level, and put things, individuals and places in different historically specific relations to each other.[11]

Making up a necessary fundament, vagrancy was precisely therefore putting particular pressure on the social institution of reciprocity, and was, accordingly, a field restricted by both social control and legal device. As pointed out by several scholars in Romani Studies (Lucassen et al. 1998, Mayall 1988, Bancroft 2005, Pulma 2006, Tervonen 2010), the gradual institutionalization of social concerns furthered public measures to control vagrancy, and was effected by laws regulating the areas of mobility, poverty and labour. From the Swedish context a core example is the transformation of the poor relief system during early mediaeval time. Poor relief was then gradually taken over by the town governances from religious parties, which in turn brought the establishment of a crucial distinction between the 'legitimate poor', that is, those being part of the resident population, and the 'illegitimate poor', that is, those lacking local connection. This distinction resulted in sedentary dwelling being put up as a prerequisite for poor relief but, subsequently, also resulted in the ban of alien, illegitimate poor from the towns (Lucassen et al. 1998, p. 55ff, Montesino Parra 2002, p. 89, Tervonen 2010, p. 42). The nineteenth-century Swedish Vagrancy laws (cf. below) can be understood as related to this legal distinction based on the varying stability of the individual's relation to place.

Since the national border of Sweden was relatively open before the twentieth century, few attempts had been made to regulate immigration through ordinances: movement across the borders was in practice difficult to observe (Svanberg and Tydén 2005, p. 216). The gradual development of the nation-state gave increased importance to the status of citizenship, furthering an institutionalization of the category 'foreigner'. In the early 1900s it was feared that poor immigrants would burden the poor relief system (Montesino Parra 2002, p. 92). Launched in the wake of massive mobility caused by an accelerating industrialization, urbanization and emigration, the nineteenth-century Vagrancy laws aimed at first place at a marking of the limits for public responsibilities. In legal terms a 'vagrant' was defined as someone without employment or means enough to manage livelihood, and under this Act those lacking domicile were defined penal and could be held in custody until identity and residence were identified (Montesino Parra 2002, pp. 88–90, Selling 2013, p. 45). The last Vagrancy law, declared in 1885, was in practice as late as until 1964.

Against the background of an increasing spatial mobility and some Vagrancy laws, Sweden in 1914 implemented two new laws that came to have particularly devastating consequences for the Roma population. The Immigration law explicitly prohibited foreign Roma from entering into Sweden. For the Swedish Roma the Immigration law had severe consequences since it put them in total isolation from family and friends abroad.

But apart from that, the Immigration law also effectively prevented people from seeking refuge in Sweden during the Second World War and thus had fatal outcomes for those Roma who were denied immigration (Montesino Parra 2002, pp. 95–96, SOU 2010:55, pp. 140–141, Tervonen 2010, p. 87). The Immigration law was in use until 1954. The other law of 1914 was instead directed towards people without citizenship but who were living within Sweden. It prohibited 'foreigners' (such as the Roma) to conduct itinerant crafts, pedlary, trade and sales of other kind. Taken together these 1914 laws effectively restricted the mobility of the Swedish Roma population.

In 1923, the Poor Law [Fattigvårdslag] opened up for state measures far more crude. This law enabled for each municipality to decide on its own whether or not it would insert a special unofficial paragraph in the local ordinances. If, and where, this paragraph was inscribed, anyone could be evicted from camping after a three weeks stay at the same location/municipality (SOU 2010:55, p. 142). This law made eviction of Roma settlements legally approved. The sharpening of legal devices was foreshadowed in the preceding investigation: 'regulations will provide the right of the police authority to evict gypsies from private land, to deport foreign gypsies and to, with penalty, prohibit landowners to lease land to travelers and gypsies' (SOU 1923:2, p. 347).

Many municipalities implemented the three weeks camping restrictions, which forced the Roma to move from town to town about once a month. From the 1920s onwards the Swedish Roma therefore had small chances to obtain housing. The continual evictions brought that many Roma came to favour bigger towns offering better sustenance opportunities and where one accordingly could make better use of a short stay. After two decades, around the mid-1900s, a gradual process of urbanization of Roma becomes salient, especially for Stockholm.

Eventually and as a consequence of the state offer to the Roma to obtain Swedish citizenship in 1952 (a process outside the scope of this paper), the Roma were allowed to settle permanently within the municipalities. Although this was a dramatic regulatory change, the housing situation was solved only by the 1960s huge state-and-municipality's joint effort to fund and facilitate construction of housing in order to fight the persistent housing shortage on a national scale (Montesino Parra 2002, p. 118).[13]

Through the lens of regulation and from a historical perspective, we have shown how very particular conceptions of 'local belonging' gradually became embedded in legal devices that prohibited vagrancy as such, and only in the early nineteenth century became transformed into regulations aiming in particular towards Roma settlement. During the period of our study (late nineteenth century until settlement in the early 1950s) these devices kept Swedish Roma on the move and brought severe difficulties in obtaining permanent dwelling.

On historical dwelling practice of Roma

Dwelling practice has since long been at core within research related to issues of identity, belonging and place-making (Brun and Setten 2013). In accordance, this is the departure also for Cottaar's (1998, p. 175) study of the nineteenth-century Dutch travellers: 'the form of housing and identity of the residents were coupled with each other inextricably'. Nevertheless this field of study still has many lacunae since it, for example, is very difficult to distinguish the Roma mobile dwelling from other itinerant groups', or to give voice to insider's narratives.

When it comes to Swedish conditions, the general understanding is that the Roma primarily stayed in camps and were separated from the rest of society (SOU 1956:43, Tillhagen 1961, 1965, Taikon 1963, Takman 1976, Demetri, Dimiter-Taikon, Olgaç et al. 2010, SOU 2010:55). A rare account from an insider is the Swedish Rom Katarina Taikon's (1963) account in the 1960s of the camp dwelling of her childhood in the 1930s. The camp was organized in the shape of a circle with the openings of the tents and caravans pointing towards the centre. The central fireplace was used as space for socializing and work. Taikon recalls the oldest type of tent, a small size 'three-top tent', with an oblique pole supported by struts holding up the canvas, and tells that they were replaced by bigger box-shaped tents and furnished caravans around the 1940s.

A certain seasonality in moving in between rural and urban places seems characteristic of Roma historical dwelling: cities were preferred in winter, while in spring the settlement moved to the outskirts of the city or the countryside (SOU 1956:43). In an interview of 2013, a Swedish Roma woman in her 80s recalled her childhood's seasonal itineraries from rural to urban places: 'Often we went back to Skåne [in the south of Sweden] in summertime and then, perhaps, we went back to Gothenburg [on the west coast] in winter.' The advantages with coming to Gothenburg had to do with earning one's living: 'It was a big town and my brothers traded cars [...] and here [in Gothenburg], there were lots of car dealers.'[14] The pattern of seasonal movement is confirmed by studies in other national contexts. Historically many British Travellers moved into rural areas in summer because of the demand for farm workers, or simply because of the climate (Okely 1983, p. 125). Later, in the late nineteenth-century British Roma tended to take up more urban and sedentary dwelling habits: the Roma used 'winter lodging in houses and flats' located in so called 'low localities in [...] large towns' (Mayall 1988, pp. 18–20).

Thus, the seasonality in movement is closely related to opportunities to earn one's living, but must also be put in the context of shifting technologies and the transformation of material devices. In a study of Dutch itinerant groups, Cottaar (1998) has discussed precisely the relationship of the construction and successive extension of hard-surface roads between urban and rural areas, and the timing of the introduction of the wooden caravan. In England and France the wooden caravan came in use around the 1860s, in the Netherlands and in Germany it was introduced somewhat later and in Sweden not until the 1930s (cf. above). The wooden caravan could enable for year-around outdoor living, and thus could dramatically change the patterns of movement. During colder periods itinerant groups now became much less dependent upon the sedentary population.

Before the wooden caravan was introduced, several different types of dwelling were in use. English nineteenth-century Gypsy travellers[15] had tents, covered carts and wagons (Mayall 1988, pp. 23–27); the Dutch itinerant population[16] is reported to make use of rooms to rent or lodging houses in cities, while farm sheds could provide shelter in the countryside (Cottaar 1998).

Dwelling at the mobile–immobile nexus: Gothenburg's Roma sites before 1952

In searching for historical Roma urban settlements and sites for dwelling in Gothenburg before 1952, we were at first sensitive for anything that could relate to 'camps' or 'commons'. We did indeed find some sites of this kind, but very soon came to learn that these categories were far from sufficient. Roma dwelling could only be unfolded by the addition of categories of a general kind more or less equivalent with ordinary divisions of tenure (ranging from owner occupancy to squatting[17]). In order to understand Roma urban dwelling we thus needed to leave behind the preconceptions that obscured the variety of tenure.

In the next section Gothenburg's Roma dwelling is presented in the temporal order in which they occur and with regard to the different kinds of tenure: (1) squatting, (a) agreed or conventional or (b) neither agreed nor conventional; (2) long-term tenancy/hotel; and (3) owner occupancy. The study identified ten distinct sites of this kind in use for longer or shorter periods of time from the end of the nineteenth century until year 1952. These places have been projected onto a Gothenburg map of 1921.

Some particularities must be noted already initially concerning the results of the study. First, that there is a persistent deficit of reports from 'insiders', that is, Roma, on the issue of concern.[18] Second, that the public reports, although produced from the perspective of state regulation, convey the richest accounts of Roma settlements in Gothenburg (an instantiation of ambivalence); and finally, that the accounts by contemporary popular historians offer a striking outspokenness of the moral, symbolic status of the places connected to Roma dwelling (Gregory 1994, Holmberg 2006) (Figure 1).

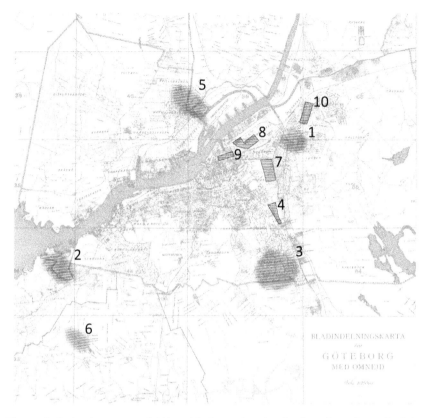

Figure 1. Gothenburg map of 1921 with Roma sites for dwelling from the end of the nineteenth century until 1952. Roma sites for dwelling are marked with numbers 1–10 and hatched areas. Faded contours are used where the exact location is uncertain and the name refers to a larger area. The strong line surrounding the city is the boundary of 1921. Before 1922 the city was little extended eastwards, which means that numbers 1, 3 and 4 – all in use before 1922 – were located outside or close to the city boundary. Numbers 9 and 10 are streets. Map by Södergren 1923: Gothenburg with surroundings in 1921, 1:25000 (Part of the atlases for the celebration of Gothenburg's 300 year anniversary). Map reproduced with permission by Gothenburg City Planning office, sub graphics by Erika Persson March 2014.

Dwelling as squatting-in-fields[19]

Interviews with Gothenburg citizens made in the 1920s reveal memories of Gothenburg's Roma places back in the late 1800s and early 1900s.[20] It is not easy to make sure whether or not the records relate to places of conventional use on common grounds or to literally squatted places, it is however likely that urban open fields were used for various temporary needs by many people during seasonal periods when no crop was growing. A kind of natural seasonality must thus have been the usual order, which in turn turns squatting of this kind of land into an activity with varying reception over the year. We have found eight fields in Gothenburg that were used as camps by Roma.

A non-Roma oral account from the early twentieth century recalls a childhood memory of Roma camping in a park called Gubberoparken (#1) located along the eastern main road. Sometimes the Roma stayed there for a whole month, fetching water from a well that belonged to a house nearby, earning their living 'through begging, dramatizing weddings and through horse trade and divination'. The Gubberoparken was at this time located just outside the city border at short distance from the city centre (the area was incorporated into Gothenburg only in 1922). Another account is very clear on the location of Roma sites: 'gypsies couldn't settle inside town' but had to stay outside the city at places such as 'Nya Varvet and Krokslätt'.[21]

Krokslätt (#3), the area mentioned, is located along a small river which in turn is parallel to the main road entering Gothenburg from the south. At this time an outskirt of the city with scattered cottages and small industrial establishments, it is described by a local historian as follows: 'on one side of smaller and larger factory complexes, large and small houses, rustic fences … the houses are mostly poor' (Fredberg 1922–1924, p. 400). The road itself is bordered by 'riffraff and rabble' and the characters' virtues are not abundant: 'the millers' farmhands driving their loads were not mother's best children' (Fredberg 1922–1924, pp. 400, 391).

We have found several accounts on Roma camps in and around this area. Roma, staying in Fredriksdal (#3 within Krokslätt) are in 1923 reported to having obtained permission to set up amusements: 'a roller coaster, shooting range, as well as a chain carousel, a couple of air swings and automobile lanes' (SOU 1923:2, p. 370). Also at the meadow called Getebergsäng (#4) close to Krokslätt, Roma had raised a camp while making performances in town. Although not indicated, we draw the conclusion that this Roma camp must have been set up before 1890, since the meadow of concern was exploited this year. Elsewhere it is reported that this meadow annually was used for livestock market and that 'horse dodgers were on the go' in the old days (Krantz 1943, pp. 25–27, 32). Accordingly, this meadow could have been a regular common and the Roma's tenure could thus be of conventional kind; unfortunately such information cannot be derived from the sources (Figure 2).

While the information on the Gothenburg's Roma campsite mentioned are found in interviews and texts, we also have found photographic depictions, the earliest ones shot in December 1923 by a local newspaper. The caption is clear on the characters as well on the geography: 'Gypsies on Kvillebäcksvägen', that is in the area Backa (#5). The photo shows people gathered in a ring looking at two small children in the middle of a camp with a few 'threetop tents' raised in an open field (Kamerareportage, BbankG151602). A description of this camp in a Government Official Report of 1923 – the earliest found – supplies us with details: 'Josefsson [coppersmith and musician b. 1880] and

Figure 2. This photo of December 1923 is the earliest photographic depiction of a Roma camp in Gothenburg. The photo, taken in Backa (#5) shows many people gathered in front of a 'three top tent', a type commonly in use before the introduction of the wooden caravan. A contemporary report tells how performances, with admission charges for the public, were organized by Roma precisely at this site. Some of the people shown in the photo may be locals.
Photo from the press archive Kamerareportage, number BbankG151602. Reproduced with permission by Kamerareportage.

his family usually traveled in the company of [...] three gypsy families, namely Taikumer, Demeter and Taikon,[22] all of which now reside in Backa, close to the city of Gothenburg'. There is also information about dwelling conditions, saying that the Roma 'dwell in tents, carried along either by their horses and vehicles or by rail'. We learn that 'the four gypsy families were living together in a big tent' but when and if 'the weather was particularly cold they usually procured temporary indoor housing'.

What we learn from here is a very flexible relation to dwelling, bringing many activities around fixing the tents, moving indoors when cold and caring for the transport of tents to other places. The report also tells more precisely about interaction with locals:

> Occasionally the party conducted horse trade [...] but nowadays the party mostly earned their living by organizing performances in the tent, with admission charges for the public [...] Every now and then, the party demonstrated the ceremonies of a gypsy wedding. The fees paid at the performances would be sufficient for the gypsy party. (SOU 1923:2, p. 370)

The site of concern is a meadow just at the city's border and next to the northern main entrance road (on Hisingen, an island on other side of the river Göta Älv). The area around the meadow is known for its early industries (but does not figure in local descriptions) and is traversed by a small river. The area, just at the fringe between urban structures and the hinterland, was a key to the city. We have found records also from the 1950s telling about Roma camps in this area, which suggests that the meadow in Backa has continuously been used as a Roma campsite (Aftonposten 1952, 11 March and 1952, 31 July). Squatting, most probably in the original sense and without permission, could enable for many kinds of interaction with people passing. What we see from these reports is that here dwelling evolved over time and that the Roma could make use of a site where many people passed but where land not yet exploited and city planning not yet had been implemented.

The Government Official Report of 1923 contains a record also about Roma living in Grimmered (#6). At this time a small village located just outside the city border southwest of Gothenburg, Grimmered had commons and also a small tarn. The report tells about Johan Kaldaras Columber, born in Hungary 1877, and his strategies to earning a living and dwelling.

> Up until three or four years ago, Columber had earned his living by coppersmith work why he had travelled from one place to another. Thereafter he engaged with amusement park business. During wintertime Columber also traded iron and scrap-metal. For some time now and for a fee he has provided air swings tours, roundabouts and shooting range to the public in Grimmered / ... /. In summertime, Columber and his family lived in tents, and during winter they stayed in single housing trailer owned by Columber. When extremely cold, Columber and his family rented indoor housing [...] The Columber family does not have a fixed residence. In the near future, the family will leave [but it] is not yet decided upon where they are going next. (SOU 1923:2, p. 385)

In this example, as well as in the last, there are no hints at all on disturbance or trouble, but instead the report gives an important contribution to understanding the different kinds of interactions between multi-sited dwellers and locals that enfolded around the Roma dwellings in the urban landscape. The interaction of concern is reported with neutral objectivity (Figure 3).

There are reports on Roma family at yet another meadow, named in a press photography caption of 1949 as 'Gypsy-camp at Levgrens äng' (Kamerareportage BbankG172021). The photo shows that the camp at Levgrens äng (#7) was placed along a small road and consisted of two caravans supplemented by a small tent. The children in the family are out playing. Levgrens äng, a meadow, was until 1958 an unexploited spot, located slightly east of central Gothenburg. According to local narratives it was known as a refuge for thieves and bandits (Fredberg 1922–1924, chapter 12).

From interviewing a Roma woman born in the 1930s and who stayed at this camp when being a child, we learned that the meadow was particularly

Figure 3. Roma family camping at Levgrens meadow (#7) in 1949 showing two wooden caravans of quite modern design and a small box-shaped tent. At the time this meadow was an unexploited lot close to many junctions and just outside central Gothenburg. Photo from the press archive Kamerareportage, number BbankG172021. Reproduced with permission by Kamerareportage

suitable because of its closeness to Heden, the main motor market of the period and the site for the family's main source of income. She also recalls another camp, situated behind the central railway station, and explains how this location was particularly useful during the Second World War when the Roma often had to move by train because of the reduction of horses available. The location of a camp near the central railway station gave the advantage of access to washing rooms, water and heated indoor (Figure 4).

This camp, located behind the railway station on the street Kruthusgatan (#8), was the target of a Swedish National Television's visit in 1944. The report from the 'gypsy campsite' reported twenty people living in caravans and large box-shaped tents. Children are playing in the street and a young woman stands in the small kitchen inside of a caravan. The reporter notes that the camp is cleaner and better equipped than at earlier visits (Swedish

Figure 4. The inside of a well-equipped caravan of 1944 found at Kruthusgatan (#8) close to the central station. The photo was shot by a reporter from the Swedish National Television. Photo from the press archive Kamerareportage, number G120400. Reproduced with permission by Kamerareportage.

National Television 1944, 13 November; Kamerareportage Scagn-71, Scang-73 and Scg-72, G120400).

Some years later, in March 1952, local newspapers report that a Roma family was evicted by the police ordinance from their camp at the park Bergslagsparken, located at one end of Kruthusgatan (Holmberg 2010, Aftonposten 1952, 11 March, Kamerareportage BbankG140638). This eviction happened the same year as the Roma were accepted Swedish citizens, but while still the local ordinances were going. Photographs from the day of eviction show aspects of the complex situation: a group of policemen are talking to the Roma family in the park, some policemen and members of the family sit down on chairs; and a caravan is parked in the otherwise desolated park. As shared in the self-biography of Hans Caldaras, Rom, writer and artist, the camp at the central railway station is part of his childhood memory in the years around 1951. He recalls and describes the eviction as traumatic (Caldaras 2005, pp. 87–88, presentation at the City Museum of Gothenburg 20130525).

Dwelling as tenacy-in-hotels[23]

As mentioned above, one of the Roma families used to stay indoors in winter, which we understand as some kind of tenure. Not knowing where such tenure occurred, we were very happy to find several reports on Roma tenure in the 1923 Government Official Report. The locations were all very central and specified as either the street Postgatan #9, adjacent to the central railway station, or as a register in Christinae församling, one of the central parishes. From the mid-1800s and into the 1900s this street was particularly known for countless hotels and inns, 'room for travelers', boarding houses, cafes and emigrant offices (Lönnroth 2003, p. 444). Emigrants going overseas or travellers to elsewhere, those waiting for the next ship or for relatives to join, all stayed in Gothenburg's district with cheap hotels for shorter or longer periods.

> [T]he streets are dark and narrow, the houses are old-fashioned, the yards often terrible. The traffic of peasants and emigrants runs through the neighborhood. In this area arises a particular kind of individual more distinctly than elsewhere: the vagabond. Nowhere but here a richer sample of vagabond types occurs: tricksters, dodgers, drinkers, idlers, has-beens – some of them with the particular elegance of the has-been, some more broken, and many with a more or less pronounced predatory physiognomy. (Fredberg 1922–1924, p. 410)

The addresses particularly mentioned in the report were located towards the east, a part with many simple hotels and beds as bunks along the walls (Krantz 1943, p. 150). Here we meet some Roma families that stayed for longer or shorter periods on tenure in hotels. One Roma family consisted of spouses and nine children, but also within their realm another ten named individuals of different ages (SOU 1923:2, p. 371).[24] Another family of spouses and two children was reported as registered in the same parish and as having stayed at Postgatan for only some weeks during winter, but was then evicted. The conditions of yet another Roma family are extensively reported and hence of particular interest in the context of assembling 'Roma urban places in Gothenburg before settlement'.

Horse trader Maximilian Karl Hiller of catholic religion and born in Schlesien 1808, and his housekeeper Antonie Elisabet Winkler born 1868 in Oppeln, Ober-Schlesien, moved into Christine Parish, house No. 41 Postgatan on 1 February 1916, and moved to Bans parish, Malmöhus län, on 2 January 1920. It is told that:

> They had arrived at hotel Victoria with 7 children on th 12th of January 1915 […] They informed that the reason for their arrival was travelling in order to perform music. On the 6th of May all of them have left the hotel, stating that

they headed for Uddevalla. Members of this family have later stayed at the same hotel and other hotels in Gothenburg [but only before the] 27th of March 1917. […]

While living in Gothenburg, the older Hiller had traveled around to markets and traded horses. All family members had behaved particularly well and there had not been any reason for remarks. Two daughters went to school from April 14th to May 15th [. .] one son was skilled in reading and writing. In the beginning of 1915, Hiller, who had resided in this country since about 15 years, settled in Post-gatan No 41, where he immediately appeared to be inscribed in the national and local registers, and thereafter mainly has resided in the town mentioned until fall 1915. Thereafter Hiller, in the company of a Roma [zigenare] called Karl Axel Johansson, for two years had travelled around on the countryside of the Swedish midlands to perform horse trade whereby not staying at one place for more than 14 days. During this period, Hiller had often visited Gothenburg, but not stayed for more than a couple of days. (SOU 1923:2, p. 372)

What we learn here is that this family is a story of subordination and strategy. The report uses extensive space telling circumstances that do not conform to hegemonic discourse. It declares an instance of ambivalence and thus gives an important contribution to understanding the variety of relations between the Roma and the majority prevalent in the urban context, a history of co-habitation.

The street Postgatan was brought up again later. A newspaper of 1942 reports of Roma, that had never before been registered by local authorities, suddenly were registered at a non-existing hotel on the address Postgatan 25, which is all explained as related to food restrictions (permanent residence being a prerequisite for access to food cards): '53 Roma were revived from nowhere' (Göteborgs Handels och sjöfartstidning 1942, 05 May) (Figure 5).

Tenure of rooms for longer and shorter periods of time in more or less simple hotels crowded with ordinary travellers, migrants and 'vagrants', in the urban centre but close to the railway and the ships. This is one important site enabling for Roma dwelling within the urban centre. In these reports, tenure does only denote renting for certain longer periods, and we learn that some were considered to manage this situation as well as any other, and that some were not.

Dwelling as owner occupancy[25]

In 1920, a Roma man with horse trading as provision was reported staying at a hotel at Postgatan for one night. For several reasons we assume that he is identical to a person mentioned as the purchaser of a property at Ånäsvägen No. 13 the same year (SOU 1923:2, p. 372). The street Ånäsvägen (#10) situated north east of the town and fairly close to Gubberoparken (#2) of above was planned and constructed in the early twentieth century. He is called 'the Nor-wegian horse trader' and it is reported that he and his wife with four children

Figure 5. Dwelling as tenancy-in-hotels was common as winter lodging. From 1910s until 1942 there are several reports that tell of Roma people renting rooms in the hotels on Postgatan (#9) in the district Östra Nordstan. In the end of the nineteenth and beginning of twentieth centuries, this part of the city was Gothenburg's major emigrant district and disrepute for its many cheap hotels. It was packed with hotels, inns, 'room for travelers', cafés and emigrant offices. Postgatan is located close to the central railway station and to Kruthusgatan (#8). Photo from the press archive Kamerareportage, number BbankG0037607. Reproduced with permission by Kamerareportage.

fulfilled the parish registration when the purchase was settled. While it seems as if the family never moved into the house (but some months later moved to the municipality of Kungsbacka) in this report we have indications that some Roma individuals in Sweden in the early decades of the nineteenth century had a wider spectrum of relations to dwelling and tenure than hitherto known. Although the sources are rare, we find this report a key to wider explorations of the relations of Roma to majority society and, in particular, to dwelling in contemporary times of overt racism.

Ephemeral topographies of Roma urban dwelling

Much research that concern the Roma have been carried out within the specialist sphere of Roma studies, which means that the Roma very seldom have been of interest within mainstream social or cultural theory (Mayall 2004, p. 25ff). Robins (2010) argues that this lack of recognition has led to a large neglect of their contributions to a changing Europe. Departing from

Robins' account, this paper comprehends Roma history as integral to the place where they have been, which means that the paper focuses on how Roma historical dwelling is entangled in connections and interactions at, but also beyond, the location of concern. Hence, this paper does not designate the sites found as 'belonging' solely to Roma urban history (as a kind of 'Swedish Roma urban landscape' apart and detached from other landscapes), and does not even understand these sites as being particularly related to dwelling practices of a certain nomadic groups (cf. Miggelbrink *et al.* 2013) or to issues such as migration.

Although the continual forced vagrancy around the turn of the last century produced many short-term sites for dwelling, we can discern some emerging topological patterns[26]: camping in open fields and meadows (commons) while using the legal boundary of the city as a node; long-term rent of hotel rooms in the way in the wrinkles of the dense urban fabric while mingling well with other migrants and itinerants; squatting as an unintended use of planned areas and interstices (railway complexes, parks, junctions). The Roma have made use of what Saltzman (2009) calls 'interstices': in-betweens and ephemeral zones where territories and regulation is ambiguous.

The locations of concern can be related to the gradual expansion of the city and the sites therefore moved around over the time period studied. Until the beginning of 1900s the Roma sites mostly were situated south and east of the city, along the entrance roads. This changed as the municipal borders were dislocated through the successive expansion of Gothenburg through incorporation of adjacent parishes. The first record of a campsite north of town, on Hisingen in 1923, foreshadows the later 1950s many Roma settlements in this area. When industrial plants spread in the northern districts, this part of the city seems to having been favoured by the Gothenburg's Roma as the campsite location.

The different historical contexts have enabled for varying and particular dwelling strategies that relate differently to the mobility–immobility axis over time and space. While the Roma generally seem to have practised a seasonal mobility between rural and urban sites in the nineteenth century, the twentieth century brought an increasing urban dwelling. This often took place 'in less privileged spaces', but also as a hybrid system made up by a combination of objects, technologies, socialities and affects (Hannam et al. 2006, pp. 12, 14).

Conclusion

As argued in this paper, knowledge of Roma urban dwelling needs to be understood as related to varying historical contexts, sometimes harsh regulation by governmental control and sometimes conditioned within general concerns for social stability, but all the time sited within locality and made up by connections between here and elsewhere, and between social and corporeal subjects. In framing the argument of this paper we contend that the fact of the Roma per se being targets for control, surveillance and expulsion is crucial but, while at heart of mobility studies, that it does not alone enable for embracing the full multifacetedness of Roma urban dwelling before 1952. We stand with findings that point out the fact of a topography of Roma urban dwelling before settlement; we have traced some aspects of the genealogies of repression and of circumscription of Roma dwelling; we find ambivalent accounts the Roma in the discourses that make up the very fundament for repression. In resisting on bringing a self-sustained and coherent interpretation of the findings, the paper nevertheless tries to reach beyond mere description and to bring forth a counter-history: one of urban co-habitation. The sites found can in this perspective be 'sites of resistance' not only for its users and dwellers, but also for its contemporary interpreters.

The assemblage 'Roma urban places before settlement' has departed from the notion of the Roma as corporeal and geographical subjects partaking in the continually evolving transformation of the urban landscape. The many Roma places for dwelling found in the empirical material give witnesses to an urban reality of co-habitation that consists of many different and heterogeneous kinds of subjects, trajectories and interactions (whereof the Roma are but one).

The study revealed all in all 10 different sites that were in use during varying periods and each with different interrelations with society. The sites, in and of themselves, show in what ways the urban spatial and material topography of different time-periods has been able to comprise and hold different subjects and phenomena, and even those understood as 'problematic' within hegemonic discourse. The sites reveal not only the heterotopicality and interconnectedness of urban landscapes, but also the very shifting reality of Roma dwelling. This dwelling not only shows similarities with the conventional tenure spectrum but also shows some particularities related to duration, position and kinds of connection.

From the assemblage perspective, the connections exposed at these sites are not only between different people, places, materialities, things and flows over space and time, but also between these entities and the very sources that the study has made use of. While much of the empirical material is produced as registers of control, it is nevertheless obvious that it also can reveal that Roma dwelling in Gothenburg was a situation of connection and co-habitation. In giving another and different picture of Roma everyday historical dwelling, knowledge of these places per se take us well beyond hegemonic discourse, into ambivalence and also into the politics of future possibilities.

Note

1. The first evidence of Roma presence in Sweden is found in year 1512 when a group of 'tatare' arrived in Stockholm (Almquist & Hildebrand 1931, p. 272). A regulation of 1637 says that all 'tartars' should be driven out of the country, and yet another law (the Hang law) stated that all Roma men should be to be hung without trial. During the same century all Roma present in Sweden were relegated eastwards (today Finland) (SOU 2010:55, pp. 137–173).
2. But cf. the illegal and covert police register, uncovered in September 2013 by a Swedish newspaper (Orrenius 2013).
3. Cf. Liégeois (2012) on the terminology deployed by the Council of Europe.
4. Within the Swedish minority politics there are several different groups and among them those who often refer to themselves as Resande, i.e. Travellers. Among the travellers there are some that do regard themselves as part of the Roma minority and others who do not (SOU, 2010:55 p.81–82:113). For more details on terminology and difficulties, see Council of Europe (2011), Hancock (2002), Lucassen et al. (1998), Svensson (1993, p. 87).
5. It should be noted that before the turn of the last century, occasionally, the historical term 'zigenare' also comprised the historical term 'tattare' (Montesino Parra 2002). In our study this complication has been handled.
6. An exception is found among our interviewees (Personal communication, 19 Dec 2013).
7. In this study it has not been feasible to find and deploy a differentiated endonym terminology of the kind suggested by Hancock.
8. It is often stressed that that many people did not define themselves as Roma only for the sake of escaping discrimination or persecution.
9. With exception for the Sámi and Sverigefinnar, these small numbers are similar to the other Swedish national minorities. For statistics on Swedish minority groups, see SOU 1997:193. For historical numbers, see Svanberg & Tydén (2005).
10. The growing numbers have been explained as related to a growing awareness among the Roma of their particular situation, an extended identification with related groups, an official recognition of the numbers offered by Roma organizations. Although the numbers of Roma officially identified have been at least tripled over the last ten years, the numbers are largely unsettled since many countries, among them Sweden, do not register ethnicity, cultural- or language-based groups while other countries do (or do rely on numbers offered by Romany representatives).
11. See, for example, the historical works of Le Roy Ladurie (1981, 1997) that explore both local ambivalences around mobility (the village of Montaillou) and mobility as a strategy (The Platter's family). For a recent account of the centrality of understanding the past through the lens of mobility also in the context of the study of pre-historical times, see Leary (2014).
12. The political debate in Gothenburg in the 1950s regarding Roma housing is referred in Selling (2013, p. 138).
14. Personal communication with a Swedish Roma woman, 19 December 2013.
15. Mayall's study compares the dwelling practices of English 'Gypsy-travellers' with other itinerant groups, constantly stating that it is difficult to be completely sure of which group the facts refer to: itinerant beggars, tents- and van-dwellers or strolling outcasts, etc.

16. In Cottaar's study, 'itinerant population' refers to all kinds of people and groups and includes travellers (but not 'gypsies').
17. http://en.wikipedia.org/wiki/Housing_tenure.
18. All names used in the text are quoted from printed material. When personal communication is referred, no names are specified.
19. Numbers 1–8 on map.
20. As a results of over a hundred years' work with documenting popular culture, the archive at the Institute for Language and Folklore in Gothenburg holds a large collection of through interviews and question lists.
21. A 1914 photograph caption in a local newspaper also confirms this location: 'gypsies at Nya Varvet' (Kamerareportage BbankG129761).
22. Personal names have not yet been replaced or modified in citations. Definite decision regarding the use of personal names in this article will be done before publishing.
23. Numbers 9–10 on map.
24. It remains unclear if these individuals also are church registered in Gothenburg or if they only were living at the same address.
25. Number 10 on map.
26. But cf the discussion on fluid, gel-like and flickering topologies in Hannam *et al.* (2006, p. 14).

Disclosure statement

No potential conflict of interest was reported by the authors.

References

Aftonposten (1952) 'Sorg hos zigenarna vräks av nazister', *Aftonposten*, 11 March.
Aftonposten (1952) 'Zigenarlägret som anlitar telefonväckning', *Aftonposten*, 31 July.
Almquist, J. A. & Hildebrand, H. (1931) *Stockholms stadsböcker från äldre tid. Ser. 2:4, Stockholms stads tänkeböcker 1504–1514*, Stockholm, Kungliga Samfundet för utgivandet av handskrifter Skandinaviens historia.

Bancroft, A. (2005) *Roma and Gypsy-Travellers in Europe: Modernity, Race, Space, and Exclusion*, Aldershot, Ashgate.

Brun, C. & Setten, G. (2013) *Hus, hjem og sted. Geografiske perspektiver på vår samtid*, Trondheim, Akademika forlag.

Caldaras, H. (2005) *I betraktarens ögon*, Stockholm, Pan.

Cottaar, A. (1998) 'Dutch travellers: dwellings, origins and occupations', in *Gypsies and Other Itinerant Groups: A Socio-Historical Approach*, eds. L. Lucassen, W. Willems & A. Cottaar, Basingstoke, Macmillan, pp. 174–189.

Council of Europe (2011) *The Council of Europe: Protecting the Rights of Roma*. Strasbourg: Council of Europe Publishing, [online] Available at: http://www.coe.int/ AboutCoe/media /interface/publications/roms_en.pdf (accessed 20 January 2014).

Demetri, M., Dimiter-Taikon, A., & Olgaç, C. R., *et al.* (2011) 'Romernas okända kulturarv', I & M: invandrare & minoriteter, Norsborg, Stiftelsen Invandrare & minoriteter, vol. 38, no. 6, pp. 16–20.

Dimitrios, Z. (2011) 'Sedentary Roma (Gypsies) the case of Serres (Greece)', *Romani studies*, vol. 21, no. 1, pp. 23–56.

Faist, T. (2013) 'The mobility turn: a new paradigm for the social sciences?', *Ethnic and Racial Studies*, vol. 36, no. 11, pp. 1637–1646.

Fredberg, C. R. A. (1922–1924) *Det gamla Göteborg: lokalhistoriska skildringar, personalia och kulturdrag*, D. 3. Göteborg.

Gregory, D. (1994) *Geographical Imaginations*, Cambridge, MA, Blackwell.

Göteborgs Handels och Sjöfartstidning (1942), 'Kors i ring under deklarationsblanketten!', *Göteborgs Handels och Sjöfartstidning*, 05 May.

Hancock, I. F. (2002) *We are the Romani people = Ame sam e Rromane džene*, Hatfield, University of Hertfordshire Press.

Hancock, I. F. (2010) *Danger! Educated Gypsy: Selected Essays*, Hatfield, University of Hertfordshire Press.

Hannam, K., Sheller, M. & urry, J. (2006) 'Editorial: mobilities, immobilities and moorings', *Mobilities*, vol. 1, no. 1, pp. 1–22.

Holmberg, I. M. (2006) *På stadens yta: om historiseringen av Haga.* PhD thesis, University of Gothenburg, Göteborg, 2006, Göteborg & Stockholm, Makadam Förlag.

Holmberg, I. M. (forthcoming) 'On the 'limes' of heritage: handling Roma subalternism in official heritage practice', in International Journal of Heritage Studies.

Kamerareportage, photo-id: BbankG172021, BbankG151602, BbankG140638, BbankG129761, BbankG0037607, Scagn-71, Scang-73 och Scg-72, [online] Available at: http://bildarkiv.kamerareportage.se/fotoweb/Grid.fwx (accessed 14 March 2014).

Krantz, C. (1943) *Idyll och sensation i 1800-talets Göteborg*, Göteborg, Gumpert.

Leary, J. (2014) *Past Mobilities: Approaches to Movement and Mobility*, Abingdon, Ashgate Publishing.

Le Roy Ladurie, E. (1981) *Montaillou: Cathars and Catholics in a French Village, 1294–1324*, Harmondsworth, Penguin. (Originally published 1978)

Le Roy Ladurie, E. (1997) *The Beggar and the Professor: A Sixteenth-Century Family Saga*, Chicago, IL, University of Chicago Press.

Liégeois, J. P. (2012) *The Council of Europe and Roma 40 Years of Action*, Strasbourg, Council of Europe Publishing.

Lucassen, L. (1998) 'A blind spot: migratory and travelling groups in Western European historiography', in *Gypsies and Other Itinerant Groups: A Socio-Historical Approach*, eds. L. Lucassen, W. Willems & A. Cottaar, Basingstoke, Macmillan, pp. 135–152.

Lucassen, L., *et al.* (1998) *Gypsies and Other Itinerant Groups: A Socio-Historical Approach*, Basingstoke, Macmillan.

Lundahl, M. (2013) Keynote at 'austere histories', in *International Symposium*, University of Linköping, Linköping, November 28–29.

Lönnroth, G. (2003) *Hus för hus i Göteborgs stadskärna*, Göteborg, Stadsbyggnadskontoret.

Marsh, A. R. N. (2008) No promised land: history, historiography and the origins of the Gypsies. PhD thesis, University of Greenwich.

Mayall, D. (1988) *Gypsy-Travellers in Nineteenth-Century Society*, Cambridge, Cambridge University Press.

Mayall, D. (2004) *Gypsy Identities, 1500–2000: From Egipcyans and Moon-Men to the Ethnic Romany*, London, Routledge.

Miggelbrink, J. *et al.* (2013) *Nomadic and Indigenous Spaces: Productions and Cognitions*, Abingdon, Ashgate Publishing.

Montesino Parra, N. (2002) *Zigenarfrågan*: intervention och romantik. PhD thesis, Socialhögskolan, Lund, Univ.

Okely, J. (1983) *The Traveller-Gypsies*, Cambridge, Cambridge University Press.

Orrenius, N. (2013) 'Över tusen barn med i olaglig kartläggning', *Dagens Nyheter*, 23 September, pp. 8–9, [online] Available at: http://www.dn.se/nyheter/sverige/over-tusen-barn-med-i-olaglig-kartlaggning/ (accessed 2 May 2014).

Palosuo, L. (2009) *En inventering av forskningen om romer i Sverige*, Uppsala, Centre for Multiethnic Research.

Pieris, A. (2013) 'Out of place: postcolonial traces of dynamic urbanism', in *Landscapes of Mobility: Culture, Politics, and Placemaking*, eds. A. Sen & J. Johung, Burlington, VT, Ashgate Publishing Company, pp. 185–206.

Pulma, P. (2006) *Suljetut ovet: Pohjoismaiden romanipolitiikka 1500-luvulta EU-aikaan*, [Closed doors: Nordic Romani policy from the 16th century to the EU era], Helsinki, Suomalaisen Kirjallisuuden Seura.

Reading, A. M. (2012) 'The European Roma, an unsettled right to memory', in *Public Memory, Public Media and the Politics of Justice*, eds. P. J. Lee & P. Thomas, Basingstoke, Palgrave Macmillan, pp. 121–140.

Reading, A. M. (2013) 'Europe's other world: Romany memory within the new dynamics of the globital memory field', in *Memory, Conflict and New Media: Web Wars in Post-Socialist States*, eds. E. Rutten, J. Fedor & V. Zvereva, pp. 21–31.

Robins, K. (2010) 'Why Roma? A brief introduction', *City: analysis of urban trends, culture, theory, policy, action*, vol. 14, no. 6, pp. 637–642.

Said, E.W. ([1979] 2003) *Orientalism*, London, Penguin.

Saltzman, K. (2009) *Mellanrummens möjligheter. Studier av föränderliga landskap*, Göteborg & Stockholm, Makadam Förlag.

Selling, J. (2013) *Svensk antiziganism: fördomens kontinuitet och förändringens förutsättningar*, Limhamn, Sekel.

Sen, A. & Johung, J. (2013) *Landscapes of Mobility: Culture, Politics, and Placemaking*, Burlington, Ashgate.

Sheller, M. (2011) *Mobility*. Sociopedia.isa 2011.

Söderström, O. (2014) *Cities in Relations: Trajectories of Urban Development in Hanoi and Ouagadougou*, Oxford, Wiley-Blackwell.

SOU 1923:2 (1923), *Förslag till lag om lösdrivares behandling m. fl. författningar*, [Swedish Government Official Reports 1923:2], Stockholm.

SOU 1956:43 (1956), *1954 års zigenarutredning. Zigenarfrågan: betänkande* [Swedish Government Official Reports 1956:43], Stockholm.

SOU 1997:193 (1997) *Steg mot en minoritetspolitik: betänkande*. Europarådets konvention för skydd av nationella minoriteter. Minoritetsspråkskommittén, 1997 [Swedish Government Official Reports 1997:193], Stockholm, Fritze.

SOU 2010:55 (2010) *Romers Rätt: en strategi för romer i Sverige. Delegationen för romska frågor* [Swedish Government Official Reports 2010:55], Stockholm, Fritze.

Spivak, G.C. (1988) 'Can the subaltern speak?', in *Marxism and the Interpretation of Culture*, eds. C. Nelson & L. Grossberg, Houndmills, Macmillan Education, pp. 217–313.

Svanberg, I. & Tydén, M. (2005) *Tusen år av invandring: en svensk kulturhistoria*, 3rd edn, Stockholm, Dialogos.

Svensson, B. (1993) Bortom all ära och redlighet: tattarnas spel med rättvisan, PhD thesis, Lund, Univ.

Swedish National Television (1944). [online] Available at: http://www.svtplay.se/klipp/132649/lager-med-nybyggda-husvagnar (accessed 13 November 1944).

Taikon, K. (1963) Zigenerska, Stockholm, Wahlström & Widstrand.

Takman, J. (1976) The Gypsies in Sweden: a socio-medical study, PhD thesis, Uppsala, Univ.

Tervonen, M. (2010) 'Gypsies', 'travellers' and peasants. A study on ethnic boundary drawing in Finland and Sweden, c 1860–1925, PhD thesis, European University Institute.

Tillhagen, C. H. (1961) "Thet folket, som fara omkring", in Fataburen: kulturhistorisk tidskrift, Stockholm, Nordiska museet, pp. 37–60.

Tillhagen, C. H. (1965) *Zigenarna i Sverige*, Stockholm, Natur o. kultur.

Multi-local lifeworlds: between movement and mooring[†]

Nicola Hilti

Departement Architektur, ETH Wohnforum – ETH CASE, ETH Zürich, Zürich, Switzerland

ABSTRACT
Multi-local living is on the rise. This development was the starting point for my considerations. The term describes the long-term living arrangements across two or more residences. This is by no means a new social phenomenon, but it has been undergoing a fundamental change due to the ever-faster social changes in late modernity. It interacts with numerous social fields of action, for example with the infrastructures of housing and transport, settlement trends, civic commitment, social relationships (partnership, family, or neighbourhood), or investment behaviour. The present paper is based on a study which above all aimed to explore the phenomenological breadth of multi-local living. The study design puts a strong emphasis on the multi-locals' practices of everyday life. The issues raised relate to action patterns in and meanings of multi-local arrangements, focusing on the relationality of the housing locations. The methodological core of the study consists of 31 qualitative interviews with multi-local actors (and some of their partners) in Switzerland. The main findings resulted in a real-world typology of the lifeworlds of people living multi-locally. Based on the present analysis of multi-local living, a phenomenon emerges that cannot be attributed to a specific academic research field but must be regarded as a distinctive socio-spatial strategy.

'Room wanted for 2–3 days a week' or: why multi-local living is relevant

When browsing rental ads, a particular form of living arrangement has become striking in recent times: living in multiple places. On the demand side it says, for example: 'Room wanted for 2–3 days a week' or 'Homesick Viennese looking for attic room'. On the supply side we may read: 'Looking for occasional flat mate' or 'Short-term rental flat (by week or by month)'.

[†]This article is based on a study conducted for my Ph.D. thesis 'Here – There – Between. Lifeworlds of Multi-local Residents between Movement and Mooring' (ETH Zurich, 2011) and on further considerations.

Such adverts can be found in great numbers and they reflect a socio-spatial practice that is gaining increasing attention and focus from diverse actors of research and practice: multi-local living. However, we are aware of a growing discrepancy between social interests, perception of the problem, and qualified understanding of this phenomenon.

The great attention currently being paid to multi-local living is based on the everyday life observation that more and more people are using multiple residences and that the forms of use are becoming highly diversified. The apparent ubiquity and the direct or indirect individual experience with multi-local living sometimes even results in regarding multi-local living as a new 'megatrend', as a major long-term driving force of social transformation (swissfuture 2012). Yet it is often ignored that multi-local living is in no way an entirely new social development, but rather existed in various pre-modern forms, such as the upper-class summer retreats, seafarers, migrant labour, the Swabian children (i.e. children taken from poor Alpine farmers to work on German farms), or members of the armed forces (Bendix and Löfgren 2007, p. 8f, Hilti 2009, Weichhart 2009). It is, however, a late-modern novelty that multi-local living is not restricted to social elites or marginalized groups, but – as qualitative research on the phenomenon has shown (Rolshoven 2009, Hilti 2013) – includes broad levels of society. Yet in discourses, the issue is still frequently reduced to either social elites in terms of 'job nomads' or to forced mobility of less privileged population groups, triggered by economic necessities. Multi-local living turns out to be a 'projection screen' for opposed concepts and attributions. Even in research, we note a preference to focus either on the individual suffering of a mobile way of life caused by economic constraints (Sennett 2000) or on the culturally productive or even subversive force of multi-local living (Rolshoven 2007). In fact, however, multi-local living is a dynamic social phenomenon that flourishes in a complex structure of controversial fields and, thus, resists dichotomous attributions. Such a controversial field that is specifically reflected by multi-local living is represented by mobility and mooring: People living multi-locally are located in more than one place and are repeatedly and simultaneously mobile between these places of residence. What applies to housing as a practice in general finds its particularly striking expression in living in multiple places: Housing is 'always immobile and mobile at the same time', even if it 'appears to be static, reified, enclosed' (Breckner 2002, p. 145).

Because of its increasing quantitative and qualitative significance, its complexity and dynamics, multi-local living has far-reaching consequences for numerous social fields of practice and, on the individual level, has a great impact on various spheres of life such as housing, working, leisure, or social relations. What is more, multi-local living is a definite, actively chosen way of shaping one's life and its actors are engaged in close interaction with the processes and conditions of late-modern western society, relating for example to: globalization and Europeanization, migration and transnationalization, changes in working conditions, development of new technologies of information, communication and transport, the emergence of (international) mass tourism, and female emancipation. On the structural level, multi-local living, therefore, is interrelated in manifold ways with other social fields of action and systems, all of which are also responsible for the framework of this way of life and relating to: economy (e.g. the changing working world, transnational companies, housing industry), politics (e.g. political participation, exercising civil rights), laws (regarding e.g. taxes, residence permits, voting), and planning (architecture and settlement development, spatial and regional planning, transport). Multi-local living and its ever-growing significance as an option of one's conduct of life have thrown up a number of complex social, political, economic, administrative, and planning questions. Therefore, it seems to make sense to regard and explore multi-local living as an independent socio-spatial strategy (Weichhart 2009, p. 7).

With this in mind, the paper aims to raise awareness of the lifeworlds of people living multi-locally. It is assumed that a comprehensive lifeworld understanding will only be possible when the different housing situations[1] are related to one another, specifically regarding their respective attribution of meaning, practices, and materializations. Moreover, depending on the context of origin of the multi-local living arrangements and on the self-concept of the multi-locals, specific types of multi-local lifeworld may be identified, which may be distinguished through the relationship of the housing situations. Based on a completed qualitative-explorative study of multi-locals in Switzerland, this hypothesis is scrutinized. To start with, the following considerations include a brief outline of the state-of-the-art research as well as the theoretical and methodological concepts of the study.

The concept of the study

The study is based on a subject-oriented, lifeworld approach. This subjective perspective is theoretically embedded in phenomenological sociology, which focuses on the structure of everyday lifeworlds (Peuckert 2006). The actors produce social reality through their actions; the analysis aims to uncover the hidden subjective meaning and reconstruct the relevant frames of meaning and reference (Schröer 1997, Lueger 2000). Qualitative exploration pays attention to the phenomenological range of the forms, relevance, and practices of multi-local living. The analysis of lived experience enhances the understanding of this way of life and may explain the actor's 'meaningful action' (Alasuutari 2000, p. 2). The research questions revolve around: the motives and purposes of a multi-local way of life, coping strategies, the relevance of multi-local living for place and group attachment and for local ties (e.g. feeling at home/mooring, social contacts, or civic involvement), the significance of being mobile and housing as well as their relationship to each other, and the interaction of the housing situations constituting the multi-local living arrangement.

The methodological key element of the study presented here in parts consists of 31 qualitative interviews conducted with 36 people living multi-locally in Switzerland, among them five partners. These interviews make up the methodological core of the study. Furthermore, a number of additional sources were collected, to illustrate the wider context of multi-local ways of life, such as: interview transcripts, research memos, short questionnaires, photos, (media-based) discourses, and secondary data statistics.

In accordance with the exploratory approach, the target group was defined very widely as: people who have more than one place of residence, at least one of which has to be located in Switzerland. These residences are used on a more or less regular basis. Their common feature is living in several places, which, by exercising a substantial influence, is a relevant structural element of the conduct of life.

The interviews followed the technique of the problem-centred interview (Witzel 2000). It includes questions and narrative inputs which are directed towards revealing biographical data relating to a specific issue. Characteristic features of the method include the orientation on a socially relevant issue, orientation of the methods employed on the object, and process orientation (Flick 2002). The respondents are regarded as experts of their everyday lives. Owing to its methodological and theoretical principles, the problem-centred interview is suitable to describe and reconstruct the motives, contexts of reasoning and action patterns of people living multi-locally; the data collection may also encourage the elaboration of theoretical concepts.

In the beginning, respondents were recruited quite unsystematically via independent contact networks, which, by employing the method of snowball sampling, gave access to new contacts. Moreover and quite surprisingly, an enquiry at my home municipality's residents' registration office rendered a list of people living multi-locally and, hence, potential respondents. Furthermore, I used Internet portals with real estate adverts such as 'Homesick Appenzeller looking for a second home' to gain access to users of second homes. Additionally, I addressed specific target groups of multi-locals via gatekeepers. That was how, for instance, I managed to interview owners of static caravans. Parallel to the progress in analysis, the search became increasingly systematic to close gaps in the respondents' group and ensure structural variance. The selection aimed at grasping the heterogeneity of the field of study (Schlehe 2003, p. 83) and at uncovering the relevant dimensions and variants of multi-local living. In order to achieve these objectives, theoretically relevant combinations of characteristics were considered as comprehensively as possible (Kelle and Kluge 1999, p. 53). Therefore, the composition of the interview partners must be understood as an exemplary selection based on the principles of heterogeneity and structural variance.

To begin with, the variance systematically observed in the selection refers to the structural characteristics of the multi-local living arrangements which should also include extremes, for example: the distance between the living arrangements: Two respondents lived alternately in flats that were only a 15-minute bus ride apart. On the other hand, I talked to a man who alternately lived in Switzerland and in the USA, in other words in two places a 12-hour flight apart. These examples include various other characteristics which are reflected by the sample, such as national and transnational cases. This is connected with the rhythm of living in several places, which ranges from annual intervals to seasonal, weekly and even shorter ones and which vary in the degree of regularity of the movements between here and there. Furthermore, the patterns of multi-local living differ in their complexity: Some of the cases belonged to the 'classic' weekly commuters, while others are spatially and functionally interwoven by combining the multi-local arrangement with other forms of mobility (e.g. with daily commuting). Other characteristics which may vary relate, for instance, to the form of housing and housing tenure (e.g. ownership, rented homes, room in a shared flat, hotel, caravan, the couch of a relative, or office folding bed) as well as to the (apparently) major reasons for living multi-locally (e.g. working, leisure activities, partnership, mixed forms). Even though I did consider variations of personal socio-structural characteristics, such as social position, gender, age, and occupational groups, I did not make too many restrictions in order not to obstruct our view of the unexpected.

With a few exceptions, the interviews with the multi-locals were conducted at one of their residences and with their partners at their single residence. Choosing a familiar setting for the interview creates a favourable influence on the dialogue atmosphere. Several authors have pointed out the advantage of a 'natural field situation' in terms of the closeness to the lifeworld (Lamnek 1995, p. 103). Moreover, gaining insight into the residences serves as an important additional source of information (Lang 1998, p. 92).

Evaluation of the data, which consisted primarily of interview transcripts, followed various suggestions from literature which, on the one hand, rely on reconstruction technique (Froschauer and Lueger 1992, Lueger 2000, Froschauer and Lueger 2003) and, on the other hand, comprise descriptive approaches – a combination considered highly useful by the hermeneutic sociology of knowledge, which is closely related to phenomenological sociology.

The text analysis is based on a hermeneutic approach, which adapts the rough analysis to the exploration of complex social systems (Froschauer and Lueger 1992, Lueger 2000). This method comprises four steps: First, what has been said is reduced by paraphrasing it. Second, the question is raised which intentions the respondent pursues with their answer. The third level refers to the conditions of context under which the statements have been made. These contexts are twofold: In the interviews, aspects are included that are directly related to the text production (in this case the interview), such as the potential influence of the interviewer. The reflection of the context of development is highly important for second-order data. As Lueger (2000, p. 212) has pointed out, the second context refers to the lifeworld represented in the text and the milieu as major object of research. For this purpose, the interpreters picture the structural framework conditions of the respondent's action field. The action conditions, then, allow for drawing conclusions on a 'hypothetic cause-effect relationship' (Lueger 2000, p. 212). The action sequences thus obtained become the guiding perspective for the subsequent interpretations. This way, I succeed in (re)constructing the observation schemes included in a text and constituted in an action field in the course of everyday practice. Furthermore, I also reconstruct the associated, collectively constituted horizons of meaning of an action field (Lueger 2000, p. 215).

The particular characteristic of the relationship between here and there may be matched with specific features of the relevant dimensions of the multi-local way of life: The time axis includes the context of origin and self-concept, the social axis refers to the social conduct of life, and the spatial axis relates to (spatial) mooring and place attachment. All three dimensions interact with one another; regarding them separately, however, makes sense as this serves the abstraction and theorization of the phenomenon. They refer to the central topics which are discussed in research on and practice of multi-local living: Who are the multi-local residents and which are their motives and purposes to pursue this way of life? What are the effects of multi-local living on social relations? How does multi-local living relate to (spatial) mooring and place attachment?

Based on selected empirical material, I have designed a typology of the lifeworlds of multi-local residents, which helps structure this heterogeneous and complex phenomenon, systematize it and make it comprehensible (Kluge 2000).

Lifeworlds of multi-local residents

Parallel worlds: a compromise

Paul is a forest manager, 45 years old, married and father of three children. Since he could not find any adequate employment in the surrounding area of his native village in Eastern Switzerland and did not want to leave the place, he has been a weekly commuter for 11 years. Twenty-nine-year-old Ivan is a Ph.D. student and lives with his wife and child in the Tyrol. From Monday to Thursday or Friday he stays in Zurich, his place of study, where he has sublet a room from an elderly lady. Maurice is a lawyer, 35 years old and lives with his cohabitee in Zurich. From Monday to Friday he rooms in a flat share in Berne, where he works for the federal administration.

The above-mentioned multi-local arrangements have emerged from job-related requirements and mediate in terms of a compromise between different needs which cannot be satisfied at the primary place of residence. However, it is the aim of the people involved to terminate the arrangements and their personal ideal is to live at a single residence. Among others, this is expressed by the practised hierarchy of the housing situations (primary and secondary residences), which manifests itself in the rigorous demarcation between private life and work life and in the divergence of social relations. It is a particular challenge of this way of life to establish balance and continuity, especially of the relationships, with the structuring of time being a possibility of conflict. Both Paul and Ivan explicitly regard only one place of residence as primary residence and home of their families. The hierarchy of relevance is also reflected by the physical design of housing: The set-up at the secondary residence is very basic and purely functional, whereas the primary residence has a 'homely' atmosphere so that, according to Paul, 'actual living' only takes place there. The use of the places also displays a marked difference: at the secondary place of residence, it is reductive; at the primary one, it is extensive. Paul suffers from his multi-local way of life, especially from the separation from his family, because, as he points out: 'I miss out so many things.' Ivan, on the other hand, takes the (temporary) arrangement relatively easy – even though it is certainly not ideal for him – because it is a key to advancement on the career ladder and to personal achievement. According to Ivan, the office folding bed, for instance, serves the purpose to avoid a 'not-so-good CV'.

In this case, the relationship of the housing situations to each other is characterized by a marked differentiation and hierarchizing, which finds expression on all levels relating to self-conception, the social conduct of life, and the physical equipment. This pattern may be conceived as the lifeworld type of *parallel worlds*, which may be divided into two subtypes: The subtype 'dissatisfaction' displays an overall negative attitude to the multi-local living arrangement. On the other hand, the subtype 'ambition' sees some positive aspects by defining multi-local living as a necessary, yet endurable way to jump up the career ladder.

Counter worlds: happy with contrasting places

From spring to autumn, 54-year-old Barbara and her 60-year-old husband manage a camping site in Basel, where they live in a flat provided by the employer. The winter season they spend at their house on the Costa Blanca, Spain. Marta, a 68-year-old retiree, lives in a flat in the surroundings of Zurich, and owns a small flat in a block of flats in Ticino where she has come to relax for several days for many years. Karl, a 69-year-old retired teacher, owns a house together with his wife in the surroundings of Zurich, as well as a simple hut in a small alpine village, which can only be reached by a private cable car. The couple always spends there several days or weeks a year.

All these cases have in common that the multi-local living arrangements allow them to live a 'different' life at another place, which suits their personal lifestyles because they 'like both' (Barbara). The examples show that job-related and private reasons and motives overlap. The relationship between the housing situations complementing each other is egalitarian. Multi-local living offers a temporary or thrilling distraction from everyday (work) life, which combines the notion of gaining freedom. Another relevant feature is the temporary escape from the narrowing milieu of origin and, as it were, the reverse, the recollection of some past place of desire. Contrast as major characteristic refers to the social conduct of life, which is coped with in a spatio-temporally divergent way. As regards the possibility of social conflicts, one option is staying away for some time so that 'the storm of quarrel sub-sides' (Marta). On the other hand, the contrasting ways of life here and there contain a special potential for generating conflicts because of the quickly changing social environment and the totally different expectations involved. Feeling at home in several places is another facet or, as Barbara puts it, 'being at home there in winter and being at home here in summer'. Making the experience of two contrasting housing situations is intensified by the differences in materialities and infrastructures so that the change of location is often felt as a brake which requires some time of adjustment and getting used to the other place, which, for example, lacks appliances like a washing machine or dishwasher and where there is 'no dancing, but wood to chop' (Karl).

The above-mentioned examples show that contrast marks the key feature of the relationship of the housing situations to each other; therefore, this type may be described as *counter worlds*.

Double worlds: 'birds of a feather flock together'

Besides his parents' home in Switzerland, Peter, a 29-year-old radio host, musi-cian, and music producer, also has a flat in Los Angeles, where he wants to boost his art career. He lives there for several months a year and, moreover, travels widely throughout the world. He works at both places and at others. Monika is 37 years old, chief executive and politician and lives with her husband and their child in the canton of Lucerne. She has rented an additional flat in Coire, where she works for the cantonal healthcare authority. This way she avoids the incompatibility between her work and her political activities. Robert, aged 26, is an engineer and shares a flat with one of his colleagues in the canton of Zurich, from where he starts for his highly mobile job assignments which frequently require month-long business trips in Europe. From time to time he spends a few days in Berlin, his former place of study, where he has recently rented a flat, or visits his parents in a German small town.

All three afore-mentioned persons have in common that they live very similar lives in different places and do not make a clear distinction between here and there. Two or more similar and equivalent conducts of life stand side by side. Furthermore, in these cases, private and job-related reasons and motives overlap. The social conduct of life is convergent; the networks of relations coincide between and accord with the places of residence. Taking the example of Monika, both places are equally places of work, leisure, and family due to the structure of everyday life (the whole family commutes according to an elaborate rhythm). It is also typical that Monika actively takes part in the local political groups and the local theatre society. The duplicate nature of the arrangements also becomes apparent through the similarity of the rented flats: Both are about equal in size and are situated in Old Towns of Lucerne and Coire, respectively, about a 20-minute walk from the respective station. Here and there, the family highly appreciates the charm and atmosphere of the renovated flats in old buildings. Moreover, the size of the houses and the number of tenants (two and three, respectively) are very similar. As Monika points out about the flat in Coire, 'It's a house with only a few flats; so here, too, everybody knows each other.'

The different relationships between mobility and mooring represent a peculiarity of these empirical cases, which is mirrored in two ways: On the one hand, there is Peter, who makes his highly mobile 'getting around' in the world a matter of personal life principle. On the other hand, the longing for mooring becomes manifest, which is realized through the multiple homes, or exists only as the wish of an individual feeling like 'the man outside'.

Monika explicitly points out that she feels at home in multiple places when she says: 'My heart is for both places' and she considers multi-local living to be a privilege, which allows her to keep up everyday life relationships, biographically shaped, with the places relevant to her identity. Peter, on the other hand, finds 'inner fulfilment' to live a life across an extended possibility space. Taking advantage of the different assets (Weichhart 2009) and the commitment at the various places are manifold. Sometimes a family member's practice of multi-local living even becomes 'contagious' to other family members.

The above-mentioned notion of 'feeling at home' is contrasted by a multi-local housing situation which constitutes an obstacle to the longing for spatial rootedness. The respondents feel, neither here nor there, at home; according to Robert, 'there is no place' for them. They refer to themselves as uprooted, always 'getting the short end of the stick' (Robert). Their conducts of life are marked by extremely high mobility and many changes of location.

People like Robert, who is 'always on the go' and whose identity comes under pressure because of the high mobility, sometimes need to validate themselves and contemplate where 'home' is. However, even these specific cases cannot be associated with a total lack of some kind of 'feeling at home': Although the places of the multi-local living arrangements and the respondents' current ways of life do not convey the feeling of rootedness, other moorings which are not connected with a specific location may play an important role, such as religious beliefs, the co-mobile family, or even the virtual world.

This said, the major feature of this type relates to the interrelationship between the housing situations, which is characterized by the duplication of both the conduct of life and the material world; I, therefore, have called this type *double worlds*, which may be divided into the subtypes 'privilege' and '(spatial) homelessness'. The former relates to the positive interpretation of extended opportunities, the latter to the lack of or negatively experienced place attachment.

In-between worlds: meaningful space between here and there

Thomas, a 37-year-old architect, has arranged life over three locations: He spends the weekends in his flat in Berne; near his workplace in Coire, he has rented another accommodation. Once a week, when he is at his other workplace in Basel, he stays overnight at his parents' house in the Basel agglomerations. He keeps a spare suit at all three places because 'there's always some reason somewhere why I need to wear a suit'. Besides, he faces the challenge to use the time he spends on the road as efficiently as possible; therefore, he has started to learn Chinese by listening to compact discs in the car in order to be even better prepared for his globalized scope of activities. Marta, who is still very active after her retirement, is used to having dinner in the restaurant carriage on her weekly way back from her workplace in Berne: 'It's become a habit of mine since my husband doesn't live anymore. That way you don't have to eat alone; and yes, there's always something going on.' To Susanne, the railway compartment is more than a 'cocoon for movement'; it is rather a bit of a private living room, 'an extension of the living room', as it were. On her weekly trips from Zurich to Ticino, she regularly meets a young, good-looking man in this compartment; they smile at each other, greet and say good-bye to each other – and that is all. The tension between closeness and distance in the moving space fires Susanne's imagination: 'I've fancied that he'd work in television, or that he'd be an editor or a journalist.' She even imagines getting involved intimately with this man or another, yet only in the moving space. The relationship 'would be something almost unreal' and quite ephemeral: 'It comes from somewhere, it takes you with it, and then it goes on.'

Combining the advantages of several places within a living arrangement requires, on the one hand, the physical crossing of space, on the other hand, the individual effort to connect and master the transitions from here to there. As life shows, the function of the trip is frequently not limited to the tedious and, hopefully, quick crossing of space. Being on the road fulfils complex functions in the transition from one place to the other. The transitions reveal active and manifold patterns.

The special type of *in-between worlds* follows this line of thought, but runs somewhat transversely to the other types. In-between worlds are included in any multi-local living arrangement so that they need to be interpreted as characterizing the significance of the space between here and there and its design by the multi-local actors. They are 'places of flows' (Beck 2008, p. 34), yet are also built of immobile materialities (Wöhler 2008), from which ambivalent social processes emerge and new mobilities, stabilities, and consistencies arise. Analogous to the heterogeneity of multi-local living as such, in-between worlds display a broad scope of routinized and ritualized actions all of which mark the transitions between here and there and, as such, reveal the consistencies in the inconsistencies. Yet, we also find the reverse, the conscientious breaking with the same old patterns of action or, as Susanne puts it, 'doing something with a twist', for example, by changing the route. Travelling between the places of residence evokes a variety of emotions, ranging from hardship to pleasure and the experience sometimes works, in Peter's words, as 'reset button' which 'neutralizes'. The travel time is often seen as useful, especially on the train, the dominant means of transport in this study – be it in terms of productivity or relaxing, without facing any expectations. 'A three-hour train ride's no problem', says Maurice because the train turns into 'an office with a view', as Anton[2] points out. The actions related to the in-between world are determined by the spatio-temporal intervals of travelling, in other words, the stops along the routes structure the multi-locals' activities in the mobile space, particularly on the train. The in-between world is a space in which diverse forms of mobility (physical, virtual, communication-related, and mental ones) are intertwined. With the dimension of social interaction in mind, the in-between worlds are determined by both constraints and freedom so that we observe strategies of isolation as well as the emergence of particular social relations, which, in terms of a 'jester's licence' (Susanne), is only possible in the mobile space. The interaction of closeness and distance follows specific norms and rules which aim to reduce the potential for conflicts among highly diverse social groups, arising from temporary interaction. The type of in-between worlds is strongly affected by the transit infrastructure. A hybrid space between privacy and the public emerges from the multi-locals' dealing with the materialities, which are both enabling and restricting at the same time. This and the organization of everyday things – taken along or left behind – are indicators of the degree of competence in multi-local living, for instance, when the learning process advances 'from the huge suitcase to the backpack' as Fabian[3] explains.

Conclusion and outlook

The present study relies on the theory of lifeworld (Schütz 2003, Schütz and Luckmann 2003 [1975]) and puts focus on the phenomenological range of multi-local living, giving particular attention to the relationality between here and there. One of the major research questions dealt with the interrelationships of the housing situations within the multi-local living arrangements. Based on the relevant literature, the assumption was that the lifeworlds of multi-local residents can only be understood through the relational consideration of the entire living arrangement. The qualitative data analysis served to establish a real-world typology which turns the spotlight on relationality.

The established typology of multi-local lifeworlds is the result of organizing, systematizing, and analysing the available empirical material. The typology aims to provide deeper insights into the phenomenon of multi-local living, its diversity, and multi-layering. The types evolved from condensing the many individual cases, their action strategies and structures of meaning; yet they reveal an inner branching. The typology is based on a sample which was deliberately kept heterogeneous and was selected beyond the usual criteria of differentiation, relating, for instance, to work and education versus leisure or forced arrangements versus voluntary activities.

The results demonstrate that the relationship between the respective housing situations is decisive for the practiced and perceived multi-local arrangement. The relationality of the housing situations and the involved conducts of life in and between the respective places prove to be highly relevant because a multi-local arrangement only makes sense to the individual in its complex referential context. It is this methodological and empirical evidence which provides the major result of the study: a real-world typology of the lifeworlds of multi-local residents which comprises the types of parallel worlds, counter worlds, double worlds, and in-between worlds.

The empirical view of the scope of manifestations of multi-local living reveals the surprising complexity, ambivalence, and dynamics of the phenomenon. Above all, it is the grey areas which are the key to the practice of multi-local living and which are given special attention in the study. However, even the results are ambivalent. The phenomenon resists simplifying assessments along opposed terms such as work versus leisure, force versus voluntariness, or mobility versus mooring. Thus the insight gained already by a number of researchers is confirmed that (late-modern) social phenomena cannot be explained and understood through a dichotomous world-view (Latour 2000). Instead, multi-local living is a 'melange phenomenon' (Beck *et al.* 2004, p. 27), which emerges in manifold controversial fields and, at best, can be located along continua.

Thus, multi-local living has many facets: It is the expression of a highly mobile lifestyle which combines diverse forms of mobility. Yet as is the case with relocation mobility, it represents a strategy not to bow to the occasionally exhausting social mobility demands, at least for some time. In this example, multi-local living serves to maintain the familiar – at least partly and temporarily – and, related to this, place attachment and mooring, as shown for instance by the own house in a leafy setting or the continuity of the children's education. Last but not least, multi-local living provides the opportunity to keep up former ties. This refers to the temporary continuity of relevant spatial relationships of everyday life or the episodic return to places of desire which remind us of the past.

Furthermore, the diversity of multi-local living expresses the growing challenge for the individual to establish stabilities and reliability of expectations. As mentioned above, this finds its way in patterns of multi-local conducts of life, which are determined by the pursuit of traditional ways of organization. Thus, elaborate controversial fields emerge which include manifold inner and outer conflicts for the multi-locals, their partners and/or families. If, however, all those involved succeed in finding new forms of establishing stability and reliability, the multi-local living arrangements may be considered a blessing rather than a load.

Special insight was gained from empirical cases with overlapping different motives, which may be condensed to multi-layered frames of action and meaning. This opens a new perspective on key concepts and terms relating to lifeworld, housing, and mobility. One of the central tasks of future considerations about multi-local living will concern the re-thinking of and connecting these issues under dynamic, process-based, and multi-local aspects. Focus needs to be put on the diversity of structural reasons, the individual motives and manifestations as well as on the social, economic, and political consequences of multi-local living. In order to achieve these goals, the application of relational approaches (Law 1999, Massey 2005, Murdoch 2006) seems highly promising. It seems important to intensify the consideration of physical materialities and technical tools, as it is suggested by the mobilities studies (Urry 2000, p. 133f) and to emphasize the processual character of the interactions between the elements involved (e.g. the homes) (Verne 2012, p. 28f). Viewed under this perspective, relational spaces emerge from the respective practices and the associated relationships (Murdoch 2006, p. 91).

To date, research on this phenomenon has combined the assumptions on the afore-mentioned frames of multi-local living with a number of social fields of action. Housing is not to be conceptualized as something static but as a multi-faceted and mobile practice. Moreover, 'identities exist in the structural possibilities of mobility and stability' so that 'we need a sense of place that is complex, permeable, and flexible' (Grossberg 1997, p. 290). This way, the practices of multi-local residents are opposed to the rigid social structures.

Nonetheless, multi-locals are not only mobile, but also located and thus, an increasingly important group of consumers in the housing market. Their specific, quite heterogeneous needs still need to be fathomed. It has become evident, however, that a number of social challenges have arisen, for example in terms of the social integration of neighbourhoods which have to deal with the temporary presences and absences and which may require new settings for establishing contacts. Moreover, multi-local households some-times have specific needs for housing as not only does their composition change in the chronological course of life, but also cyclically due to the pre-sences and absences of household members. Last but not least, it is most important to deal with issues of social disparities and the consumption of resources, which are part and parcel of the phenomenon. At least in Switzer-land, there is strong evidence that multi-local living heavily depends on assets and income and, related to this, on a high consumption of resources in com-parison with the total population. This refers particularly to the consumption of housing space (Schad *et al.* 2015). If social disparities worsen, we may risk the worsening of housing and mobility practices.

Notes

1. The term 'housing situation' refers to the term 'situation', which is firmly rooted in socio-logical action theories and which can be traced back to the Thomas Theorem (Thomas and Thomas 1926 cited Treibel 2000, p. 113). It says that each individual is always con-fronted with a particular situation which they need to define. Situation refers to the respective action context, which is enabling, yet is restrictive at the same time.
2. Anton, 70 years old, is a former teacher and politician and currently political advisor. He lives with his wife in the canton of Zurich. Six of his 10 adult children have estab-lished an organization to maintain the family-owned mountain chalet in the canton of Grisons. For many years, Anton has spent several days or weeks there in order to relax or work without disturbance.
3. Fabian, aged 36, is a doctor and has three residences: In Berne, his place of work, he has rented a room in a shared flat; his cohabitee, who is also a doctor, has a flat in Freiburg, Germany. In-between, in Basel, both have rented a flat which they use, above all, for being together at weekends and sometimes in midweek.

Disclosure statement

No potential conflict of interest was reported by the author.

References

Alasuutari, P. (2000) *Researching Culture. Qualitative Method and Cultural Studies*, London, Sage.

Beck, U. (2008) 'Mobility and the cosmopolitan perspective', in *Tracing Mobilities. Towards a Cosmopolitan Perspective*, eds W. Canzler, V. Kaufmann & S. Kesselring, Aldershot, Ashgate, pp. 25–35.

Beck, U., Bonss, W. & Lau, C. (2004) 'Entgrenzung erzwingt Entscheidung. Was ist neu an der Theorie reflexiver Modernisierung?', in *Entgrenzung und Entscheidung. Was ist neu an der Theorie reflexiver Modernisierung?*, eds U. Beck & C. Lau, Frankfurt a. M., Suhrkamp, pp. 13–64.

Bendix, R. & Löfgren, O. (2007) 'Double homes, doubles lives?', *Ethnologia Europaea. Journal of European Ethnology*, vol. 37, nos. 1–2, pp. 7–17.

Breckner, I. (2002) '"Wohnen und Wandern" in nachindustriellen Gesellschaften', in *Lebenslandschaften. Zukünftiges Wohnen im Schnittpunkt zwischen privat und öffentlich*, eds P. Döllmann & R. Temel, Frankfurt a. M., Campus, pp. 145–153.

Flick, U. (2002) *Qualitative Sozialforschung. Eine Einführung*, Reinbek bei Hamburg, Rowohlt.

Froschauer, U. & Lueger, M. (1992) *Das qualitative Interview. Zur Analyse sozialer Systeme*, Wien, WUV.

Froschauer, U. & Lueger, M. (2003) *Das qualitative Interview. Zur Praxis interpretativer Analyse sozialer Systeme*, Wien, WUV.

Grossberg, L. (1997) *Bringing It All Back Home. Essays on Cultural Studies*, Durham & London, Duke University Press.

Hilti, N. (2009) 'Multilokales Wohnen. Bewegungen und Verortungen', *Informationen zur Raumentwicklung*, vols. 1/2, pp. 77–86.

Hilti, N. (2013) *Lebenswelten multilokal Wohnender. Eine Betrachtung des Spannungsfeldes von Bewegung und Verankerung*, Wiesbaden, VS Verlag.

Kelle, U. & Kluge, S. (1999) *Vom Einzelfall zum Typus. Fallvergleich und Fallkontrastierung in der qualitativen Sozialforschung*, Opladen, Leske + Budrich.

Kluge, S. (2000) 'Empirisch begründete Typenbildung in der qualitativen Sozialforschung', *Forum Qualitative Social Research*, vols. 1/1, [online], Available at: http://www.qualitative-research.net/index.php/fqs/article/viewFile/1124/2498 (accessed 15 July 2014).

Lamnek, S. (1995) *Qualitative Sozialforschung 2. Methoden und Techniken*, Weinheim, Beltz.

Lang, B. (1998) *Mythos Kreuzberg. Ethnographie eines Stadtteils 1961–1995*, Frankfurt a. M., Campus.

Latour, B. (2000) *Die Hoffnung der Pandora. Untersuchungen zur Wirklichkeit der Wissenschaft*, Frankfurt a. M., Suhrkamp.

Law, J. (1999) 'After ANT: complexity, naming and topology', in *Actor Network Theory and After*, eds J. Law & J. Hassard, Oxford & Malden, MA, Blackwell Publishers, pp. 1–14.

Lueger, M. (2000) *Grundlagen qualitativer Sozialforschung. Methodologie, Organisierung, Materialanalyse*, Wien, WUV.

Massey, D. (2005) *For Space*, London, Sage.

Murdoch, J. (2006) *Post-Structuralist Geography. A Guide to Relational Space*, London, Sage.

Peuckert, R. (2006). 'Soziologische Theorien', in Grundbegriffe der Soziologie, eds B. Schäfers & J. Kopp, Wiesbaden, VS Verlag, pp. 280–300.

Rolshoven, J. (2007) *Wohnbewegungen. Dynamik und Komplexität alltäglicher Lebenspraxen,* [online], Available at: http://www.unigraz.at/johanna.rolshoven/jr_wohnbewegungen.pdf (accessed 16 September 2010).

Rolshoven, J. (2009) 'Kultur-Bewegungen. Multilokalität als Lebensweise in der Spätmoderne', *Österreichische Zeitschrift für Volkskunde,* vol. 112, no. 2, pp. 285–303.

Schad, H., Hilti, N., Duchêne-Lacroix, C. & Hugentobler, M. (2015) 'Multilokales Wohnen in der Schweiz – erste Einschätzung zum Aufkommen und zu den Ausprägungen, mobil und doppelt sesshaft', in *Mobil und doppelt sesshaft. Studien zur residenziellen Multilokalität, Abhandlungen zur Geographie und Regionalforschung, Bd. 18,* eds P. Weichhart & P. A. Rumpolt, Wien, Schriftenreihe des Instituts für Geographie und Regionalforschung der Universität Wien, IfGR, pp. 176–201.

Schlehe, J. (2003) 'Formen qualitativer ethnographischer Interviews', in *Methoden und Techniken der Feldforschung,* ed. B. Beer, Berlin, Dietrich Reimer, pp. 71–93.

Schröer, N. (1997) 'Wissenssoziologische Hermeneutik', in *Sozialwissenschaftliche Hermeneutik. Eine Einführung,* eds R. Hitzler & A. Honer, Opladen, Leske + Budrich, pp. 109–129.

Schütz, A. (2003) *Theorie der Lebenswelt 1. Die pragmatische Schichtung der Lebenswelt,* Konstanz, UVK.

Schütz, A. & Luckmann, T. (2003) *Strukturen der Lebenswelt,* Konstanz, UVK.

Sennett, R. (2000) *Der flexible Mensch. Die Kultur des neuen Kapitalismus,* München, Goldmann.

swissfuture – Schweizerische Vereinigung für Zukunftsforschung. (2012) *Wertewandel in der Schweiz 2030. Vertiefungsstudie: Wohnformen 2030,* Luzern, swissfuture.

Treibel, A. (2000) *Einführung in die soziologischen Theorien der Gegenwart,* Opladen, Leske + Budrich.

Urry, J. (2000) *Sociology Beyond Societies. Mobilities for the Twenty-First Century,* London & New York, Routledge.

Verne, J. (2012) *Living Translocality. Space, Culture and Economy in Contemporary Swahili Trade,* Stuttgart, Franz Steiner.

Weichhart, P. (2009) 'Multilokalität – Konzepte, Theoriebezüge, Forschungsfragen', *Informationen zur Raumentwicklung,* vols. 1/2, pp. 1–14.

Witzel, A. (2000) 'Das problemzentrierte interview', *Forum Qualitative Sozialforschung/ Forum Qualitative Social Research,* vol. 1, no. 1, [online], Available at: http://www.qualitative-research.net/fqs-texte/1-00/1-00witzel-d.htm (accessed 20 February 2014).

Wöhler, K. (2008) 'ZeitRaumBilder und Realitätsverlust. Anmerkungen zum "mobility turn"', *Kuckuck. Notizen zur Alltagskultur. Zeiträume – Raumzeiten,* vol. 1, pp. 4–7.

Dwelling in different localities: Identity performances of a white transnational professional elite in the City of London and the Central Business District of Singapore

Lars Meier

Institute for Employment Research (IAB), Nuremberg, Germany

ABSTRACT

Besides being mobile, migrant professionals dwell at specific localities. It is in this article that identity performances of one social group with equal identity dimensions, white, male German financial manager, are compared in two different local contexts of their dwelling: in the City of London and in the Central Business District of Singapore. This article demonstrates that by comparing similar social groups in different localities, the effects of locality become clearly visible. As the managers are temporal migrants, their dwelling practices are to arrange themselves with locality for the time of their delegation. Everyday practices and the specific symbolic labelling of localities are expressions and producers of identity. The mobile managers encounter the two localities with unique images rooted in the colonial period; as a centre and an outpost, respectively. As these images have an impact on their identity performances today, this article demonstrates that the mangers perform whiteness and being transnational elite with different emphasis regarding locality.

Introduction

Mobile finance managers are coined as examples par excellence of global mobility with border crossing network activities (Vertovec 2002, Larsen *et al.* 2006, Nowicka 2006). As those with the most of 'network capital' (Elliott and Urry 2010), they are a transnational elite (Sklair 2001). But besides being mobile in transnational spaces, the managers dwell locally and perform their social identities in specific local contexts of cities. Dwelling is not limited to a house or an apartment but is to make the city a home by specific identity negotiations that are related to the local context of the city. By analysing the identity performances of a similar social group in different local contexts, the article makes it possible to compare the performance of identities in relation to the respective local context of dwelling. The focus here is on German finance managers' performance of whiteness and being a transnational elite in the City of London and in the Central Business District (CBD) of Singapore.

Social identity as performances

By conceptualizing social identity as performances, this article draws on dynamic identity concepts, which do not consider social identity to be a stable, monolithic entity. A person's social identity consists of multiple dimensions such as class, ethnicity and gender which come into being through everyday practices and through discourses whereby the relation of self and other is constructed and differences are named (Brah 1996, Skeggs 2004).

Identities are performed in everyday life because they are not naturally given but are expressed and constructed by discursive practices, for example by defining the self in comparison to another (Butler 1993) when for example whiteness is self-defined and represented in difference to others in specific kinds of communication (Jackson 1999, Jackson and Simpson 2003, Tierney and Jackson 2003) or by adjusting one's activities (McDowell 1997) to the supposed expectations of what suits a specific interaction. Performances are not a person's masquerade; rather, such performances are what form and express a person's identity. Identities are not only performed by bodily activities but also by narrations (McDowell 1997). By presenting the self in a spoken interaction to the other, like in an interview situation, identity is performed by giving everyday activities a meaning and through a narrative's story line; 'we talk ourselves into being' (Gubrium and Holstein 2000, p. 101). Erving Goffman has stated:

> I am suggesting that often what talkers undertake to do is not to provide information to a recipient but to present dramas to an audience. Indeed, it seems that we spend most of our time not engaged in giving information but in giving shows. (…) when an individual says something, he is not saying it as a bold statement of fact on his own behalf. He is recounting. He is running through a strip of already determined events for the engagement of his listeners. (1974, p. 508)

It is with regard to this argument that identity is considered in this paper as performed through narrations in an interview situation that includes narrations of everyday activities like clothing. The interviewed finance managers perform their identities through a narrated construction of images of the cities and the other and how they fit with their images. The managers' narrations are expressions of learned cultural models and the internalization of discourses (Strauss and Quinn 1997). The concept of performance is used to consider German finance managers' identity dimensions of being white and a member of the transnational elite (Sklair 2001) out of their everyday practices and in relation to the banker's narrated images of localities and of the others – people with different identities – whom they encounter while dwelling in two financial districts: the City of London and the Central Business District of Singapore.

The managers are considered a transnational elite as they have large amounts of economic, cultural and social capital in the form of a general privileged access to resources, as they are members of a dense social network and as they are discursively considered an elite (Woods 1998). And whiteness refers to 'a location of structural advancement', 'a standpoint, a place from which white people look at ourselves, others' and to 'a set of cultural practices' (Frankenberg 1993, p. 1). With respect to a growing literature on whiteness in the last 20 years (Frankenberg 1993, Dyer 1997, Garner 2007, Windance Twine and Gallager 2008, Reay 2008, Lundström 2014) the whiteness of the German bankers is displayed as a performed racialized subject position that is seen here as intertwined with a class identity as transnational elite. Identity dimensions are intertwined. Garner (2007, pp. 63–79) illustrates this on class and whiteness and demonstrates that whiteness is therefore a contingent hierarchy. A specific identity dimension can have more relevance in identity performance than the others. As this article demonstrates it is with regard to locality that the importance of each dimension in the performance of identity is shifting. Locality is a constellation of processes rather as a stable entity (Massey 2005). Consequently the City of London and the Central Business District of Singapore are not analysed by using objective criteria but how they are experienced and perceived by the German financial managers. London and Singapore were selected for this research project because both rank in top positions in urban hierarchies as well as connected world cities (Friedmann 1995, Taylor 2004, Derudder *et al.* 2010). Their financial quarters are considered to be major hubs within transnational financial networks ranked by their competitiveness in the small group of global leaders with regard to the number of highly qualified personnel, the overall economic situation and the general market access (Z/Yen Group 2013). Furthermore, both cities have developed in a close relationship with economic linkages and intertwined histories within the world system as imperial city and colonial city with Singapore as an outpost for the economic interests of the British Empire in the region (King 1990, Yeoh 1996). German financial managers come to the City of London and the Central Business District of Singapore with certain expectations which have their roots in the colonial period and are central elements in performing whiteness. They attribute specific qualities to these localities and other people and adapt their performances of whiteness and being transnational elite to these expectations. The manager's national identity as Germans is also of relevance for the identity performances.

The transnational elite, global cities and financial quarters: the relevance of locality and identity

Research on the transnational elite in global cities is done from two different perspectives. The first and dominant perspective characterizes highly mobile financial managers and international financial quarters both by their connectivity within the global network. These jet-setting bankers are seen as builders of global networks, and financial quarters are considered as global hubs in global cities. However, the impact of the unique locality on the everyday life of the transnational elite and their social identities is largely lost in these abstract concepts. As a consequence of their global connectivity, localities such as financial quarters which are considered to be essential centres of global networks are treated as non-places (Augé 1995) lacking any local features. By focusing on global connectivity, like in concepts of transnationalism or in research on global city and world city networks (Friedmann 1995, Taylor 2004, Alderson *et al.* 2010) the local loses its significance for the everyday activities of people who are integrated in this network. Managers in particular are imagined to exist in a world society primarily constituted by communication processes which override locality (Luhmann 1997; Meyer *et al.* 1997) due to their frequent everyday use of communication and transport technologies that drive 'time-space compression' (Harvey 1990). Consequently, these managers are considered to be a placeless global or transnational class (Van Der Pijl 1998, Castells 2000, Sklair 2001, Carroll and Fennema 2002) or as members of a 'global high technology professional culture' (Knorr Cetina and Bruegger 2002, p. 906). Their status as a transnational elite moreover provides privileged access to resources, which are mainly defined by their high level of connectivity and integration in transnational social and professional networks (Woods 1998). Hence within this strand of research they are viewed mainly from the perspective of 'transnationalism from above' (Willis *et al.* 2002, p. 505), as attendants of international financial flows and business networks (Salt 1997, Yeung 1998), and are characterized by their frequent emigration to the financial districts of different global cities as 'transient migrants' (Beaverstock and Boardwell 2000) who 'hop[ping] from one expatriate enclave to another' (Ley 2004, p. 157). Managers are primarily defined by their incorporation into transnational networks, as a transnational elite, so it comes as no surprise that dimensions of identity such as gender, national identity or ethnicity are usually neglected.

A second strand of research criticizes the perception of the transnational elite as a homogenous group (Forster 2000, Butcher 2009) that is defined by their embeddedness in transnational networks and is disconnected from locality. Against the backdrop of a critique of globalization theory the transnational elite is not only seen as transients moving from location to location. Research exists which considers identity dimensions of the mobile transnational elite (Sakai 2000, Willis and Yeoh 2002, Moore 2005, Fechter and Walsh 2010, Colic-Peisker 2010, Lan 2011, Lundström 2014); however, the relevance of locality for these identities is not clearly seen. In those studies which investigate highly qualified migrants in a specific city (Findlay *et al.* 1996, Beaverstock and Smith 1996, White 1998, Beaverstock 2002, Beaverstock 2005, Scott 2004), the cities themselves are considered more as passive backgrounds for activities without particular consequence for everyday practices and identity formation (but see Meier 2015). Recently some research was done considering a specific city as an element for identity formation of whiteness. Fechter has demonstrated this in an ethnographic study on white expatriates in Jakarta (2007); Leonard (2007, 2010, 2013) demonstrates the relevance of workplaces for performing whiteness in Hong Kong and Knowles and Harper (2009) focus on expatriates' routes through Hong Kong, their residences and leisure activities; Farrer (2010) writes about white expatriates in Shanghai and the narratives of their personal relationship to the city that is influenced by a postcolonial nostalgia for an old Shanghai and takes also reference to today's ideal of 'new Shanghainese'; Walsh (2009, 2011) and Coles and Walsh (2010) examine white British expatriates' lives in Dubai today with reference to the imperial relationship of Great Britain to Dubai. But there is a dearth of research which analyses the specific effects of locality that becomes especially visible by comparing similar social groups in different localities. Ethnicity, class and national identity become visible in this paper as the focus is not on white expatriates in general but on a specific group of expatriates. With the comparative research focus presented in this article, the particularities of single cases will be used to analyse and display the local specific relevance of ethnicity (whiteness) and class (being transnational elite) in a city that was once colonized and the city that was the centre of the Empire.

Research method: comparative research on identity performances

This article is based on interviews and ethnographic research conducted on site in London and in Singapore. Interviews were conducted with 40 German financial managers, half of whom live and work in Singapore, the other half in London. The interviewees were recruited with the help of the companies' human resources management departments, German schools, acquaintances with contacts to finance managers and subsequently with the snowball system. With the help of a cover letter sent by email the potential interviewees were asked to participate. Hereby and again later before the start of the interviews the interviewees were informed that the project is to analyse the everyday lives and activities of German finance managers abroad. It was later that I noticed through coding and analysing the data that patterned differences of identity performances are obviously linked to locality. In general this research and the data analysis are based on the principles of grounded theory and the aim of the research was gradually developed out of the data (Glaser and Strauss 1967, Hammersley and Atkinson 1995).

To secure comparativeness I used an interview guide for the in-depth interviews in London and Singapore. Besides general data like age, education, family and job position, the questions cover topics like the reason to migrate to London or to Singapore, the arrival, the course of a usual working day, social contacts and descriptions of personally relevant localities in the respective city. The questions allowed the interviewees to develop long narratives and the interviews lasted between two and four hours. In addition to those guided questions that led the overall structures and content of the interviews, the interviewer referred to the interviewees' narrations and asked additional questions. This allowed me to refer directly to the personal narrations and to deepen my understanding of issues mentioned by the interviewees. As data collection and analysis were based on grounded theory, I also took the opportunity to ask additional questions developed through the ongoing analysis of the data gained. After the end of the interviews data were also collected through observations and ethnographic interviews (Spradley 1979) in the interviewees' apartments and houses, in restaurants or pubs and by joining them in driving or walking around the cities. Data were analysed by the grounded approach of coding in three stages (Glaser and Strauss 1967). The following open coding themes emerged. In axial coding I organized these initial codes around major categories, whose conceptual relationships I then analysed in the process of selective coding.

The interviews were conducted in London and Singapore as part of the research project that started in 2004 and ended in 2008,[1] shortly before the Lehman crash and the start of the financial crisis. The sample covers mostly male interviewees (17 interviews with males and three with females each in London and in Singapore) who work in different hierarchical levels in banks and insurance companies. All 40 interviewees hold a German passport and are white but for one interviewee. In each city 12 interviewees occupy senior managerial positions as General Managers, Chief Executive Officers or as Heads of Department while eight are in upper middle management positions like Associate Manager or Underwriting Manager. Hence the subjects in both cities were of different ages (ranging from 24 to 63) and are employed in 11 different German financial companies. Age-related differences in the interviewees' leisure and family activities can be seen but their identity performances of whiteness and of being transnational elite depending on locality are similar.

Most of the interviews were done at the interviewees' offices. Interviews with those not in a senior position and therefore not equipped with their own office were taken in small conference rooms and in some cases outside the office building in nearby cafes or pubs.

In addition, localities mentioned in the narratives as being of particular relevance in the daily lives of the interviewees were observed and field notes were taken. Everyday practices and clothing styles of the managers at those localities were recorded.

Comparative research is mostly centred on one city and investigates different social groups. Recently research has been published which argues that locality must be considered in comparative migration studies (Glick Schiller and Çağlar 2009) and urban studies (Robinson 2011). By doing a comparative study in two financial quarters in different cities, this study has been designed to strengthen and qualify the central argument that the local context is of particular relevance to identity performance.

Dwelling in the centre: being challenged and rewarded by the City of London

The central part of London called the 'City of London' has been the traditional centre since the foundation of the Roman settlement Londinium in 43 AD. Due to its preferred location on the Thames it was the capital of the Roman province of Britannia. As an international trading centre London was an important destination of immigrants including a German community of traders since the fifteenth century. The City gained importance immensely during the British Colonial period and became the main financial centre of the whole Empire. Since the Big Bang, the deregulation of the finance sector in 1986, the City has increased its importance as a global finance centre. Today the City area of 2.6 km^2 is only a small segment of the 1572 km^2 of London. But with its high number of financial institutions (2.510 enterprises including the London Stock Exchange, the Bank of England, Lloyds of London and the major German banks) and a total of 368,200 employees the City contributes to the national income of Great Britain with an outstanding percentage of 3.7 percent (City of London 2013).

The German finance managers interviewed consider the City as the 'navel of the world', the 'center of finance', or as the 'world city'. They frequently directly relate its recent powerful position to its history as the urban centre of the British Empire (King 1990). For them the City is a centre with a 'real' tradition, which they put in contrast to traditions of other cities by taking reference to historical buildings. The following interview quotation provides a good example: 'It is fascinating to be here. If you compare this to Paris; in Paris there are also many nice old buildings, like Versailles. But that is all a museum, yes. Here it is not a museum, it is real' (male, 47 years, investment banker).

The bankers' specific perspective on the City of London is conditioned by their regular encounters with the City's self-presentation; a unique arrangement of architecture and smaller features confirms its historical importance. The bankers' impressions of the City are influenced by historical edifices such as Tower Bridge or St. Paul's Cathedral, the 'symbolic heart of Empire' (Jacobs 1996, p. 49) and verify the banker's image of the City as centre of tradition. These buildings are emphasized in the cityscape by careful city planning which, amongst other things, has restricted the height of new buildings and still ensures that St. Paul's is visible from several viewpoints. The cityscape arrangement pushes into the banker's view and fit well with their image of the City as the 'navel' of the world, of a centre perpetuating its importance with 'real' tradition. This is true even if today restrictions are visibly relaxed with the new skyscrapers 'the Gherkin' and 'the Cheesegrater', plus a debate about further additional skyscrapers (Guardian 2014). The historical buildings are present in the bankers' narratives of their daily arrivals in the City and in their presentation of themselves as being successful since entering the City. One German banker has described his experience to arrive in the following self-confident words:

> You see the City of London, on the left side you see Big Ben and the Houses of Parliament. That is a moment when I think: it is so great to work in the City. It is so impressive that I made it, that I can work in the City. (…) I am perfectly suited to the City. (male, 37 years, investment banker)

On entering the City, the bankers are impressed by historic buildings and by being a person who is 'entering the heart of the economy'. It makes them proud that they have 'made it' as the ones who have gained entrance to the centre. For the German financial managers, achieving entrance into the City of London is a distinction in their personal record. It seems that they transpose their image of the city as a centre of economy onto themselves. Having worked in London is regarded as a testimony to being able to survive harsh competition, a highpoint in their curriculum vitae. To this effect, a banker told me: 'Of course it was a step forward in my career. Working for one or two years in London comes across really well in your personal record'.

By their very presence in the City, the finance mangers feel they have become a part of this centre. Gaining entrance into the centre is seen as a proof of their own resilience and personal strengths. It is their opinion that only those who can 'meet the demands' (male, 50 years, head of credits) ever gain entrance. The German bankers interpret their own success in working in London to mean that they have unique personal characteristics that make them 'perfectly suited to the City'. The interviewees explain that they are able to work in the City because they possess qualities like courage, purposefulness, diligence, enthusiasm, social competence, social networking ability and adaptability. Having these abilities is what differentiates them from those bankers who are not as successful and who are still working in Germany rather than in the 'real' centre. From the bankers' perspective, only those who can adapt to the demands of the City will fit into the City. Adapting to working and living in the City is a constant theme in their narratives. Presenting these qualities is part of their class identity performance as a member of the transnational elite. An interview partner talked of the exceedingly high expectations concerning work performance on entering the City: 'That level of performance is expected and if you don't achieve it then they come to you and tell you: "Look out, if you continue like this, our time together will be over". This never happens in Germany' (male, 47 years, investment banker).

Even if this quotation is over the top it demonstrates that the bankers' image of the City creates particular expectations that they consider they must meet to be integrated in this financial centre. Therefore, their narratives of everyday life are only complete if they refer to the very high workload they must cope with. For them, being here is directly linked with hard work and long hours. One explained: 'In Germany it is seen more as a job, a thing that you have to do. But your life outside of work is of more importance. ... Here in London people live for their work during the week' (male, 37 years, investment banker). The macabre relevance of this statement was demonstrated by the death of a young German student in 2013 working in a 'culture of extreme working hours' (Guardian 2013) for Merill Lynch.

Seeing the City as the centre of the world is related to the bankers' expectations that their time must be characterized by a necessary adaptation to a particularly high level of efficiency. As an outcome of their image of the City, those working in the centre feel obliged to render particularly outstanding performances and feel under pressure to adapt in order to fulfil this expectation. Stories about adapting to the high levels of work are a constant theme in the bankers' narratives. They feel under pressure to adjust, to act in accordance with a certain image and to present themselves as particularly industrious. Their sense of being in the City, a location which deserves exceptional performance due to its central importance and their subordination to the requirements of the City correspond with their everyday experiences and lead them to adapt their actions. Their actions become hectic: they are ignoring the pedestrian traffic lights, walking quickly and purposefully along the streets and giving up the German tradition of a lunch break for a quick bite at work. One states with exaggeration that for him the City is defined by: 'Work. In comparison, Germany was a walk in the park' (male, 50 years, head of credit).

For the managers, certain qualities of everyday life – such as unsmiling faces on the street, the single-minded concentration on work, lack of distraction and irritation by the other, and the lack of quite areas on the street – make the City an exclusive and unfriendly locality where competition is all.

They feel that they are in a locality where everything is designed to serve the correct functioning of the financial system and where they have to adapt their performance as transnational elite to this function. One explained: 'Banks are its life-blood and the people who work here and everything else is really just focused on serving this'.

In the City of London one is surrounded by similarly dressed people: men and women in dark suits. Even if the bowler hat is less common than it once was, upon entering the City one is immediately confronted with distinct clothing rules and codes (McDowell 1997, p. 189). If the German managers have not prepared for the traditional and formal clothing style, their first visit to the City will make it clear that they must conform. For example, a young banker told me that he could not wear the light-coloured suits that he wore in Germany because he felt the need to adapt his clothing style to that of the City. On his arrival his clothes became unwearable and after his first working day he bought new suits exclusively in black and dark blue. By adapting their clothes the bankers fulfil a tacit but always visible demand to accept the City's clothing norms. The uniform clothing of other managers is evident on the streets and in the office and is a clearly seen in its class difference to the clothes worn by the others like construction workers, waiters and baristas. In addition, one simply has to walk through the streets to be continually confronted by the clothes in the shop windows of local boutiques that display the approved dark suits, coloured shirts, ties and cuff links over and over again. The clothing norms are powerfully urging the bankers to comply. As Germans in London the bankers are eager to assimilate themselves to the dress and style of the City as passing with a generic 'European identity' is for them much more pleasant and unproblematic than standing out as German in the UK context. This is also because the German bankers still consider themselves as being potential targets of 'kraut-bashing' (Weber-Newth and Steinert 2006, pp. 19–21) by the British, as a follow-up to the Nazi-German bombings of the City of London, which led to vast destructions and 32,000 dead people in the Second World War. These events produced a still continuing 'Germanophobia' in British society that has resulted in the exclusion of Germans from the Baltic Exchange (Leyshon and Thrift 1997, p. 311). The German banker's eagerness to assimilate themselves stands in a tradition of Germans concealing their national identity in everyday life after the war (Weber-Newth and Steinert 2006, p. 195). The bankers try to avoid openly expressing a German identity. The German finance manager's identity performance is dominated by their class identity as transnational elite, a privileged segment within the 932 thousand highly skilled immigrants in 2005 (OECD 2011). Performing this in its different facets superposes the performance of whiteness in the City. This is because the managers are included in the major ethnic group (59.7 percent of the population is classified as 'White'; see Office for National Statistics 2012). Frankenberg has demonstrated that whiteness matters even when it is not overtly problematized. It is besides a location of structural advantage a standpoint from which one considers society with the social position of oneself and others (Frankenberg 1993, p. 1). This is also true for the German bankers in London. They consider whiteness in the City as the norm that is not reflected in their narratives as an own identity dimension or as their privilege. As the next section demonstrates this is different in Singapore.

Dwelling in the outpost: being a desired and undisputed foreign talent in the CBD of Singapore

Singapore's 716 km^2 is nearly half the size of London, but with its 5.4 million inhabitants and its 7,541 inhabitants per square km the city state is more densely populated than London (5,285 inhabitants per km^2). Financial institutions are concentrated in the south of the Island along the shore of the Singapore River and around Raffles Place. The commercial and business area was enlarged by several land reclamation projects since the 1970s. Due to its location at the Strait of Malacca, Singapore has developed to an important harbour since the fourteenth century. With its inclusion into the British Empire Singapore was developed and restructured 11,000 km away from London (Yeoh 1996) as a main harbour on the trading route between India and China. With the growth of trade in the nineteenth century German traders settled in Singapore as well. Like the British they were engaged in preferred social positions in the colonially ruled ethnic division of Singapore. In 1965 Singapore gained independence from the British Empire but with an ongoing economic dependence on foreign trade. Due to huge investments in the qualification of the population, Singapore has developed since the 1970s from a location for low wages in industrial mass production to an export-orientated economy with knowledge-based complex products and high wages. Especially since the 1990s the city-state has developed as a major centre in the international bank, insurance and service sector. Singapore's prominent position is visible by the landmark skyscrapers at the United Overseas Bank Plaza, the Bank of China Building or the Maybank Tower. In 2012, 5,000 companies in the financial and insurance sector were located here and employed 150,000 residents. In 2010, Singapore's per capita gross national income (GNI) of 45,418 USD is more than the per capita GNI of Great Britain with 36,840 USD (Department of Statistics Singapore 2013). Today Singapore is similarly ranked to London according to its competitiveness as one of the four top Global Financial Centers (Z/Yen Group 2013) and has the second largest container harbour in the world after Shanghai (Journal of Commerce 2012).

A pole apart from the City of London, the German finance managers regard Singapore in light of its historical role as a colonial outpost. Their identity performances are dominated by whiteness accompanied by a Eurocentric view that widely determines their performance of class as transnational elite.

For them, the Central Business District in Singapore lacks the central role in the world economy which they attribute to the City of London. They consider Singapore to be a centre, but more as a subordinated regional centre in Asia. And Asia from their eurocentric perspective is remote from the truly important events. German bankers in the CBD see themselves as 'out here'. 'Out here' in Singapore, the bankers consider themselves to be somewhat more independent and somewhat less important than in the City of London, because they are not in the 'real' centre. One said: 'Out here, you are a bit more your own master and boss. (…) Out here, you are much more independent than you can be at the headquarters' (male, 48 years, general manager, bank).

This feeling of independence is part of the bankers' self-image as adventurers and contrasts greatly to those in London who feel under pressure to adapt themselves to the high demands of the City of London. Bankers emigrate to the imagined outpost of Singapore in order to 'experience something different' as one (male, 38 years, chief information technology officer, bank) put it.

The financial managers' feelings of success which result from being endorsed to work in the City of London can be contrasted to their feelings about moving to Singapore. Moving to Singapore is also linked with success as it demonstrates that one is part of the flexible and active elite. Nevertheless, it has different connotations from moving to London.

In the City of London, German bank managers feel themselves to be part of the centre. It is the 'real' centre where many other managers work – managers who are considered to be the transnational elite by German bankers. From their perspective, if one works in London, at the 'navel of the world', one is automatically part of the transnational elite. There they have the feeling that they are in a challenging locality of competition and are under pressure to fulfil the demands of the City. In contrast, bankers in the CBD of Singapore feel they are in a locality where they are required for their qualities as 'foreign talent'. They see themselves as members of a small group of western expatriates who they consider to be the transnational elite.

Besides its 3.8 million residents Singapore has a large number of 1.5 million people with the status as non-residents (Department of Statistics Singapore 2013). Within this group 12 percent are high skilled foreigners, like managers or professionals holding the Employment Pass (EP). This group is treated more liberally by the Singaporean State as lower qualified foreigners. These highly qualified non-residents count for 3.4 percent (186,000 people) of the inhabitants and include also expatriates from Europe and North-America. The Singaporean statistics is very eager to classify people into ethnic groups. While there are no official data on the ethnic composure of the non-residents the majority of the permanent residences are classified as 'Chinese' (74 percent), 'Malay' (13 percent) and 'Indians' (9 percent). Different to the

City of London where the majority of residents are labelled 'White' in Singapore only 3.3 percent permanent residents are classified as 'Others' (Department of Statistics Singapore 2013).

The German managers' identity performance is dominated by whiteness and it refers to the colonial history of Singapore where the whites have been in a superior social position. In Singapore the managers differentiate themselves as the transnational elite from those managers who come from Asian countries. The non-white Asian managers are viewed by the German bankers as dependent, inflexible and uncreative. They do not correspond to the image which the white Germans have of themselves as members of a transnational elite. One interviewee contrasted himself in regards to Asian managers in the following way: 'Here they are so fixated on what gets drummed into them three, four times every day by the newspaper, by the government etcetera. I think that makes them quite dependent' (male, 62 years, assistant general manager, bank).

With respect to a perspective of whiteness as culturally superior the German managers consider Singapore's economic progress to be largely a result of expatriates' work. In their opinion, the creativity of white expatriates improves the economic development of Singapore and likewise was a prerequisite for the progress of the city-state.

The German bankers thus consider themselves to be part of a desired and required social group that is pampered by a Singaporean society that recognizes its dependence on the expatriates' qualities. The construction of the Esplanade, for example, a cultural centre and concert hall where popular western orchestras perform, is interpreted as the Singapore government's attempt to make life for the valued expatriates as pleasant as possible. As one said: 'They especially want to attract foreign talent, as they call it here. They want to make this place a bit more of a home for them, so that these people feel comfortable and stay longer' (male, 48 years, general manager, bank). Another banker expresses a feeling of being preferred over the Asian managers: 'We are treated completely differently, and this is what our Singaporean colleagues complain about' (male, 32 years, regional manager, insurance company).

The German managers' sense of being desired in Singapore does not only arise from their knowledge of the politics used to recruit members of the transnational elite; they experience it on an everyday basis. They experience it not only in the ease with which they are granted access to exclusive buildings based on their whiteness, but also in the helpfulness and kindness shown to them by Singaporean people.

Clothes are usually, as material culture (Küchler and Miller 2005), a form of everyday differentiation from other people (Bourdieu 1987) and are significant for the German bankers in the City of London as an element of class-related differentiation to others, as there whiteness can also mean one is a worker or a pauper. 'Clothes are artefacts "create" behavior through their capacity to impose social identities and empower people to assert latent social identities' (Crane 2000, p. 2) For the German finance employees in Singapore there is less need to differentiate by means of clothing. The difference through whiteness in the outpost is felt by them to be as obvious as and equivalent to a distinction by clothes. For them, being white in Singapore means being part of the transnational elite. Therefore, many of the bankers wear more casual clothes at work than they would in London. In Singapore a specific distinction through clothes is unnecessary in the way it is in London. One said: 'There is normally no need for a jacket' (male, 56 years, assistant general manager, bank).

The temperature in tropical Singapore varies around 30 degree Celsius; the climate is also a factor for not wearing a jacket. But this is marked by the interviewees not as being the only reason. Another banker explained:

> If I am leaving for home after work, I take off the tie and put it there into the drawer [he opens the drawer with different ties in it]. I have five others there and tomorrow morning I'll choose one to wear. In the evening I don't go home with a tie; there is nobody who knows me outside, and if there was somebody who knows me, it would be all the same to me (he laughs). (male, 62 years, assistant general manager, bank)

The German bankers perform as transnational elite in the CBD of Singapore by wearing casual clothes. Because they see themselves with their white abilities as in demand as 'foreign talents' in the imagined outpost and so perceive 'no demand' to wear formal clothes. Their performance as transnational elite in the City of London is different because the German bankers feel a strong need to adapt themselves to the demanding centre where they feel to be in competition. Being a part of the centre is expressed for them through their ability to adapt to the needs of the 'real' centre, performed by wearing formal clothes.

For the German bank managers, a move to Asia expresses two things. Firstly, they consider themselves to be in an economic boom region. Secondly, they consider themselves to be experiencing an adventure in Singapore, with the possibility of acquiring features of a white transnational elite. They are displaying flexibility, readiness to take risks, a willingness to go the extra mile for their career and enthusiasm for new situations (Hannerz 1996). They are thus proving that their careers take priority over their private lives. They integrate the story of expanding their personal horizons – by becoming acquainted with something new and foreign – into an explanation of the benefit of these qualities in succeeding in professional competition. The stories told of their courage in moving to Singapore become at the same time a personal differentiation of their professional abilities. These tales of adventure provide evidence to support the adventurous image they enjoy back home in Germany which is consequently attributed to them as an advantageous professional quality. These German finance managers expect that the price necessary to pay for this distinction is paid by their stay in Asia and by their everyday experiences of a foreign and uneasy locality where they have to experience adventures. However their expectations of an Asian city are confounded on their arrival in Singapore. Once they have hands-on experience of the city they are amazed. An interviewee said about the confounding of their preconceptions upon direct contact with Singapore: 'I was surprised how comfortable it is' (male, 38 years, chief information technology officer, insurance company). Another manger said: 'We were astonished. You can get everything here' (male, 37 years, chief human resource officer, insurance company). This surprise arises from the contradiction of the manager's preconception of Asia. They thus conclude that Singapore is 'not the real Asia'. In their contact with the city they realize that Singapore is no longer part of what Edward Said conceptualized as the Orient (Said 1978). On their arrival, mysterious Singapore transforms into a western island. From their perspective, developed areas cannot be a part of the Orient and is therefore seen as being western. One banker said:

> For me Singapore is Asia light. It is not the real Asia. It is actually like a western island in Asia. (…) there are so many things now which are so heavily influenced by the West that I see this place in fact as a western island in Asia. At least, western culture has a big role in everyday life and in the way things are done here. The behavior and the cultures are different in what I would call hardcore Asian countries like Thailand or China. Compared with Singapore, they are worlds apart. Behavior like burping or whatever is commonplace in China, because it is part of the culture. Here there are many Chinese, but the influence of the West has such a big impact that people just give those things up. They say, okay it is not proper to do this. Therefore it is much easier here, because you don't need to worry about someone spitting at your feet as you're walking along. (male, 38 years, chief information technology officer, insurance company)

Suddenly, from the perspective of the German bankers, Singapore seems less an Asian city and more a 'western island' in Asia where everyday life for the German expats is very easy. As they consider themselves to be on a 'western island', they do not have to adapt to the CBD. Instead, it is seen as the duty of the Asian managers to adapt to this 'western island'. From the German bankers' point of view Singapore is not 'real', like the City of London. Moreover, they consider the colonial buildings differently, as proof of Singapore's dependent development and as evidence of a traditional role as a colonial outpost. As successors to those who built them, only they can fully appreciate the significance of these buildings, in their opinion:

> The historical centre of Singapore with City Hall, St Andrew's Cathedral and Chijmes, I find that pleasant. It is nice to walk there because you can see

buildings that have messages and that show a bit of history. Not just buy, buy, buy or eat, eat, eat. Yes, it's nice. (male, 32 years, regional manager, insurance company)

They present their own interest in historical buildings as being different from what they see as the interests of the Singaporeans. They refer to a central element of whiteness. What is conceptualized as their own culture is set as superior. German bankers consider themselves different to the Singaporeans because of their interest in buildings 'that have messages and that show a bit of history'. These buildings are predominantly those which were constructed by the former white British colonial rulers. The bankers' identity of whiteness develops out of their interest in historical 'buildings that have messages'. The interests of others are presumed to be different to their own. The white Germans regard themselves as being able to appreciate historical buildings and understand their significance in a special way. This ability is placed in contrast to the abilities of the others, the non-white Singaporeans. For instance, an interviewee said: 'Culturally, we are playing on different levels in any case'. In Singapore, they see themselves as the group which is capable of understanding and developing an interest in culture. The bankers particularly regard the historical buildings of the former British colonial rulers as being cultural and so consider themselves to be the group which can understand these buildings. This demonstrates that the colonial history of the City-state is of importance for their white identity in Singapore today.

The German bankers experience Singapore today with reference to its history, and their white identity is constructed according to Singapore's past as a colonial city. It refers to a city that gained 'culture' from white colonialists. Today that 'culture' is specially constructed, as they see it, for the satisfaction of their cultural needs. Thus some consider the newly established Esplanade concert hall as an effort on the part of the Singaporean state to fulfil the cultural needs of white expatriates. The German bankers' identity formation as transnational elite is intertwined with their whiteness. Their class performance as transnational elite is dominated by performing a white identity in Singapore. For the finance manager, the dependency of the CBD on the distant centre is expressed through their own move to Singapore. This is the reason that they considered working here; their special abilities are required in this dependent city. In contrast to those in the City of London, they do not regard the CBD as an exclusive locality. Here in the outpost, the others are omnipresent, not only the Asian managers but also those people shopping in the malls, eating in the hawker centres or resting in the cafés along the Singapore River. German managers feel less stressed by the demands of the CBD. The availability of shady spots for relaxation, air-conditioned shopping centres and regular lunch breaks all add to their sense of living and working in a locality where their well-being is of importance. This feeling of being desired in the CBD because of their abilities as a white transnational elite goes hand in hand with an impression of being out of the rat-race; instead, they feel secure and unthreatened.

This goes along with the frank presentation of a German identity. This is because the German bankers in the CBD consider their national identity as valued by the Singaporeans. In this context they do not consider their German identity as a burden resulting from a history of aggression. In the CBD of Singapore the German bankers do not feel any discomfort with expressions of their national identity. They consider this possible in contrasting their national background with that of the former colonialists, the British. In the account of a German banker some Singaporeans demonstrate this through the naïve consideration of the German history. One of the German bankers said: 'It can happen that a cab driver says to you "Ah you are German. (...) Hitler gut" and then I say: Hey forget about it' (male, 40 years, general manager, bank) He expressed that Germans have a very good reputation in Singapore and explained this in contrast to the national identities of some other expatriates: 'Because we handle them decently. The British sometimes have a colonialist mentality and the US Americans are sometimes without sensibility' The German bankers are considered to have a more reputable national identity than the British or US American. For them this difference enables them to perform their national identity in Singapore openly, for example by going to traditional German pubs or by putting a German flag on the gate of their house.

Conclusion

The motivation to move to Singapore is different from the motivation to move to London. Overall, the decision to move abroad – either to London or to Singapore – is seen as creating an advantage in the competition for better positions. For the managers the move abroad is evidence of their ability, flexibility and courage. As a consequence of taking this step, they consider themselves to have risen into the group of the transnational elite. Richard Dyer has demonstrated in his groundbreaking book on 'white makings of whiteness within Western culture' that whiteness is represented as normality with the 'assumption that white people are just people whereas other colours are something else, is endemic to white culture' (Dyer 1997). My article has argued that it is important to analyse the performance of whiteness by taking reference to the specific local context; in London where 'white people need to learn to see themselves as white, to see their particularity' (Dyer 1997, p. 10) and in Singapore where whiteness is not the invisible, unmarked and universal identity.

By dwelling the managers perform their social identities of whiteness and being transnational elite today with reference to specific local contexts (with colonial histories) and related cognitive models. The German bankers' images of the City of London as the centre and of the Singapore CBD as an outpost refers to the interconnected histories of both cities as imperial city and colonial city. It is also relevant for the finance managers' everyday encounters both with these localities and with the others at these localities today. This is expressed not only by a specific way of talking about the locality and the others at these localities, but also by unique activities such as selecting clothes at the finance quarters. In the CBD of Singapore their performance of transnational elite is dominated by whiteness while for their identity performances in the City of London class has more importance. Whiteness for German bankers' performance of being transnational elite in the City of London is different. This is because whiteness in London is more about competing forms of whiteness between elite and less-elite spaces (Gardner 2007). Within the elite space of the City of London the dress code distinguished the elite from the non-elite whites.

As members of the transnational elite in London they present themselves as being in continual competition with others who are also capable of working in the centre, and are therefore also part of the transnational elite. In consequence, their work in London is mostly presented as being very strenuous; they are adapting themselves to the supposed demands of the City. Having the opportunity to work in the City and therefore to be a part of the centre is considered to be a mark of honour by the German bankers. They feel part of a select group that suits the City because of their ability to adjust their daily actions to the City's demands, such as the strenuous workload, the hectic atmosphere and the tacit rules regarding formality of clothing.

In the CBD of Singapore performing as transnational elite is different: they do not feel themselves to be in constant competition with each other. From their point of view the others, the non-white Asian managers, lack the qualities of the white transnational elite, which the German bankers possess. They feel secure because they consider themselves to be desired by and necessary to Singaporean society. This sense of being desired for their advanced qualities is reminiscent of the position of the white rulers in the past colonial period. For German bankers today, being in Singapore is less a mark of honour than it is a mark of their courage to enter a foreign world. Here, the bankers feel unchallenged in their social position as transnational elite because they consider themselves as whites both desired and required for the development of Singaporean society. They feel that their white, transnational elite identities make them welcome like it is with their German identity that is unloaded with a problematic history as it is in London.

Note

1. For this article data that have been published in parts within a German monograph (Meier 2009) are employed to develop a new article.

Disclosure statement

No potential conflict of interest was reported by the author.

References

Alderson, A. S., *et al.* (2010) 'Intercity relations and globalisation. The evolution of the global urban hierarchy', *Urban Studies*, vol. 47, no. 9, pp. 1899–1923.

Augé, M. (1995) *Non-places – Introduction to an Anthropology of Supermodernity*, London, Verso.

Beaverstock, J. (2002) 'Transnational elites in global cities – British expatriates in Singapore's financial district', *Geoforum*, vol. 33, pp. 525–538.

Beaverstock, J. (2005) 'Transnational elites in the city: British highly-skilled inter-company transferees in New York city's financial district', *Journal of Ethnic and Migration Studies*, vol. 31, no. 2, pp. 245–268.

Beaverstock, J. & Boardwell, J. T. (2000) 'Negotiating globalization, transnational cooperation and global city financial centres in transient migration studies', *Applied Geography*, vol. 20, pp. 277–304.

Beaverstock, J. V. & Smith, J. (1996) 'Lending jobs to global cities – skilled international labour migration, investment banking and the City of London', *Urban Studies*, vol. 33, no. 8, pp. 1377–1394.

Bourdieu, P. (1987) *Distinction – A Social Critique of the Judgement of Taste*, Cambridge, MA, Harvard University Press.

Brah, A. (1996) *Cartographies of Diaspora – Contesting Identities*, London, Routledge.

Butcher, M. (2009) 'Ties that bind. The strategic use of transnational relationships in demarcing identity and managing difference', *Journal of Ethnic and Migration Studies*, vol. 35, no. 8, pp. 1353–1371.

Butler, J. (1993) *Bodies that Matter*, London, Routledge.

Carroll, W. K. & Fennema, M. (2002) 'Is there a transnational business community?', *International Sociology*, vol. 17, no. 3, pp. 393–419.

Castells, M. (2000) *The Rise of the Network Society*, Vol. 1, 2nd edn, Oxford, Blackwell.

City of London. (2013) *Economic Research and Information. Statistics. Frequent asked questions*, London, [online] Available at: http://www.cityoflondon.gov.uk/business/economic-research-and-information/statistics/Pages/Research%20FAQs.aspx (accessed 11 November 2013).

Coles, A. & Walsh, K. (2010) 'From 'Trucial State' to 'Postcolonial' city? The imaginative geographies of British expatriates in Dubai', *Journal of Ethnic and Migration Studies*, vol. 36, no. 8, pp. 1317–1333.

Colic-Peisker, V. (2010) 'Free floating in the cosmopolis? Exploring the identity belonging of transnational knowledge workers', *Global Networks*, vol. 10, no. 4, pp. 467–488.

Crane, D. (2000) *Fashion and its Social Agendas. Class, Gender and Identity in Clothing*, Chicago, University of Chicago Press.

Department of Statistics Singapore. (2013) *Singapore in Figures 2013*, Singapore.

Derudder, B., *et al.* (2010) 'Pathways of change. Shifting connectivities in the World City Network 2000–08', *Urban Studies*, vol. 47, no. 9, pp. 1861–1877.

Dyer, R. (1997) *White*, London, Routledge.

Elliott, A. & Urry, J. (2010) *Mobile Lives*, London, Routledge.

Farrer, J. (2010) 'New Shanghailanders' or 'New Shanghainese'. Western expatriates' narratives of emplacement in Shanghai', *Journal of Ethnic and Migration Studies*, vol. 36, no. 8, pp. 1211–1228.

Fechter, A. M. (2007) *Transnational Lives. Expatriates in Indonesia*, Aldershot, Ashgate.

Fechter, A. M. & Walsh, K. (2010) 'Examining "expatriate" continuities – postcolonial approaches to mobile professionals', *Journal of Ethnic and Migration Studies*, vol. 36, no. 8, pp. 1197–1210.

Findlay, A., *et al.* (1996) 'Skilled international migration and the global city – a study of expatriates in Hong Kong', *Transactions of the Institute of British Geographers*, vol. 21, pp. 49–61.

Forster, N. (2000) 'The myth of the 'international manager', *International Journal of Human Resources Management*, vol. 11, no. 1, pp. 126–142.

Frankenberg, R. (1993) *White Women, Race Matters – The Social Construction of Whiteness*, Minneapolis, University of Minneapolis Press.

Friedmann, J. (1995) 'Where we stand – a decade of world city research', in *World Cities in a World System*, eds. P. L. Knox & P. J. Taylor, Cambridge, Cambridge University Press, pp. 21–47.

Garner, S. (2007) *Whiteness. An Introduction*, London, Routledge.

Glaser, B. G. & Strauss, A. L. (1967) *The Discovery of Grounded Theory – Strategies for Qualitative Research*, New York, Aldine de Gruyter.

Glick Schiller, N. & Caglar, A. (2009) 'Towards a comparative theory of locality in migration studies – migrant incorporation and city scale', *Journal of Ethnic and Migration Studies*, vol. 35, no. 2, pp. 177–202.

Goffman, E. (1974) *Frame Analysis. An Essay on the Organization of Experience*, New York, Harper & Row.

Guardian (2013) *Bank of America Intern's Death Puts Banks' Working Culture in Spotlight*, 21st August 2013, [online] Available at: http://www.theguardian.com/money/2013/aug/21/bank-intern-death-working-hours (accessed 9 September 2014).

Guardian (2014) *The London Skyline Debate*, [online] Available at: http://www.theguardian.com/cities/series/london-skyline-debate (accessed 9 September 2014).

Gubrium, J. F. & Holstein, J. A. (2000) 'The self in a world of going concerns', *Symbolic Interaction*, vol. 23, pp. 95–115.

Hammersley, M. & Atkinson, P. (1995) *Ethnography – Principles in Action*, London, Routledge.

Hannerz, U. (1996) *Transnational Connections – Culture, People, Spaces*, London, Routledge.

Harvey, D. (1990) *The Condition of Postmodernity – An Enquiry into the Origins of Cultural Change*, Cambridge, Blackwell.

Jackson, R. L. (1999) 'White space, white privilege. mapping discoursive inquiry into the self', *Quarterly Journal of Speech*, vol. 85, pp. 38–54.

Jackson, R. L. & Simpson, K. (2003) 'White positionalities and cultural contracts: critiquing entitlement, theorizing and exploring the negotiation of White identities', in *Ferment in the Intercultural Field*, eds. W. J. Starosta & G. M. Chen, Thousand Oaks, Sage, pp. 319–326.

Jacobs, J. (1996) *Edge of Empire – Postcolonialism and the City*, London, Routledge.

Journal of Commerce (2012) *The JOC Top 50 World Container Ports*, [online] Available at: http://www.joc.com/sites/default/files/u48783/pdf/Top50-container-2012.pdf (accessed 12 November 2013).

King, A. D. (1990) *Urbanism, Colonialism, and the World-economy – Cultural and Spatial Foundations of the World Urban System*, London, Routledge.

Knorr-Cetina, K. & Bruegger, U. (2002) 'Global microstructures – the virtual societies of financial markets', *American Journal of Sociology*, vol. 107, no. 4, pp. 905–950.

Knowles, C. & Harper, D. (2009) *Hong Kong. Migrant Lives, Landscapes and Journeys*, Chicago, University of Chicago Press.

Küchler, S. & Miller, D. (eds) (2005) *Clothing as Material Culture*, Oxford, Berg.

Lan, P. C. (2011) 'White privilege, language capital and cultural ghettoisation. Western high skilled migrants in Taiwan', *Journal of Ethnic and Migration Studies*, vol. 37, no. 10, pp. 1669–1693.

Larsen, J., Urry, J. & Axhausen, K. (2006) *Mobilities, Networks, Geographies*, Aldershot, Ashgate.

Leonard, P. (2007) 'Migrating identities. Gender, whiteness, and Britishness in postcolonial Hong Kong', *Gender, Place and Culture*, vol. 15, no. 1, pp. 45–60.

Leonard, P. (2010) 'Work, identity and change? Post/colonial encounters in Hong Kong', *Journal of Ethnic and Migration Studies*, vol. 36, no. 8, pp. 1247–1263.

Leonard, P. (2013) 'Making whiteness work in South Africa: a translabour approach', *Women's Studies International Forum*, vol. 36, pp. 75–83.

Ley, D. (2004) 'Transnational spaces and everyday lives', *Transactions of the Institute of British Geographers*, vol. 29, pp. 151–164.

Leyshon, A. & Thrift, N. (1997) *Money/Space. Geographies of Monetary Transformation*, London, Routledge.

Luhmann, N. (1997) 'Globalization or world society: how to conceive of modern society', *International Review of Sociology*, vol. 7, pp. 67–79.

Lundström, C. (2014) *White Migrations. Gender, Whiteness and Privilege in Transnational Migration*, Basingstoke, Palgrave.

Massey, D. (2005) *For Space*, London, Sage.

McDowell, L. (1997) *Capital Culture – Gender at Work in the City*, Oxford, Blackwell.

Meyer, J., et al. (1997) 'World society and the nation state', *American Journal of Sociology*, vol. 103, no. 1, pp. 144–181.

Meier, L. (2009) *Das Einpassen in den Ort. Der Alltag deutscher Finanzmanager in London und Singapur*, Bielefeld, transcript.

Meier, L. (ed.) (2015) *Migrant Professionals in the City. Local Encounters, Identities, and Inequalities*, London, Routledge.

Moore, F. (2005) *Transnational Business Cultures. Life and Work in a Multinational Corporation*, Aldershot, Ashgate.

Nowicka, M. (2006) *Transnational Professionals and their Cosmopolitan Universes*, Frankfurt/Main, Campus.

OECD (2011) *OECD Regions at a Glance 2011*. Skilled immigration in OECD regions, Paris, [online] Available at: http://www.oecd-ilibrary.org/sites/reg_glance-2011-en/03/10/

index.html; jsessionid=632otcnevfac.delta?contentType=&itemId=/content/chapter/
reg_glance-2011-15-en&containerItemId=/content/serial/19990057&accessItemIds=
/ content/book/reg_glance-2011-en&mimeType=text/html (accessed 16 November
2013).

Office for National Statistics (2012) *2011 Census: Key Statistics for Local Authorities in
England and Wales*, [online] Available at: http://www.ons.gov.uk/ons/rel/census/
2011-census/key-statistics-for-local-authorities-in-england-and-wales/rft-table-
ks201ew.xls (accessed 13 November 2013).

Reay, D. (2008) 'Psychosocial aspects of White middle-class identities', *Sociology*, vol. 42,
no. 6, pp. 1072–1088.

Robinson, J. (2011) 'Cities in a world of cities – the comparative gesture', *International
Journal of Urban and Regional Research*, vol. 35, no. 1, pp. 1–23.

Said, E. W. (1978) *Orientalism – Western Concept of the Orient*, London, Penguin.

Sakai, J. (2000) *Japanese Bankers in the City of London – Language, Culture and Identity in
the Japanese Diaspora*, London, Routledge.

Salt, J. (1997) 'International movements of the highly skilled', International Migration
Unit Occasional Papers, No. 3, Paris, OECD.

Scott, S. (2004) 'Transnational exchanges among skilled British migrants in Paris',
Population, Space and Place, vol. 10, pp. 391–410.

Skeggs, B. (2004) *Class, Self, Culture*, London, Routledge.

Sklair, L. (2001) *The Transnational Capitalist Class*, Oxford, Blackwell.

Spradley, J. (1979) *The Ethnographic Interview*, New York, Wadsworth.

Strauss, C. & Quinn, N. (1997) *A Cognitive Theory of Cultural Meaning*, Cambridge,
Cambridge University Press.

Taylor, P. J. (2004) *World City Network – A Global Urban Analysis*, London, Routledge.

Tierney, S. & Jackson II, R. (2003) 'Deconstructing whiteness ideology as a set of rhetori-
cal fantasy themes: implications for interracial alliance building in the United States',
in *International and Intercultural Communication Annual, Volume XXV, 2002:
Intercultural alliances: Critical transformation*, ed. M. Collier, Thousand Oaks, Sage,
pp. 81–107.

Van Der Pijl, K. (1998) *Transnational Classes and International Relations*, London,
Routledge.

Vertovec, S. (2002) 'Transnational networks and skilled labour migration', *ESRC transnational communities programme working paper*, WPTC-02-02, Oxford.

Walsh, K. (2009) 'Geographies of the heart in transnational spaces. Love and the intimate lives of British migrants in Dubai', *Mobilities*, vol. 4, no. 3, pp. 427–445.

Walsh, K. (2011) 'Migrant masculinities and domestic space: British home-making practices in Dubai', *Transactions of the Institute of British Geographers*, vol. 36, no. 4, pp.
516–529.

Weber-Newth, I. & Steinert, J. D. (2006) *German Migrants in Post-war Britain. An Enemy
Embrace*, London, Routledge.

White, P. (1998) 'The settlement patterns of developed world migrants in London',
Urban Studies, vol. 35, no. 10, pp. 1725–1744.

Willis, K. & Yeoh, B. (2002) 'Gendering transnational communities – a comparison of
Singaporean and British migrants in China', *Geoforum*, vol. 33, pp. 553–565.

Willis, K., Yeoh, B. & Fakhri, S. (2002) 'Introduction – transnational elites', *Geoforum*, vol.
33, pp. 505–507.

Windance Twine, F. & Gallagher, C. (2008). 'The future of whiteness: a map of the 'third
wave', *Ethnic and Racial Studies*, vol. 31, no. 1, pp. 4–24.

Woods, M. (1998) 'Rethinking elites – networks, space, and local politics', *Environment and Planning A*, vol. 30, pp. 2101–2119.

Yeung, H. (1998) *Transnational Corporations and Business Networks*, London, Routledge.

Yeoh, B. (1996) *Contesting Space – Power Relations and the Urban Built Environment in Colonial Singapore*, Oxford, Oxford University Press.

Z/Yen Group (2013) *The Global Financial Centres Index 14*, London, [online] Available at: http://www.longfinance.net/images/GFCI14_30Sept2013.pdf (accessed 11 November 2013).

Dwelling-in-motion: Indian Bollywood tourists and their hosts in the Swiss Alps

Sybille Frank

Department of Sociology, Technische Universität Berlin, Berlin, Germany

ABSTRACT

Until recently, tourist routes typically led from 'the West' to the so-called 'rest' of the world, and travel guides and travel novels were the essential media for planning a journey. In recent years, however, the intensified circulation of place images through global communication media has connected more and more places with more and more imaginations, while the price reductions in and the expansion of travel offers as well as the economic upswing in parts of the global 'East', 'Middle East', and 'South' have set a rising number of these places within potential reach for ever more people. This paper investigates the places and performances of Indian Bollywood tourists and their hosts in and beyond a small town hotel in the Swiss mountains. The Swiss Alps are quite a 'traditional' destination of Indian tourism, as they were discovered by the Indian Bollywood film industry as a filming set as early as in the 1980s. Today, many Swiss towns display a comprehensive tourist infrastructure that specifically cares for the services needs of Indian tourists. Building on ethnographic field research and based on recent tourism mobilities studies, this paper explores the practices of Indian tourists in a transitory mode of dwelling and in a place familiar to them through the images produced by the film industry. Moreover, it retraces the way in which the Indian tourists' practices of dwelling-in-motion have been co-produced and received by service and sales personnel as well as the local population, and how rather immobile imaginations rooted in colonial times structure both the discourses and interactions in the local tourist space.

Introduction

Thin-soled shoes skid across the ice. Snowballs fly. Delighted squeals can be heard as soon as the furrowed slopes upon which it is possible to slide down a few metres into the snow have been discovered. Saris flap in the wind, camera phones and video cameras are set up. A text message home from the 3,200-metre-high peak of Mount Titlis in Central Switzerland is something of a compulsory component of the touristic programme. Then the Indian tourists all gather for lunch at the Indian group restaurant at the

145

peak station. The Indian tour group has a stay of three hours at the Titlis peak during their European package holiday. That is longer than in London or in Paris, for example (Gasser 2011). Yet for the Indian travellers it is not Paris, like for many Europeans, but Mount Titlis which epitomizes the idea of love and romanticism and therefore forms one of the highlights of every trip through Europe (Wenner 2003). 'The global Indian holidaymaker has arrived and is now a force to be reckoned with'[1] – this is how the Indian market leader for European trips, SOTC (Sita Online Tourism Corporation), sums up the latest power shift in the field of tourism (Frank 2012a).

Until recently, long-haul international tourist routes typically led from 'the West' to the so-called 'rest' of the world ('The West and the Rest', Hall 1992, Cohen and Cohen 2014), and travel guides and travel novels were the essential media for planning a journey. In recent years, however, the intensified circulation of place images through global communication media has connected more and more places with more and more imaginations, while the price reductions in and the expansion of travel offers as well as the economic upswing in parts of the global 'East', 'Middle East' and 'South' have set a rising number of these places within potential reach for ever more people.

This paper asks what makes travellers from India go to Switzerland and which place images and mutual perceptions structure the performances of Indian tourists and their hosts within the local tourist space. First of all, the background of the rising Indian tourism boom in Switzerland will be examined, placing particular emphasis on the imaginations the Indian tourists bring with them. Then there will be an overview of more recent tourism mobility studies, and the here presented research will be situated in this context. On this basis, the local specific crossover of (im)mobilities of humans, objects, images, imaginations and perceptions will be worked out by the example of the small municipality of Engelberg in Central Switzerland and the local Hotel Terrace. Finally, the Indian guests' practices of dwelling-in-motion as well as the latter's coproduction, perception and commenting on by the local population will be analysed regarding the question of which everyday knowledge stocks and categories of social inequality are mobilized to structure the local tourist space and to (re)establish tourism-related power positions.

In doing so, this paper analytically and methodologically connects to recent tourism mobilities research that has put performances, imaginations, places and social inequalities centre stage in the field of tourism research. Regrettably however, this young research tradition has up to now paid little attention to the relatively new phenomenon of the increasing international long-haul travel from the global 'East', 'Middle East' or 'South' to the 'Western world' (Cohen and Cohen 2014). Accordingly, this paper is meant to provide answers to the question of how encounters within the tourist space happen if no longer 'the West' tours 'the rest', as it has been practiced for centuries (Said 1978, Hall 1992), but when the so-called 'rest of the world' starts to knock, in the role of tourists to be served, on Western doors in order to consume both the vernacular 'Western' culture and their own heritage in place. The first question to be addressed now will be this one: What brings the Indian tourists to Switzerland?

Bollywood and the Swiss Alps

The reasons for the great interest in Switzerland among Indians are Indian Bollywood films. By now the flourishing commercial Indian Bollywood film industry produces around 1,000 films per year. This is much more than Hollywood.[2] In terms of content, most of the films vary between three large topics: the victory of good against evil, the dream of upward social mobility, and romantic love stories that overcome political, social, religious and language-related barriers (Follath 2006). The films are supposed, in the first instance, to entertain, but they should also deal with great emotions, address people's yearnings and help to cope with conflicts between modernity and tradition, all matters which occupy Indian society to a great degree. Since the 1980s these conflicts have been managed, above all, by means of 'new definitions of marriage, love, family and partnership' (Wenner 2003, p. 135) – successfully, as attendance figures of up to three billion people per film demonstrate.

However, because of the strict moral ideas that still dominate much of Indian society, the directors have been unable to show any explicit love scenes. This is why they seek recourse in romantic song-and-dance scenes (Shedde 2002). These are elaborately staged clips, similar to music clips, which interrupt the film's action by a kind of dream sequence. There are usually at least six of such sequences per film (Schneider 2005). In these scenes a young couple, desperately in love, sings and dances, preferably in front of an idyllic mountain landscape where their dreams of closeness and eroticism are fulfilled. The fantasy scenes are bound to neither time nor place; in other words, costumes and locations are changed abruptly, and heavy rainfall or storms appear out of nowhere, so that the actors' clothing clings seductively to their bodies (Follath 2006). How the story between the two protagonists continues is left to the viewers' imagination, helped along by telling fade-outs or veils that waft in front of the camera (Shedde 2002).

In India, the idea of romantic love is closely linked with the names Krishna and Radha (Dwyer 2002, Schneider 2005). The love story between the blue-skinned god Krishna and the dairy maid Radha has been told time and again for centuries in paintings, songs and poetry; how he once watched the beautiful dairy maid while bathing, and how he seduced her. The romantic relationship between the god and the girl consists of 'a series of amorous episodes which always take place against pastoral backgrounds, specifically: in a blooming, fluvial, verdant and hilly paradise' (Wenner 2003, p. 136). The song-and-dance scenes of Indian Bollywood films adopt these themes in a popular manner, but paradise-like landscapes are indispensible.

In the 1950s and 1960s, the preferred locations for such song-and-dance inserts were the mountain meadows of the snow-covered Kashmir ranges (Shedde 2002). However, as it became too dangerous to film there because of the conflicts with Pakistan that broke out in the 1980s, Bollywood producers went looking for alternatives (Keller 2005). And they discovered similarities in landscape between Kashmir and the Swiss Alps (Dwyer 2002). In particular, Mount Jungfraujoch in the Bernese Highlands and Mount Titlis in the Central Swiss Alps became popular filming locations. Numerous song-and-dance scenes were filmed there in the 1980s for movies that now count among the most successful Bollywood productions ever. In the 1990s, 'real' film scenes also began to be set in the Swiss mountains, such as around one third of the action of the 1995 film 'Dilwale Dulhania Le Jayenge' with Shah Rukh Khan, for example ('The Big Hearted Will Take the Bride'). Since the turn of the century, urban Swiss locations such as pedestrian zones, fountains, parks and trams have also been used as film backdrops (Schneider 2002, Wenner 2003).

Idyllic images of singing Bollywood stars, dancing erotically in front of peaceful, masticating cows or in sleepy villages and spotlessly clean towns made Switzerland into a paradise, into a guarantee of sun, calm, closeness to nature and happiness (Von Ascheraden 2007, p. 25). Although Indian film crews have long since discovered new filming locations in Eastern Europe, New Zealand or in the United Arab Emirates, for example, the popularity of Switzerland as a romantic destination remains unabated (Dwyer 2002, p. 98, Von Ascheraden 2007, p. 23). More and more Indians dream of travelling to the original locations of the films – and an increasing number of them can now afford the long journey to Europe.

In Europe, the Indian market is considered to be one of the most promising future tourist markets of all. The more than one billion Indians represent around 17 per cent of the world's population, yet only 1 per cent of Indians has been able to afford travelling abroad (World Tourism Organization 2011, p. 179). Thanks to the lasting economic boom in India, which has produced a growing middle class with new consumption patterns, the potential for growth is enormous. Because an Indian guest tends to spend much more money per day on holidays than an American traveller, for example (Keller *et al.* 2002, p. 389), the traditional travel destination of Switzerland, which has suffered from a decline in tourism, has developed a certain interest in meeting the film-fuelled expectations of its Indian guests. Before we start analysing how this has been achieved, at first there will be an overview of more recent tourism-related research trends, allowing for understanding tourism as a field of a complex crossover of mobilities.

The mobilities turn in tourism studies

In recent years, the so called 'mobilities turn' (Hannam *et al.* 2006, Urry 2007) and in its wake the 'new mobilities paradigm' (Sheller and Urry 2006) have increasingly found their way into interdisciplinary tourism studies. The point of view of mobilities studies was attractive for tourism research because it promised answers to a number of urgent topical and conceptual questions from the field of the scientific consideration of travelling which for a long time could not be answered by tourism research, due to a lack of theoretical further development (Rolshoven 2014). As far as into the 1990s, tourism was considered 'a series of discrete, enumerated occurrences of travel, arrival, activity, purchase, departure' (Franklin and Crang 2001, p. 6) and diametrically opposed to the everyday world. In the world of tourism, tourists appeared most of all as passive consumers of the offers made by tourism industry. Accordingly, tourism kept being characterized by fundamental dichotomies whose guiding distinctions have been summarized as oppositions such as economic vs. noneconomic, production vs. consumption, global vs. local und people vs. places (Mavrič and Urry 2009) or also home vs. away, everyday vs. holiday, host vs. guest, domestic vs. international (Cohen and Cohen 2012). 'Culture' was understood to be immobile and static, and it was located in cozy towns and villages being steamrolled by streams of mobile capital and tourists threatening with depriving them of their authenticity and integrity (Cresswell 2002). Thus, researchers implicitly categorized mobility as a threat for the 'harmonic' social order of nostalgically glorified traditional communities, as threatening the 'natural' cohesion of group, culture and space with dissolution (Lenz 2010, Frank 2016).

In an age of ongoing globalization processes these unquestioned basic assumptions proved to be epistemological obstacles. Under the impression of the cultural, spatial and postcolonial turns, in the late 1990s tourism research on the one hand turned towards questions of knowledge, meaning and representation, of the senses and the body, and of the active production of places, imaginations and experiences through tourist performances and embodiments (Coleman and Crang 2002, Jafari 2002, Edensor 2009). On the other hand there was a growing awareness of the fact that in the field of tourism one encounters the most different kinds of mobility, each being crossed over in a complex way (Sheller and Urry 2004). To be able to scientifically analyse this complexity, John Urry (2007) introduced an analytical distinction of five interdependent mobilities in the field of tourism which, however, must always be analysed 'together in their fluid interdependence rather than discretely' (Appadurai 1990, Cresswell 2006, Hannam and Roy 2013, p. 142). They are corporeal travel (people), movement of objects (goods, materials, souvenirs), imaginative travel (knowledge, ideas, media images), virtual travel (money, online information) as well as communicative travel (e-mails, mobile phones) (Urry 2007, Söderström *et al.* 2013, p. 5). Thus, analysing tourism mobilities means not restricting oneself to the touristic travel activities of humans but to just as well grasp the complex contexts within which run the transnational streams of humans, objects, imaginations and information as well as the continuous performative creation of these contexts (Lenz 2010).

As a result the new approach of 'tourism mobilities' was born. No longer did it conceptualise tourism as 'an ephemeral aspect of social life that is practised outside normal, everyday life' (Hannam and Roy 2013, p. 141) but 'as integral to wider processes of economic and political development and even constitutive of everyday life' (Wöhler 2011, Hannam and Roy 2013, p. 141). Thus travel and tourism, understood as 'significant modality through which transnational modern life is organised' (Franklin and Crang 2001, p. 3), were suddenly ontologically placed 'at the centre of social and cultural life rather than at the margins' (Hannam *et al.* 2014, p. 182).

One crucial concept of mobilities research is performance. As a reason, Mavrič and Urry give that '[e]xamining people's performances reveals how places are made and how they exist (partially) by what and how people perform within them' (Mavrič and Urry 2009, p. 649). As active interpreters and performers tourists actively contribute to the production of places, for their imagination of the place, which often, before arriving at the place, has been influenced by images and imaginations derived from travel guides, brochures, blogs, films, photos and travel reports, structures their travel performances. Thus, by way of a performative, corporeal approach it becomes possible 'to understand places as practiced, produced and performed' (Bærenholdt *et al.* 2004, p. 32).

At the same time this means that no longer places are bounded localities or homogeneous entities, fixed on the map, but that they are themselves travelling the world: 'Places can be "dislocated" since images, thoughts, photographs or memories are on the move, by means of technologies and the moving flows of people' (Mavrič and Urry 2009, p. 647). Accordingly, Bærenholdt supports conceptualizing places as 'sedimented practices requiring extensive networks and flows of mobilities in order to stabilize' (Bærenholdt *et al.* 2004, p. 10). Thus, tourist places bring together guests, hosts, buildings, objects and imaginations in such a way as allowing for the creation of certain performances.

Furthermore, it is an important concern of tourism mobilities to view at social inequalities in tourism which are said to be due to differing social status and power relations of places and actors 'located in the fast and slow lanes' across the globe (Sheller and Urry 2006, p. 207, Hannam and Roy 2013, p. 142). By grasping immobility as being constitutive for mobility, also the research of immobilities is an inseparable element of tourism mobilities. For, the mobility of some requires the immobility of others providing the tourism infrastructure such as freeways, airports, train stations, hotels, resorts, beaches, regulatory frameworks, that is the moorings of travelling. Also, a different 'motility' (Kaufmann 2002), as the 'access to means of mobility and to know-how concerning technologies of mobility' (Söderström *et al.* 2013, p. 7) is called, is said to be closely connected to the social structural categories of class, race and gender as well as to modern concepts of space which, for the time being, have been reflected on only to a limited degree (Cohen and Cohen 2014, see also Meier and Frank 2016, in this issue).

On the whole, the new mobilities paradigm calls on tourism research to analyse the 'complex combinations of movement and stillness, realities and fantasies, play and work' within trans-local contexts as well as social inequalities in tourism (Sheller and Urry 2004, p. 1) – a demand this paper is meant to meet, while at the same time enriching tourism mobilities by the previously neglected aspect of increasing international long-haul travel from the global 'East' to the 'Western world'.

Dwelling in tourism mobilities

Now, how does the practice of dwelling fit to the concept of tourism mobilities? Here we may connect to Martin Heidegger's famous, phenomenology-based definition of dwelling:

> Now, what is building? The Old High German word for building, 'buan', means dwelling, in the sense of staying, residing. […] The way in which you are and I am, in which we humans *are* on earth is […] dwelling. Being human means: being on earth as a mortal, means: dwelling.[3] (Heidegger 1952, p. 73)

In this broad sense, emphasizing aspects of protection, of security, of comfort, of communication and acceptance (Hannemann 2014), dwelling is not limited to one defined place but generally includes human practices of feeling home and making oneself feel home on earth.

Such practices can be extraordinarily studied by the example of tourism. This holds for travels by way of public (Lyons and Urry 2005) and private transport (Featherstone *et al.* 2004) and for lodging in holiday homes, on camp sites, in hotels or motels. In the latter touristic homes, a number of actors is occupied with performatively making guest areas comfortable e.g. by way of decoration (Hörz and Richter 2011), and often objects belonging to these homes are taken on the long journey back home, to be further used and/or arranged as souvenirs there (Johler 2011). Even if, for he time being, actual lodging particularly in hotels has been little researched (Pritchard and Morgan 2006), research considers hotels potential liminal spaces, where tourists 'may […] subvert social norms, challenge convention and seek adventures' which, however, are at the same time highly supervised spaces, due to 'people watching' in residence areas, CCTV cameras and electronic access codes (Pritchard and Morgan 2006, p. 762). Precisely due to the latter quality, all around the world hostels and hotels have repeatedly been used as refugee camps, which challenges traditional distinctions between mobility and immobility, of voluntary and enforced mobility, and of tourism and migration (Lenz 2010).

On the other hand, the spreading phenomenon of the permanent guest of a hotel suggests 'imagining [residing] on the stability-mobility axis and thus to also open our eyes to the various manifestations along this axis' (Bendix 2011, p. 199). More recent research aims in a similar direction, observing an 'increasing […] touristification of everyday life parallel to making travelling an everyday matter' particularly in urban contexts (Rolshoven 2014, p. 15, Wöhler 2011, p. 15). Others suggest generally grasping the touristic as a sign of our variety of presences which are characterized by urbanity, digitality and mobility, as it refers not only to movement but also systematically to practices of the symbolic and material appropriation of places (Stock 2014). In this sense, the way of residing in the world as addressed by Heidegger (1952) is these days primarily a touristic appropriation, a set of diverse practices of dwelling-in-motion.

In sum, the representatives of the new mobilities paradigm understand these shortly sketched, performatively created activities of making oneself feel home on journeys – both on the fast and the slow lane as well as during periods of immobility – as 'forms of material and sociable dwelling-in-motion' (Hannam and Roy 2013, p. 143). By this they mean the 'various practices of "domesticating" other places as well as the personalizing of very local spaces while on the move' (Mavrič and Urry 2009, p. 647).

According to Büscher et al. (2011), to be able to methodly analyse mobilities approaches must be found which are suitable for taking the interwovenness of movement and stay as well as that of humans, places, objects and imagination into consideration and enable to ask about the effects of translocal and transnational mobilities both on the social and on the societal relations. In the following, in the sense of tourism mobilities research, I will conceptualize the hotel as a node 'where various mobilities or flows intersect' (Mavrič and Urry 2009, p. 647) and where various, both appropriating and domesticating and disciplining, practices of dwelling-in-motion are performed. My method follows Gille and Ò Riain (2002) who argue that place, being such a node, is the ideal locus for studying (im)mobile social life in global times. For places, I choose the picturesque mountain village of Engelberg that remains the most popular destination of Indian travellers in Switzerland, and as a particular focus at Engelberg the Hotel Terrace and Mount Titlis. All findings presented are based on documentary analysis and on ethnographic on-site field work, comprising participant observations as well as informal interviews with local services and sales personnel, local inhabitants and also some Indian tourists[4] that I conducted during two several day stays at the Hotel Terrace in Engelberg in 2011 and 2012.[5] The following chapter will take a closer look and examine the effects the enormous tourist demand from India has had on the municipality.

Engelberg and hotel terrace, shooting stars of Indian tourism

Engelberg is a civil parish in Central Switzerland with around 4,300 inhabitants.[6] It is situated at a height of 1,000 metres in a wide upper valley at the foot of Mount Titlis (Figure 1). The next largest city, Lucerne, is 40 kilometres away. Thanks to its plentiful sunshine and its wind-sheltered position, Engelberg developed into an international health resort and climatic spa for the wealthy in the mid-nineteenth century, with regular guests from England, Germany, France and Russia. The health and beauty association was founded as early as in 1883, thus providing a professional structure for marketing the health resort around the world. In 1898 Engelberg was connected to the Swiss railway network by a rack railway, so that it could be reached reliably also in winter. Investment in the construction of sledge and tobogganing runs as well as ski slopes also made Engelberg a winter sports destination. Construction works on the cable car began in the 1910s, and Mount Titlis was connected in 1967 (Höchli 1990).

In 1990 Engelberg had more than 120 kilometres of marked ski slopes, 25 funiculars and ski lifts, 26 hotels, over 500 holiday apartments, 40 restaurants,

Figure 1. The civil parish Engelberg in Central Switzerland. Courtesy: Sybille Frank.

19 summit restaurants, almost 400 kilometres of hiking trails and more than 100 businesses. On this basis the small town has started to call itself an 'international tourist metropolis' (Höchli 1990, pp. 9, 19). Indeed, despite its low number of inhabitants the municipality can boast of many multi-storey buildings, its own pedestrian zone, a museum with art exhibition spaces, a shopping centre, a sports and golf centre, a heated outdoor swimming pool, an international university and a cinema. Seventy-six per cent of the municipality's economic performance results from tourism, while 90 per cent of the residents make a living from this field.[7] More than 9,000 guests stay overnight in Engelberg in the peak season. That's more than twice as many guests as inhabitants.

One of the most traditional accommodation establishments in Engelberg is Hotel Terrace, built in 1905 in the style of the Belle Époque. It followed the trend of the time, which was to base hotel architecture on the residences of the aristocracy (Figure 2). Correspondingly, the hotel had a palace-like façade with pillars and columns at many levels and generously sized parklands with exotic plants and fountains. Inside the hotel was furnished with large reception and dining rooms as well as luxury rooms for almost 400 guests. The hotel's own cable railway was something of a sensation, taking the guests from the station to the grand hotel, which was situated as a landmark above the town.

Figure 2. Hotel Terrace in Engelberg. Courtesy: Sybille Frank.

In the 1950s the Terrace was sold to the Club Méditerrannée and continued to be run as a typical club hotel for decades. In 1993 a Japanese company purchased the hotel with the intention of opening an international catering college there. However, because of the economic crisis in Japan the project never came to fruition. Finally, in 1998, the municipality of Engelberg took over the empty hotel in order to lease it to the local cable car society, Titlisbahnen. Because this society not only ran the cable cars to but also the peak restaurants on Mount Titlis, their involvement in the hotel business seemed well suited for providing attractive package offers to both summer and winter tourists.

But then Titlisbahnen, together with the renowned Swiss tour operator Kuoni, decided to open a base in particular for Indian package holidays in Engelberg (Keller 2005). A few years earlier, Kuoni had bought India's largest tour operator SOTC, which had specialized in cheap family package deals with all-round Indian care and support. The programme also included European tours. The peak travelling time of the Indian guests was May and June, two months when India is very hot, which is why this is the time of school holidays. In Switzerland, on the other hand, May and June belong to the pre-season, when visitor numbers are notoriously low (Keller *et al.* 2002, p. 390). Kuoni promised to book all of the Indian package tourists' overnight stays in Switzerland in the Hotel Terrace – upon which the management of the Terrace decided to provide the hotel with the official byname 'SOTC Indian Village'.[8]

Already in the first season of 1999 there were 34,000 overnight stays by Indian guests at the Terrace (Stauber 2000). The Indian groups, who often find themselves on their very first trip to Europe, usually start their European tour in London and spend an average of three to four days in Switzerland, at the Terrace. They go on day-trips from the Terrace, to the Mount Titlis of course, but also to Mount Jungfraujoch, to Lucerne or Zürich (Keller 2005, p. 283). According to information from the services staff, among the guests there are travellers at all stages of life, from the honeymoon of a newly wed couple to the journey of a large extended family encompassing three generations. After the tour groups from India in May and June, Kuoni then brings non-resident Indians to Engelberg in July and August, such as those who live in the USA or Kenya (Rutishauser 1999). Then, from September on it is the turn of the Korean tour groups who pass the baton to European, American and Israeli ski-package holidaymakers in October.

In the first year, in October only, the hotel got back its traditional name, 'Terrace'. Since the second season, however, in response to public voices criticizing that the name of this traditional hotel was connected to that of an Indian tour operator, the building is again called 'Terrace' all year round – but the idea of bringing Indian package holidaymakers to Engelberg has been expanded further. Many more hotels in Engelberg have specialized in caring for the Indian guests, so that 72,000 Indians stayed in Engelberg in 2011.[9] The Indians therefore now account for almost one-fifth of all overnight stays in the municipality. This way, the Bollywood films and their successful location placement have led to profitable balances not only of the Hotel Terrace but also of numerous other local hotel and services businesses (Figure 3). To boost Indian package tourism even further, the municipality of Engelberg has been marketed by the slogan 'Engelberg/Titlis – it's heaven!'. The offers marketed by help of this slogan showcase an idealised image of Switzerland which – according to the image of Switzerland presented in the Bollywood films – is pictured as a clean, intact natural landscape and a romantic destination for lovers (Shedde 2002, Schneider 2005, Von Ascheraden 2007).

Now, given these powerful images travelling from India to Switzerland and back again, let us ask about the spatial and social effects the described film-induced mobility of places, images, imaginations and people has had on Hotel Terrace, Mount Titlis and the municipality of Engelberg.

Hotel terrace and Mount Titlis as nodes of intersecting mobilities

Since the start of the cooperation of the local Titlisbahnen cable car society with the Swiss tour operator Kuoni and the arrival of the first package tourists from India at Engelberg in 1999 both the Hotel Terrace and Mount Titlis have

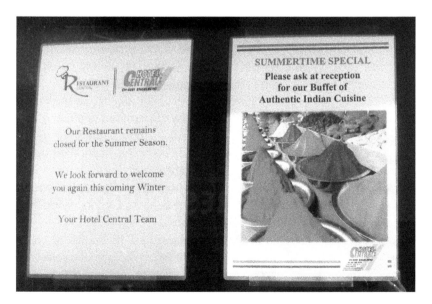

Figure 3. Announcement of Indian Cuisine at Hotel Central, Engelberg. Courtesy: Sybille Frank.

seen much change. For example, one significant novelty at the Terrace is that during the months in which the Indian tourists are on the move, travellers from other cultures are no longer hosted – with the argument, expressed by a young male Swiss receptionist, that 'no normal operation' of the hotel can take place during this time. Between May and September the hotel operations are exclusively oriented at the needs of the Indian travellers. At the beginning of the summer season this decision starts complex (im)mobilities of humans, goods, information and knowledge stocks on which further light shall be shed in the following.

Those entering the lobby of the Terrace in the summer months might believe to be somewhere in the midst of India. A clock ticks above the reception desk, showing the time in both Engelberg and Mumbai (Figure 4). Female guests in colourful saris walk around the lobby, and in the sitting areas groups of travellers from India are having their chai tea which is provided cost-free by the hotel management in the lobby during the summer months (Figure 5). Provisional signs in English show the way to the dining halls as well as to the hotel's own club, where in the evening an Indian DJ invites for Indian Disco. The culinary needs of the Indian tourists are taken care of by Indian chefs, for whom the Swiss chefs have to make way from May to September. The ingredients and cooking utensils are delivered specially from India, and the chefs are well acquainted with the strict nutritional rules of the different

Figure 4. Hotel reception with clocks. Courtesy: Sybille Frank.

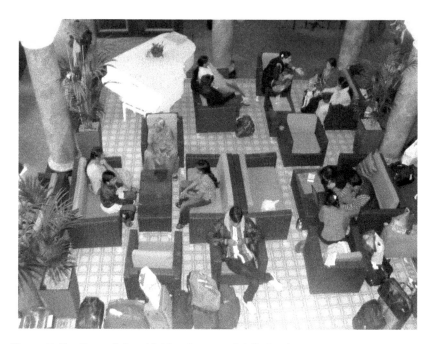

Figure 5. The Terrace's hotel lobby. Courtesy: Sybille Frank.

religions. Compared to the local taste, traditional Indian dishes are made quite spicy and are prepared mostly without lactose-laden products such as the famous Swiss cheese, and are served in the dining hall at tables that are big enough to accommodate entire families. The hotel's own 'Chandra' restaurant serves a big choice of Indian food, too, and lunch packs or Indian caterers are booked for excursions.

On their diverse bus trips starting from the Terrace, the Indian package tourists are frequently driven to places where famous Bollywood film scenes have been set. In order to remind the tourists of the scenes and to evidently locally connect the world of Indian film-making with the world of Switzerland, the Bollywood films in which the scenes are featured are often shown again on the buses taking the Indians to the places in question (Schneider 2005). At the end of each excursion, as reported by the Terrace services staff, the Indian guests receive a small photo album as a memento, with a famous scene from a Bollywood film on the left-hand side and a recreated scene on the right-hand side, with the travellers adopting the same pose as the Bollywood stars, in the exact location.

Even on Mount Titlis the operator of the Terrace, Titlisbahnen, in cooperation with Kuoni has perfectly adjusted to the services needs and imaginations of the Indian package tourists. Already at the valley station, just as later on the cable cars, the Indians are welcomed in Hindi; a huge salesroom for winter clothes is meant to adjust the guests from India to the cold temperature on the mountain, who, given the film images of lightly clad stars dancing in the snow, are often surprised of the cold on the peak, as the sales staff tells. Who nevertheless starts his/her way up to the peak, leading via several mountain stations and cable cars, wearing flip-flops is helped on the peak station by a mountain boots rental. Having arrived at the peak of Mount Titlis, the travellers from India are welcomed, against the dramatic background of the Swiss mountain landscape, by life-size cardboard cutouts of famous Bollywood actors in their well-known poses, many of the Indian travellers playfully interacting with them while being photographed and filmed (Figure 6). Apart from the cardboard figures, the snow and the panoramic view, the Indian flag waving on Mount Titlis is another sensation.

When the Indians have spent enough time on the peak, their physical well-being is taken care of at an Indian group restaurant offering Indian food. All Swiss products, such as the mineral water served there, are labelled in English or Hindi, and the ingredients are carefully declared. After lunch there is still some time for buying souvenirs of typical Swiss quality products such as watches. The most popular offer at the peak station, however, is a photo studio where the guests from India can have themselves photographed against a panoramic view of the Alps, wearing original Swiss wear and handling items such as alphorns, accordions, skis or rifles. Also this way they adopt the

Figure 6. Celebrating 'Dilwale Dulhania Le Jayenge' on Mount Titlis. Courtesy: Sybille Frank.

practices of famous visitors such as the Bollywood star Amisha Patel wearing traditional wear in the midst of a Swiss mountain landscape (Figure 7).

However, apart from the described adjustments of the local providers to the imaginations the travellers from India bring with them, the Indian guests are just as well expected to adjust to certain local conventions. Sanitary areas have proven to be important places of immobile infrastructure, but also of cultural delimitation. Because the Indian guests, most of them coming from

Figure 7. Bollywood star Amisha Patel in the photo studio on Mount Titlis. Courtesy: Sybille Frank.

urban areas (Keller 2005), are generally used to have bidets and running water in the entire sanitary areas, numerous instances of water damage have occurred in public and private lavatories (not only) at the Terrace, as told by the hotel staff. Other than, for example, the Hotel Cathrin in Engelberg which according to its owner decided in 2005 to generally equip its bathrooms with bidets and drains in the floor, Titlisbahnen has chosen to 'educate' their Indian guests at the Terrace and on Mount Titlis with the

Figure 8. Lessons in local hygiene, Hotel Terrace. Courtesy: Sybille Frank.

help of signs in the bathrooms ('please sit down'/'only toilet paper', Figure 8). Also by help of signs, at the lifts the attention of the Indian guests is attracted to the fact that they provide room for a 'maximum of six people', whereas by signs on the wall and instructions by the services staff they are again and again reminded that it is not allowed to walk barefoot in the staying areas of the hotel.

On guests and hosts: immobilities of mutual perceptions

If thus, beyond the described places and performances, one is interested in the stories the Indian travellers tell about the locals of Engelberg and, vice versa, the latter tell about their Indian guests, one finds that the contacts between the travellers from India and the locals are characterized by comparably stable mutual imaginations – even if the first package tourists from India arrived at Engelberg more than 15 years ago.

Usually, the Indians have no specific image of Engelberg. In the famous Bollywood productions Engelberg – other than Lucerne – does not play any significant role, if any at all. It is only that the sets were on the mountain meadows in the vicinity of the town or right on Mount Titlis. Nevertheless, the Indians I spoke with expressed their expectation that at Engelberg they would experience 'rural Switzerland'. As both the Bollywood productions and Engelberg tourism marketing present Switzerland as the perfect Indian film paradise (Schneider 2005), the conclusion suggests itself that the Indian travellers expect Engelberg to be an idyllic, perfectly clean place within a pastoral Swiss mountain landscape. Indeed, according to the statement by an middle-aged male Indian tourist, on the agenda of the European trip Engelberg runs as 'the countryside part'.

These aspects – also given the Indian all-inclusive service package – have brought research of recent years to the unanimous diagnosis that Engelberg's Indian guests want to experience kind of a 'home away from home' in Switzerland (Keller *et al.*, 2002, p. 391, Schneider 2002, p. 139). Basically, this statement may be correct, as e.g. it is quite a frequent finding concerning the needs of package tourists in general. Rather, it is interesting that in case of the Indian package tourists this diagnosis has opened up a discursive space which seems to legitimate certain disciplining reactions from the side of the hosts.

If once the therein hidden message 'the Indians don't want contact to us as people' has pushed through, the way has been paved for a variety of narrations referring to the 'home away from home' motif. Since long they have been counting among the everyday knowledge stock of the inhabitants of Engelberg and can be read in several reports by the local and national press. What is lamented is the ways of communication of the guests from India which are perceived as being inappropriately loud, their habit of haggling for goods, their practices of walking barefoot in public areas, or their already mentioned hygiene habits in the bathrooms. Most frequent, however, is the story of the stove. It tells that often large Indian families had set up camp stoves on the floors of their hotel rooms in Engelberg to prepare their familiar curry dishes there and eat them among the family. No direct source for this story could be identified; none of my interview partners could tell me anybody who claimed to have personally observed such an incident. Neither could it be reconstructed when and where exactly the story was supposed to have happened, nor could it be clarified why – despite Indian all-inclusive catering – these families should have done this.

These narrations may have such a long life because during their trip through Europe the Indian tourists have hardly any opportunity to see Engelberg. In most cases, after the day trips they have too little time to have a walk through the village before supper is served at the hotel. However, when strolling through the Engelberg town centre one notices that the shop windows display many items, such as Swiss knives, which are demanded by Indian travellers. Also, quite a significant number of the services and sales staff have been specially trained to react appropriately to the shopping behaviour of the Indian guests who often try to re-negotiate fixed prices. Only a few shop windows show signs like 'No bargaining!'. On the contrary, most shop owners make efforts to adjust to the holiday culture (Thiem 2001) of this new, solvent group of tourists.

Notwithstanding all practical and actual approaches, still the local and trans-local discourses on the guests from India stay connected to traditional knowledge stocks. By 'traditional' I mean those still powerful Eurocentric patterns of thought, stemming from the period of colonialism, which celebrate 'the West' as the peak of civilization and judge on the 'rest of the world' according to the criterion of this modern western world, as they have been reconstructed by authors such as Edward Said (1978) or Stuart Hall (1992). From this context there comes the everyday knowledge, which in Central Europe can be reliably referred to by way of the above described anecdotes, of loud communication, haggling, walking barefoot, appearing in large kinship groups and cooking on open fires in hotel rooms as 'primitive' and 'uncivilized' behaviour. It does not come to the minds of those telling such stories that these practices of dwelling are simply 'different', that they are simply 'other' ways of expressing social cohesion, conformal shopping behaviour or displayed snugness. Even the Indians' lacking experience with western bathrooms is considered evidence of being 'uncivilized'. However, already 80 years ago the German sociologist Nobert Elias (1969, 1982) would have interpreted the irritation of Indians by Swiss hygiene habits as an easily comprehensible problem of a 'civilized' (Indian) culture provided with higher shame and embarrassment thresholds – considering the cleaning of the genital area by hand and toilet paper a taboo – being confronted with the comparably laxer (Swiss) hygiene standards.

Thus whereas Indians, as serviced guests, are starting to conquer the global West, the representatives of the western culture, who are given the role of those providing service and telling about it, react to this shift of power in the field of tourism by Orientalizing the travellers from India (Said 1978). This may be helpful with at least discursively reconstructing a world order which, in the field of tourism, has fallen apart. However, this discourse threatens to make the knowledge of the Indian travellers disappear that Switzerland is not India – that it is no 'home away from home' – while at the same time neglecting the variety of enormous adjustment efforts by the small municipality of Engelberg, in the form of staff training and new recruitments, culinary reorientation, spatial renovations and redecorations as well as the production of new tourist destinations and performative offers in the past few years.

Social inequalities

If, for once, the travellers from India leave Hotel Terrace above the municipality to stroll through Engelberg village street and buy souvenirs, as many interviewees reported, different perceptions of serving and being served become a frequently lamented problem (Frank 2012b). These perceptions are interpreted as uncovering an 'elitist attitude' of the Indian guests towards the local service and sales staff. Most of the guests from India belong to higher castes (Keller 2005); they are comparatively wealthy – at least wealthy enough to pay for a relatively expensive trip to Europe for themselves and the members of their families. A look at the name tags of the suitcases of Indians waiting in the lobby of Hotel Terrace produced a surprisingly high share of travellers having a doctoral grade. Thus, in the summer months Hotel Terrace is inhabited by a comparably well-off social class which in the western world is seldom connected to package tours. Whereas service is a recognized profession in Switzerland, with reciprocal expressions of respect between the person serving and the one being served, the caste mindset of the Indians means that trained services and sales staff are often treated like servants. Whereas usually the class affiliation of guests and hosts does not play any role in the context of tourism in Switzerland or is dealt with professionally, the buying and customer performances of the Indian guests attribute a lower social rank to the local services and sales people, which irritates the latter's self-perception, their perception of the guests from India and their action routines.

Also, it was reported to be a problem for the local services and sales staff that many Indians flatly rejected female service staff to collect money – and that financial transactions, even if groups of women were shopping, were exclusively carried out by men. Furthermore, stories are told in the village about Indian males who, in case of 'risky' offers such as fast sleigh rides down steep slopes, at first send their wives to 'test' them before riding themselves. These stories about bad treatment of Indian and non-Indian women by Indian males make obvious that the interactions between the Swiss hosts and their Indian guests make also gender relations, apart from class relations, a local topic of discussion. From the point of view of the inhabitants, however, ethnicity – immediately identifiable with a view to skin colour and clothing (Keller *et al.* 2002, p. 390) – is the characteristic feature that testifies to the 'exotic nature' of the 'uncivilized' Indian guests.

Whereas dealing with foreign guests belongs to the history of Engelberg, inhabitants nevertheless emphasize again and again that the people of Engelberg have preserved their traditions and that it is precisely these traditions that make the place so attractive for tourism. For example, the history of the town, written by the local bookseller, a number of times points out to the fact that Engelberg is dominated by a lively local club scene and that 'staged shows for tourists […] are foreign to Engelberg's cultural institutions' (Höchli 1990, p. 15). But for many of the Engelbergerians, as mentioned before, it seems that the Indian tourists do not wish to experience Engelberg during their stays, but instead Switzerland as a perfect Indian film paradise (Schneider 2005). Therefore, a survey on the topic of 'Engelberg in 100 years', which was conducted by the municipality among some of its juvenile inhabitants in 2009, produced quite sobering results. The teenagers agreed on Engelberg continuing to be attractive as a 'fairytale land' – especially for Asian tourists (Einwohnergemeinde Engelberg 2010, p. 108). To quote a young woman from Engelberg: 'It is now August 2109. I go for a walk with my mother in Engelberg. We meet a lot of tourists from Italy, China, India' (Einwohnergemeinde Engelberg 2010, p. 109). Two other female inhabitants have a similar vision: 'There are more and more tourists in Engelberg. The residents are becoming fewer. In a hundred years the Hotel Terrace will only be there for Indians' (Einwohnergemeinde Engelberg 2010, p. 108). Expressions such as 'The inhabitants of Engelberg have been pushed out by the tourists' (Einwohnergemeinde Engelberg 2010, p. 110) appear unanimously in all of the texts submitted, and some go as far as to presenting the vision that a completely new Engelberg will have been built, to which tourists no longer have access. One sender had it as follows: 'Our native mountain farmers and residents of Engelberg are almost extinct, replaced by people of different nationalities. […] The main languages spoken are English and Chinese' (Einwohnergemeinde Engelberg 2010, p. 109). But new groups of tourists are also considered. To quote three Engelbergerians: 'The climate is getting warmer, that's why more and more Arabs are coming to Engelberg' (Einwohnergemeinde Engelberg 2010, p. 110).

The contributions presented show that the people of Engelberg have understood that global mobilities, which might bring, besides the Indians, also Chinese and Arab travellers to Engelberg, poses a challenge to many of the traditions they have grown fond of. A radio feature on Deutschlandradio summed up this discomfort as follows:

> When a wealthy Indian sees snowy mountains on the other side of the world in the cinema, all he has to do is pull out his credit card, and he can be there the following week. And if he prefers to eat Chicken Biryani there instead of Rösti, that is an utterly normal wish by a customer who understands how to use globalization. What annoys the people of Engelberg is the fact that it is completely irrelevant whether or not they agree with this. What they, the Swiss, for centuries have considered to be their identity, the insistence on what once was, is not even folklore anymore. It is simply overrun. And by tourism, of all things: their basis of life, for which they have worked so hard. (Sitzler 2005, p. 15)

All in all, the Engelbergerians seem to feel that the tourists from the global 'East' and 'Middle East' do not intend to knock on their doors – they just enter.

Conclusion

This paper has used some of the new research perspectives advocated by the still young field of tourism mobilities studies as a backdrop to investigate Indian (Bollywood) tourism into Engelberg in Central Switzerland. In doing so, it has specifically investigated how places and practices 'of material and sociable dwelling-in-motion' (Hannam and Roy 2013, p. 143) are jointly and performatively produced by both the Indian guests and their local hosts. In order to make the Indian travellers' trip to Engelberg a valuable experience and to ease perceptions of security, comfort, ability to communicate and acceptance given as being essential for dwelling by Heidegger (1952), Bollywood film-induced imaginations of Switzerland are both taken up and, by way of a variety of offers, performatively updated and localized. Moreover, this paper has delineated how places, performances and social inequalities are produced, structured and stabilized by locally specific intersections of the (im)mobilites of people, objects, places, images and imaginations.

From the above presented empirical material the following conclusions can be drawn. First, the Engelberg case directs our attention at ongoing processes of democratization in the field of tourism mobilities, where at least the touristic travel routes of humans are increasingly no longer one-way destinations from the global 'West' to the global 'East'. By the here presented case study it becomes obvious that the presence of people as tourists in the 'West' who have previously been located in faraway regions irritate previously unquestioned local notions of distance (far – near), spatial global orders (modern – pre-modern), knowledge stocks (we – you), understandings of roles (western guest – western or non-western services provider), and assumptions about motility (mobile – immobile). This process, which for the time being has escaped the attention of the sciences, challenges practiced power relations in the field of tourism in a variety of ways. Second, the Engelberg case reminds us that travelling and the power of tourists to impose specific (im)mobilities and practices of place-making on regions that have been turned into 'destinations' has always been a privilege of the wealthy – in this case of the wealthy among the Indians. Third, the disciplining of Indian tourists both in the local space and in the public discourse as it is described in this paper demonstrates that languages of ethnic superiority and of racial inferiority and, thereby, hidden assumptions of modern society itself, are still very much alive in the field of global tourism mobilities.

Disclosure statement

No potential conflict of interest was reported by the author.

Notes

1. http://www.superbrandsindia.com/images/brand_pdf/consumer_3rd_edition/SOTC.pdf, accessed 2 November 2014.
2. http://www.guinnessworldrecords.com/records-1/largest-annual-film-output/, accessed 4 November 2014.
3. German original: 'Was heißt nun Bauen? Das althochdeutsche Wort für bauen, , buan', bedeutet Wohnen. Dies besagt: bleiben, sich aufhalten. […] Die Art, wie du bist und ich bin, die Weise, nach der wir Menschen auf der Erde sind, ist […] das Wohnen. Mensch sein heißt: als Sterblicher auf der Erde sein, heißt: wohnen'.
4. Unfortunately, informal conversations with tourists from India proved to be outspokenly difficult, as many of the Indian guests – in particular women and children – were not ready to talk to me. Occasionally, when being on the car up to the peak of Mt. Titlis, I could take the opportunity of having a longer conversation.

5. For this article data that has been published in parts in two German journals (Frank 2012a, Frank 2012b) is employed to develop a new paper.
6. http://www.gde-engelberg.ch/dl.php/de/0civ5-xmpdcc/bevlkerungsstatistik_ 2012_gesamt.pdf, accessed 2 November 2014.
7. http://www.gde-engelberg.ch/de/portrait/gemeindeinzahlen, accessed 2 November 2014.
8. http://www.twai-canada.com/site/sotc.html, accessed 2 August 2012.
9. http://www.migrosmagazin.ch/leben/reisen/artikel/k%C3%A4ptn-iglu-und-die-inder, accessed 2 August 2012.

References

Appadurai, A. (1990) 'Disjuncture and difference in the global cultural economy', *Theory, Culture, Society*, vol. 7, pp. 295–310.

Bærentholdt, J. O., *et al.* (2004) *Performing Tourist Places*, Aldershot, Ashgate.

Bendix, R. (2011) 'Dauergäste. Bausteine zu einer Phänomenologie des immobilen Nichtzuhauseseins', in *Voyage. Jahrbuch für Reise- und Tourismusforschung*, vol. 9, Special Issue: *Das Hotel*, eds. N. Langreiter, *et al.*, Berlin, Metropol, pp. 198–217.

Büscher, M., *et al.* (2011) 'Introduction. Mobile methods', in *Mobile Methods*, ed. M. Büscher, *et al.*, London & New York, Routledge, pp. 1–19.

Cohen, E. & Cohen, S. A. (2012) 'Current sociological theories and issues in tourism', *Annals of Tourism Research*, vol. 39, no. 4, pp. 2177–2202. [online] Available at: doi:10.1016/j.annals.2012.07.009 (accessed 18 September 2014).

Cohen, E. & Cohen, S. A. (2014) 'A mobilities approach to tourism from emerging world regions', *Current Issues in Tourism*, vol. 18, no. 1, pp. 11–43. [online] Available at: doi:10.1080/13683500.2014.898617 (accessed 26 November 2014).

Coleman, S. & Crang, M. (2002) 'Grounded tourists, travelling theory', in *Tourism Between Place and Performance*, eds. S. Coleman & M. Crang, Oxford, Berghahn Books, pp. 1–17.

Cresswell, T. (2002) 'Introduction. Theorizing space', in *Mobilizing Place, Placing Mobility*, ed. G. Verstraete & T. Cresswell, Amsterdam, Rodopi, pp. 11–32.

Cresswell, T. (2006) *On the Move. Mobility in the Modern Western World*, New York, Routledge.

Dwyer, R. (2002) 'Landschaft der Liebe. Die indischen Mittelschichten, die romantische Liebe und das Konsumdenken', in *Bollywood. Das Indische Kino und die Schweiz*, ed. A. Schneider, Zürich, Hochschule für Gestaltung und Kunst, pp. 97–105.

Edensor, T. (2009) 'Tourism and performance', in *The Sage Handbook of Tourism Studies*, eds. T. Jamal & M. Robinson, Los Angeles, Sage, pp. 543–557.

Einwohnergemeinde Engelberg. ed. (2010) *Ängelbärger Zeyt. Engelberger Jahrbuch 2010*, Engelberg, Engelberger Druck AG.

Elias, N. (1969) *The Civilizing Process, Vol. I: The History of Manners*, Oxford, Blackwell.

Elias, N. (1982). *The Civilizing Process, Vol. II: State Formation and Civilization*, Oxford, Blackwell.

Featherstone, M., *et al.*, eds. (2004) 'Special issue: cultures of automobility', *Theory, Culture & Society*, vol. 21, pp. 1–284.

Follath, E. (2006) 'Big Bang Bollywood', *Der Spiegel*, 3 June.

Frank, S. (2012a) 'Indien in der Schweiz: Engelberg als *global-lokale Kontaktzone*', *Design & Kunst*, vol. 2, Special Issue: Destination Kultur, pp. 44–47.

Frank, S. (2012b) 'When "the rest" enters "the West": Indischer Tourismus in die Zentralschweiz', *Zeitschrift für Tourismuswissenschaft*, vol. 4, no. 2, Special Issue: Interkulturalität und Tourismus, pp. 221–229.

Franklin, A. & Crang, M. (2001) 'The trouble with tourism and travel theory', *Tourist Studies*, vol. 1, no. 1, pp. 5–22.

Gasser, H. (2011) 'Das Alpen-Delhi', [online] Available at: http://www.hansgasser.de/reportagen-alpen/reportagen-alpen-engelberg/ (accessed 3 November 2014).

Gille, Z. & Ò Riain, S. (2002) 'Global ethnography', *Annual Review of Sociology*, vol. 28, no. 1, pp. 271–295.

Hall, S. (1992) 'The west and the rest: Discourse and power', in *Formations of Modernity*, eds. S. Hall & B. Gieben, Cambridge, Polity Press, pp. 275–320.

Hannam, K. & Roy, S. (2013) 'Cultural tourism and the mobilities paradigm', in *The Routledge Handbook of Cultural Tourism*, ed. M. Smith & G. Richards, London and New York, Routlege, pp. 141–147.

Hannam, K., *et al.* (2006) 'Editorial. Mobilities, immobilities and moorings', *Mobilities*, vol. 1, no. 1, pp. 1–22.

Hannam, K., *et al.* (2014) 'Developments and key issues in tourism mobilities', *Annals of Tourism Research*, vol. 44, pp. 171–185.

Hannemann, C. (2014) 'Zum Wandel des Wohnens', *Aus Politik und Zeitgeschichte*, vol. 20–21, pp. 36–43.

Heidegger, M. (1952) 'Bauen Wohnen Denken', in *Darmstädter Gespräch. Mensch und Raum*, ed. O. Bartning, Darmstadt, Neue Darmstädter Verlagsanstalt, pp. 72–84.

Höchli, A. (1990) *Engelberg, Schweiz*, Engelberg, Verlag Buchhandlung Alexander Höchli-Délèze.

Hörz, P. F. N. & Richter, M. (2011) 'Zwischenlager: Das Motel zwischen Transit und Verortung', in *Voyage. Jahrbuch für Reise- und Tourismusforschung*, vol. 9, Special Issue: *Das Hotel*, ed. N. Langreiter, *et al.*, Berlin, Metropol, pp. 121–136.

Jafari, J. (2002) 'Tourism's landscape of knowledge', *ReVista: Harvard Review of Latin America*, Winter Issue: Tourism in the Americas, [online] Available at: http://revista.drclas.harvard.edu/book/tourisms-landscape-knowledge (accessed 4 November 2014).

Johler, B. (2011) 'Das Hotel daheim', in *Voyage. Jahrbuch für Reise- und Tourismusforschung*, vol. 9, Special Issue: Das Hotel, ed. N. Langreiter, *et al.*, Berlin, Metropol, pp. 192–197.

Kaufmann, V. (2002) *Re-Thinking Mobility. Contemporary Sociology*, Aldershot, Ashgate.

Keller, U. (2005) 'Indische Touristen in der Schweiz', *Internationales Asienforum*, vol. 3–4, pp. 279–288.

Keller, U., *et al.* (2002) 'Bollywood und der indische Tourismus in der Schweiz', *Tourismus Journal*, vol. 3, pp. 383–396.

Lenz, R. (2010) *Mobilitäten in Europa. Migration und Tourismus auf Kreta und Zypern im Kontext des Europäischen Grenzregimes*, Wiesbaden, VS Verlag für Sozialwissenschaften.

Lyons, G. & Urry, J. (2005) 'Travel time use in the information age', *Transport Research A: Policy and Practice*, vol. 39, no. 2–3, pp. 257–276.

Mavrič, M. & Urry, J. (2009) 'Tourism studies and the new mobilities paradigm', in *The Sage Handbook of Tourism Studies*, ed. T. Jamal & M. Robinson, Los Angeles, Sage, pp. 645–657.

Meier, L. & Frank, S. (2016) Dwelling in mobile times: places, practices and contestations. doi.org/10.1080/09502386.2015.1113630

Pritchard, A. & Morgan, N. (2006) 'Hotel Babylon? Exploring hotels as liminal sites of transition and transgression', *Tourism Management*, vol. 27, pp. 762–772.

Rolshoven, J. (2014) 'Mobilitäten. Für einen Paradigmenwechsel in der Tourismusforschung', in *Voyage. Jahrbuch für Reise- und Tourismusforschung*, vol. 10, Special Issue: Mobilitäten!, ed. J. Rolshoven, *et al.*, Berlin, Metropol, pp. 11–24.

Rutishauser, M. (1999) 'Das Terrace nach einer Sommersaison', *Informationsblatt der Gemeinde Engelberg*, vol. 2, p. 12.

Said, E. W. (1978) *Orientalism*, Harmondsworth, Penguin.

Schneider, A. (2002) '"Home Away From Home" oder Warum die Schweiz im indischen Kino (k)eine Rolle spielt', in *Bollywood. Das Indische Kino und die Schweiz*, ed. A. Schneider, Zürich, Hochschule für Gestaltung und Kunst, pp. 136–145.

Schneider, A. (2005) 'Die Schweiz im Hindi-Mainstream-Kino – ein "Disneyland der Liebe"', *Internationales Asienforum*, vol. 3–4, pp. 265–278.

Shedde, M. (2002) 'Die Schweiz. Ein Disneyland der Liebe', in *Bollywood. Das Indische Kino und die Schweiz*, ed. A. Schneider, Zürich, Hochschule für Gestaltung und Kunst, pp. 9–19.

Sheller, M. & Urry, J. eds. (2004) *Tourism Mobilities. Places to Play. Places in Play*, London, Routledge.

Sheller, M. & Urry, J. (2006) 'The new mobilities paradigm', *Environment and Planning A*, vol. 38, no. 2, pp. 207–226.

Sitzler, S. (2005) 'Panorama Made in Bollywood. Indische Touristen entdecken den Schweizer Ort Engelberg', *Deutschlandradio Kultur*, Menschen und Landschaften, 17 July, [online] Available at: http://www.dradio.de/download/36206/ (accessed 27 March 2012).

Söderström, O., *et al.* (2013) 'Of mobilities and moorings. Critical perspectives', in *Critical Mobilities*, ed. O. Söderström, *et al.*, London & New York, Routledge, pp. 1–21.

Stauber, R. (2000) 'Tourismus: Die Invasion der "neuen Japaner"', *Beobachter*, vol. 21.

Stock, M. (2014) '"Touristisch wohnet der Mensch". Zu einer kulturwissenschaftlichen Theorie der mobilen Lebensweisen', in *Voyage. Jahrbuch für Reise- und Tourismusforschung*, vol. 10, Special Issue: *Mobilitäten!*, ed. J. Rolshoven, *et al.*, Berlin, Metropol, pp. 186–201.

Thiem, M. (2001) 'Tourismus und kulturelle Identität', *Aus Politik und Zeitgeschichte*, vol. B47, pp. 27–32.

Urry, J. (2007) *Mobilities*, Cambridge & Malden, Polity.

Von Ascheraden, A. (2007) 'Bollywood in Switzerland', *Der Arbeitsmarkt*, vol. 6, pp. 20–25.

Wenner, D. (2003) 'Happy End in Switzerland. Warum indische Bollywood-Filme in der Schweiz spielen', in *Reflexionen der kulturellen Globalisierung. Interkulturelle Begegnungen und ihre Folgen*, ed. U. Hoffmann, Berlin, Wissenschaftszentrum Berlin für Sozialforschung, pp. 127–140.

Wöhler, K. (2011) *Die Touristifizierung von Räumen: Kulturwissenschaftliche und Soziologische Studien zur Konstruktion von Räumen*, Wiesbaden, VS Verlag für Sozialwissenschaften.

World Tourism Organization. ed. (2011) *Compendium of Tourism Statistics: Data 2005–2009*, Madrid, World Tourism Organization, pp. 179–180.

Diasporic daughters and digital media: 'willing to go anywhere for a while'

Youna Kim

Department of Global Communications, The American University of Paris, Paris, France

ABSTRACT

This study explores the paradoxes of digital media as place-making practices in the lived and mediated experiences of relatively silent or invisible groups of migrants – educated and highly mobile generations of Korean, Japanese and Chinese women in London. One of the striking features in the transformational nature of international migration today is the salience of provisionality and the nomadic symptom ('willing to go anywhere for a while'), as evident among the East Asian women in this study. Underlying the processes of circulatory migration flows, modes of social organization and transnational experiences are the accelerated globalization of digital media, Internet and its time–space compressing capacity. As this study will argue, today's circulatory migration and provisional diaspora is significantly enabled, and driven in part, by the strategic and mundane use of mediated cultural spaces, through which movements are not necessarily limited but are likely to increase in their impact, and further sustained in various transnational contexts, albeit with unintended consequences. The electronic mediation of Internet plays a significant role not just in facilitating the ongoing physical mobility and possibly maintaining its long-term durability, but also crucially in constituting and changing the way in which diasporic lives and subject positions are experienced and felt in otherwise a sense of placeless-ness. New spaces, connections and various capacities of mobility are now changing not only the scale and patterns of migration but also the nature of migrant experience and thinking, and therefore the complex conditions of identity formation.

Introduction

This study explores the paradoxes of digital media as place-making practices in the lived and mediated experiences of relatively silent or invisible groups of migrants – educated and highly mobile generations of Korean, Japanese and Chinese women in London, a place that is characterized by super-diversity and representative of vernacular cosmopolitanism of European urban centres. One of the striking features in the transformational nature of international migration today is the salience of provisionality and the nomadic symptom ('willing to go anywhere for a while'), as evident among the East Asian women in this study. Digital media and mediated networks have been instrumental in facilitating this change in contemporary movements. Thus, it is not just the increasing, nomadic flows of people that are of significance here, but also the increasing, multi-directional flows of the media, information and communication technologies that parallel the people's transnational movements creating new conditions for identity formation in diaspora. Transnational mobility of young people from Korea, Japan and China has increased massively since the 1990s, and women now constitute a considerable proportion of this cross-border flow and diasporic population (Kelsky 2001, HESA 2006, IIE 2006, Kim 2011). Eighty per cent of Japanese people studying abroad are women, an estimated 60 per cent of Koreans studying abroad are women, and more than half of the Chinese entering higher education overseas are women. Studying abroad has become a major vehicle of entry into Western countries, and East Asia continues to be the largest sending region. Every year, about 53,000 Koreans, 42,000 Japanese, and 62,000 Chinese move to US institutions of higher education; 4,000 Koreans, 6,000 Japanese, and 53,000 Chinese move to UK institutions of higher education. The majority of women make their way to the USA, with the UK rapidly becoming a popular destination. There is not much detailed and substantial empirical research on the new generations of women in East Asia and the role of gender in this particular form of transnational mobility driven by educated, skilled, middle-class and upper-class young women.

'Diasporic daughters' are the new emblems of contemporary transnational mobility – nomadic, transient, individualistic and networked, risk-taking and multiply displaced subjects (for details, see Kim 2011). At the heart of this movement is an emerging, precarious process of 'female individualization' that is limited in the gendered socio-economic and cultural conditions of homelands (for details, see Kim 2012). Free mobility is itself a deception, since the seemingly voluntary movement or the women's self-determined choice to move is a forced, gendered process mediated by larger forces that push women into different routes across the world. The choice of study abroad is not just a legitimate channel for physical mobility and displacement, but importantly involves the very nature of identity itself emerging as an increasingly popular do-it-yourself 'reflexive biography' (Giddens 1991), a self-determined yet highly precarious biographical strategy that is driven by imagined futures of individualization, work and economic power, self-fulfillment and the enlargement of the self. These new generations of women depart from the often naturalized images of Asian women as bearers of tradition, who are confined to the realm of home, domesticity and limited spatial freedom, and who can only be visible as the dependent daughters or the wives of travelling men and families but rarely seen as independently travelling social actors. This mobility is not an elite phenomenon, at least in Korea and Japan, but is firmly grounded in the middle classes, becoming an almost taken-for-granted and normal middle-class practice and expectation. The level of mobility embraced here is high, possibly continuous and open-ended. For the highly mobile transnational migrants, the migration circuit does not stop in a single destination, but rather, the site of destination can serve as a transient stop provisionally, until the next move to somewhere that is also contingent. The new pattern of circulatory migration flows, and this relatively recent and largely unexplored nomadic symptom, may involve multiple cross-border activities and multiple transnational forms, demanding a rethinking of migration, culture and identity as well as home, nation and diasporic imagination in the much more complex light of globalizing processes.

Underlying the processes of circulatory migration flows, modes of social organization and transnational experiences are the accelerated globalization of digital media, Internet and its time–space compressing capacity. As this study will argue, today's circulatory migration and provisional diaspora is significantly enabled, and driven in part, by the strategic and mundane use of mediated cultural spaces, through which movements are not necessarily limited but are likely to increase in their impact, and further sustained in various transnational contexts, albeit with unintended consequences. How do digital media, Internet in particular, open up new ways of experiencing and imagining places? How do Asian women migrants engage with digital media as place-making practices? Do they feel that they are at home? What are the consequences of place-making practices on the formation of migratory identity and belonging?

There is a need to consider the evolving nature of diasporic embeddedness and identity formation among contemporary, subordinate and especially female, nomadic subjects – who are potentially constantly on the move, mentally and physically, while developing place-making practices as part of life politics that enable them to go on with, and at times meaningfully sustain, their mobile lives within the mediated networks of meaning and mediated social relations. Processes of place-making can be conceived as a matter of embodied practices that shape identities and enable resistances (Gupta and Ferguson 1997). Place-making always involves a construction, rather than merely a discovery, of difference. Identity is a mobile, often unstable relation of difference, emerging as a continually contested domain of place and power. Place and space are both dynamic and historical, shaped by power relations or the 'power geometry' in which various social groups have hierarchical relationships and different levels of access to global capital, goods and mobility (Massey 1994). Space is a complex social construction, constituted through social relationships and made productive in social practices with multiple, hegemonic, sometimes contradictory and conflictual characters

(Lefebvre 1991). Crucially, the production of space and the practices of actively performed place-making inevitably involve the media today. People's senses of space and place are significantly reconfigured as a conse-quence of the media and communication technologies and processes of con-sumption, in the everyday practices and domestic rituals through which contemporary electronic communities are reconstituted on a daily basis (Morley and Robins 1995). Transnational mobility can bring a profound disrup-tion of day-to-day existence and an inevitable ongoing task of reorganizing senses of space and place. A critical reflection on the 'mobility turn' today offers the opportunity to bring in complex issues of spatial mobility, transna-tional social inequalities, asymmetries and power, hierarchization, social closure and exclusion, which become so visible in the movement of people across borders in a mobile world perceived to be increasingly interconnected and globally networked (Cresswell 2006, Urry 2007, Faist 2013). It brings together some of the more purely 'social' concerns of sociology with the 'spatial' concerns of geography and the 'cultural' concerns of anthropology, media and cultural studies, while inflecting each with a relational ontology of the co-constitution of subjects, spaces and meanings (Sheller 2011). Along with spatiality and materiality, the current mobility turn can critically explore how the context of mobility is itself mobilized, mediated and per-formed through ongoing sociotechnical, cultural, embodied and affective practices in relation to the gendered, raced, classed (im)mobility of different social groups in an electronically mediated world. Through practices of elec-tronic media use, place gets instantaneously pluralized, while raising ques-tions about exclusion and difference as places are frequently constructed on acts of exclusion (Moores 2012). Place-making practices are therefore key to understanding migrant claims to belonging. The dialectical sense of belonging and exclusion, self and system, is integral to the experience of media space (Couldry and McCarthy 2004) and to the formation of migratory identity. The mediated spaces, established through newer, cheaper and more efficient modes of communications and transnational ethnic media, allow dis-persed yet networked migrants to maintain transnationally their home-based relationships and to regulate a dialectical sense of belonging in host countries.

As this study will argue, the electronic mediation of Internet plays a signifi-cant role not just in facilitating the ongoing physical mobility and possibly maintaining its long-term durability, but also crucially in constituting and changing the way in which diasporic lives and subject positions are experi-enced and felt in otherwise a sense of placeless-ness. The place-making prac-tices through the appropriation of diasporic ethnic media enable migrants to create a new state and feeling of going global and simultaneously going home. New spaces, connections and various capacities of mobility are now changing not only the scale and patterns of migration but also the nature of migrant experience and thinking, and therefore the complex conditions of identity formation. This may present a profound paradox resulting from the double capacity of ethnic media use to produce and organize new space of one's own that enables quotidian dwelling 'here' and hyper connecting 'there'. Women in this study find themselves located neither quite here nor quite there; indeed, neither place is desirable any longer. They do not feel at home anywhere. This dilemma reflects the women's situation of never quite belonging anywhere ('feeling stuck in diaspora'), crossing national borders without becoming part of them. The consequences for transnational migration, narratives of displacement and the struggles at the heart of the subject, paradoxically point back to mythical notions of home and nationalism, while at the same time moving continually across national borders.

Longing to tell

This study is part of a larger ethnographic project (Kim 2011) that explores the nature of women's transnational migration, media and identity by undertaking a two-stage approach to data collection; personal in-depth interviews and diaries. Interviews were conducted with 60 Asian women (20 Koreans, 20 Japanese, 20 Chinese) who had been living and studying in the UK/ London for 3–7 years. The women's ages were between 26 and 33 years; single women of middle-class and upper-class positions. They were recruited by the snowball method of sampling, based on friendship networks of the participants, and several snowballs were used to ensure that interviews were conducted with women from different universities. Interviews were open-ended and unstructured, supplemented by some fixed questioning on the social and cultural backgrounds of the participants. Interviews usually began with a question on the women's everyday life, especially their study, work, leisure, the media, social activities and relationships. Most interviews were tape recorded, unless they requested otherwise, and each interview lasted between 1.5 and 2 hours, with 4–5 follow-up interviews on average to ensure a maximum flow of relevant data.

Their longing to tell stories or the evocation of travelling narratives from the marginal spaces of diaspora, as manifested in the interviewing context, mutually led to another method of conversation – email diaries. A panel of 30 diarists (10 Koreans, 10 Japanese, 10 Chinese) were recruited from the women interviewed; they were asked to write/email diaries about their experiences and to express in detail key issues raised by the interviews. This method was designed to generate biographical material accounts from the women and incorporate a reflexive biographical analysis.

Storytelling was felt to be central, and sometimes compulsive, for the significance of these stories women tell about themselves in various contexts of travelling worlds and circumstances gives access to an understanding of their subjective experience of migratory trajectories and social relations, inner mobility or their reflexive understanding of the self. It allows intimate access to women's 'emotion and reflexivity' and the ways in which they reflexively accounted for their own experience (also see Kim 2005, 2008). The longing to tell is intrinsically linked to a new identity potential, the heightened process of engagement with the self that may be enmeshed in, and often prompted by, these transnational encounters in an uneven social world, generating both the opportunities and the constraints of new articulations or disarticulations.

Unspeakable exclusion

> My room is small, the UK television is in my closet. It's just not interesting ... Why try to know them when they don't try to know us (Koreans)? While living abroad we look for something better. I don't belong here.
> No quality food, no caring for others' feelings ... There are differences between us (Japanese) and them ... I stop fighting (racism) because it was my choice to move here, because my English is not good enough. I cannot even express frustration to outsiders as they say, 'You live in attractive London!' My friend depressed in Paris hears the same, 'You live in Beautiful Paris!'
> I am always a foreigner, angry whenever people say bad things about China and look down on Chinese people. I come to know us (Chinese) better while living abroad ... If I have time to watch UK television, I would rather watch Chinese through the Internet. That's why my English has not improved ... The Internet is super! Every day, the first thing I do is to open the Chinese website (Sohu) and read news.

Britain was a centre of the 1990s boom in talk of cosmopolitanism, during which 'cosmopolitan Britain' became standard speech evoking a positive orientation towards European integration and engagement with the rest of the world; furthermore, commercial cosmopolitanism came on the heels of the late 1990s re-branding of Britain itself as Cool Britannia in the cultural and financial life of British cities, London in particular (Calhoun 2008). Britain can now be characterized by 'super-diversity' (Vertovec 2007), a notion intended to underline a level and kind of complexity surpassing anything the country has previously experienced. Such a super-diverse condition is distinguished by a dynamic interplay of variables among an increased number of new, small and scattered, multiple-origin, transnationally connected, socio-economically differentiated, ethnic migrants, including upper-class and middle-class international students increasingly from Asia. In a changing Europe, built on economic models of mobility and integration, mobile transnationals appear not to face discrimination; however, seductive world cities like London are also national capitals, which exclude even the most privileged of foreigners on the 'human dimension' (Favell 2008).

Many women in this study encounter an ambiguity about various and implicit forms of racism and how to interpret their diasporic existence that finds acceptance, belonging and respect difficult to attain. Everyday racism ('not like hitting but staring or just ignoring') can be a sign of rejection that one will never belong ('always a foreigner'). The sojourning attitude as a perpetual foreigner is very common among these migrant women in their mundane experience of social exclusion, with challenges more than opportunities for interaction with the mainstream of host society, since diasporic individuals and ethnic minorities are frequently reminded of their non-belonging status. The prevailing national cultures of the host society marked by mundane 'banal nationalism' (Billig 1995) alongside institutionalized racism can affect processes of global mobility and the extents of willing integration or resisting non-integration. The emergence of new racisms, subtle yet pervasive, and of new racialized identities in a multicultural city of Europe with some form of imperialist history, such as London, is often a reflection of 'fear of the unknown' that may be unreasonably hostile to foreigners of any description (Menski 2002). The experiences of new migrant communities today, including those of the highly educated and skilled, global knowledge diasporas, continue to demonstrate that racism is still endemic and systemic.

Women's confusions, struggles and painful silences on racism continue to operate in the lack of articulation and social support. Racism in its multiple forms of discrimination is felt with sharp clarity but often defies description ('cannot express but feel clearly'). Disarticulation and unsympathetic response is the predicament that they never fully resolve in daily struggles of living in a world city and coping with its glorified myth. Problems of exclusion and foreignness are often experienced as individual faults or weaknesses ('because my English is not good enough') and individual responsibilities ('because it was my choice to move here, my responsibility'). This tendency shapes a diasporic consciousness that individuals are responsible for their own choices and any unspeakable situations they happen to face and inhabit. Diasporic space is not primarily a sociable space to valorize, connect and exchange with Others, but a space of struggle to deal with societal insecurity and a tacit acceptance of individuated practice ('all on my own'). The experiences of migration and displacement manifestly present unresolved tensions in conflict with banal racism ('everyday little things'), implicitly violent communication, disrespect, isolation and loneliness ('feel so alone'), as well as a necessary need to develop empowering networks and meaningful relationships within new social spaces.

Ethnic media, ethnic enclave

When the dominant meaning system of a new culture in a new place is seen as a constant source of irritation or a daily reminder of non-belonging, migrants may decide to retreat into an ethnic enclave. It may become possible to live everyday diasporic lives without much regular social interactions with the dominant groups of the host society and with the symbolic spaces of the mainstream media, too. Everyday UK television and ethos, 'very national in its orientation' with distinctive modes of address, humanly pleasing care structures and the inflexion of a voice, may work naturally on 'those for whom it is made' (Scannell 1996); however, it is experienced differently by migrants in this study. Its defining character and image are often viewed as 'too British', 'not interesting', 'alienating', 'no connection' within the national symbolic space, which makes foreign subjects feel disengaged. 'Watching TV is another work!', sometimes a frustrating labour rather than an entertaining relaxation. The sojourner mentality and how they think about belonging to the society ('I don't belong here', 'always a foreigner') is a crucial determinant of the modality of disengagement from the UK media:

> I am always a foreigner. I come to think more about my Korean identity, rarely thought about this before in Korea ... I am suddenly addicted to our media, too much into Korean drama and music. I feel tempted to use more but consciously distance myself because it can affect my study time. Through Naver and YouTube, I read Korean news and see all sorts including how to make Korean food ... Everything is on my computer. The first thing I do every morning is to open my computer, and the last thing I do before going to sleep is to see something Korean. It feels like going home temporarily and coming back afresh.
>
> I don't bother to have a TV set because there are many alternatives, Japanese programs to entertain myself with the Internet. It is difficult for us Japanese to understand British humour or British drama on TV ... We watch Japanese comedy and variety shows with friends to exchange small talks and laugh together. We naturally understand what's so funny. It makes me feel I am really Japanese ... I use Yahoo Japan for news, and Mixi rather than Skype to keep in touch with friends in Japan. Every day I open Mixi and read my friends' diaries and regularly update my diary. Oh, my English is not improving!
>
> I read news on the Internet to know what is happening in China, and enjoy viewing Chinese people's unique blogs about cooking recipes, travels, or overseas life stories of Chinese women who are married to Western men, what are their differences. I used to have my own blog but decided to close it after hearing from an unknown visitor, 'your website is boring!' ... I watch Chinese TV drama on the Internet while eating dinner alone in my room. This familiar sound is comforting like home at the end of another hard day. Suddenly I realize I cannot imagine how to survive without the Internet.

Engagement with their own ethnic media and communicative activities becomes a logical choice that 'suddenly' gains a special meaning in the practices of place-making. Displaced subjects can find social ontological security in their own communication channels and become attached, or even more ('suddenly addicted'), to the inclusive mediated community, while becoming less interested or connected to the host society. For Korean migrants, variegated ritualistic links – via Korean social networking services, infotainment online portal Naver, food, Korean Wave drama, film, music as a constant background – are established in the structure of everyday life (also see Kim 2013). For Japanese migrants, the Internet, with multifaceted infotainment and active networks, including Japan's social networking site Mixi, music, drama, comedy and variety shows, plays a key role in amplifying the pleasure of a shared sphere of familiarity and connection. In conscious anxiety ('my English is not improving!'), a culture of relaxation is built around their own ethnic, national language media providing the capacity to participate in routine communicative activities and cultural spaces where talk and reflection allow for more pleasurable, self-referential modes of identification. Chinese migrants engage with news, online forums with the Chinese diaspora or dramas from the national homeland, affirming a sense of connection through habituation and sharing anxieties about interracial relationships, visa troubles, food interests and the meanings of home in the midst of displacement. Regular engagement with the online, Internet-enabled, ethnic media space enables migrant women to retain connections to the homeland culture by means of virtual, imaginary and ritualistic re-creations of home:

> With impressive architecture and parks, London city is beautiful if I don't have to deal with people … Unlike my beautiful room back home (Korea), my room here is plain, with no fancy decoration by me. Anyway, I don't belong here, this is not my home. My fancy computer and mobile phone are part of me wherever I go. Living in central London, I have a small room with a small window, which makes me feel depressed on a rainy day. In my country (Japan) I was used to small space, but never felt depressed or lonely … I watch Japanese comedy on YouTube to feel a sense of sharing what we (Japanese) have. This feeling is not simply missing home.
> I have moved again, but still don't feel comfortable in my room because of dirty carpets. As a Chinese tenant I was naïve to believe landlords' promise to send a professional carpet cleaner and a clean fridge … When this place feels out of my control, I console my feeling through the Chinese media. The culture here is for them, and the Chinese culture is for us.

However, it should be recognized that this sense of inclusion, self-enclosing retreat into an ethnic enclave and the imaginative spatialization of belonging, as enabled by the ethnic media space, is usually strategic and creative but also highly contradictory in its consequences. Self-exclusion, by choice or not, may be operating on a daily basis, when globally mobile migrants choose to engage with alternative spaces of belonging through their own ethnic media as coping mechanisms, not merely to cope with loneliness but also to stay out of the subtle social exclusion in operation and of the local social structures of the host society. The diasporic ethnic media space can present new dynamics and significance into the management of estrangement and dislocation, while reproducing discursive distinctions between 'us' and 'them' at the internal level in relation to differential power and domination. The search for uniqueness or unique identity becomes intense and dependent on the ethnic media space where the symbolic construction of internal and external boundaries is regularly sustained. Such mediated engagement can seek imagining of belonging in the continuity of cultural specificity and differentiation that, in turn, makes it ever more difficult to connect and share minority experiences with the mainstream culture of the host society. Migrants caught up in this contradictory situation may remain ethnically distinct, socially constrained and excluded perpetually, while constituting and inhabiting a new imaginary symbolic home that is mythical yet meaningful temporarily. This imaginary connection with home is ambiguous and paradoxical in its effects on their everyday transnational lives, both facilitating and constraining the development of a felt sense of belonging and of their subsequent actions 'here' or 'there'.

The nowhere women: feeling stuck in diaspora

I might go back to Korea when my student visa expires, but might come out again. The employment situation in Korea is not good. I read news, search job information on Internet. I feel more motivated knowing that Internet is available on the go, easy to keep in touch with family and friends. I am willing to go anywhere for a good job opportunity … Life in London is lonely. Sometimes I am totally alone and feel that nobody knows and understands me … Going home is not the same. I do not feel comfortable there. I do not fit there, do not fit here … There is no going back. I don't know where I stand, feeling stuck somewhere in the middle, though I now feel strongly Korean.

Finally I've got a job, even though it is for a short period. It is not a suitable position for my degree (in London), but I will work at a trading company overseas for a 2-year project … After that, just have to move for another job whether that is in Japan or elsewhere … I am very alone, very free in London; commitment to myself with no responsibility for anybody else, which was never like this in Japan. It's not real life. I feel more comfortable being back home … But I do not feel completely comfortable anywhere. There is no comfortable home. Don't know when I will go back home completely. After 5 years of study overseas I feel I cannot go back, but don't know where to go forward … Many Japanese men say work is life. I might look like a careerist travelling with a laptop Internet but I want to marry, definitely.

My priority is to find a job after this study (in London). I am shocked to realize that I will not be afraid wherever I go to live … I talk with family in China via online video calls. It gives me strength to stay here longer as I can regularly see my parents on my screen … Though my parents want me to marry, marriage is not the solution. I cannot make home here, cannot make home there … feeling stuck, I am a bit too Western in China and too Chinese in Western culture. I often have the feeling that I don't belong here. Everything seems temporary, not real to me. Don't care anymore whether this society accepts me or not, even though I have a British boyfriend and might marry. Deep inside, I am becoming more Chinese.

Contemporary transnational migrants, women in this study, may sojourn at any given time and place, continuing their existence somewhere between home and host countries whenever possible as a student, a worker or a tourist, and may take sojourning as an experimental prelude to settlement, thereby blurring the boundaries of sojourning and settlement. While the feminization of migration is now an increasingly acknowledged trend, this new form of transnational movement, a prolonged temporary status, a new mode of sojourning and its provisional nature should be recognized in research as well as in policy-making. Women may construct multiply displaced diasporic subjects, or become historical drifters, who are constantly on the move, mentally and physically, yet without knowing in which direction, and to which place, they can turn. The question of where exactly they are going can be an existential dilemma for mobile transnationals who can end up anywhere in travelling worlds. Many of them are not particularly keen to remain in the current place, yet this does not mean either that they have any clear ideas of when they will go home. Even if they go home, typically occurring for visa and economic reasons, this return migration or the meaning of 'going home' today can be thought of as open-ended and possibly continuous, since going home does not necessarily imply the same sense of closure and completion as the conventional modes of ultimate return by previous generations. The duration and nature of transnational migration can be understood in more fluid and provisional ways recognizing the salience of this nomadic symptom ('willing to go anywhere for a while') as a striking feature of going home.

Most significantly, women come to feel that they are not any longer completely at home anywhere. For many women who are acutely aware of the reality of foreignness and exclusion, how much they differ from the majority, their transnational lives do not easily result in emancipation. A paradox evident is that the more physically close, the more they try to remain different, distinct. To resist a Western influence is a quality that manifests itself in lived relations of difference, often as a reaction to the hegemonic racial order and denigration, as a conscious way of reclaiming status ('respect for who we are'). Although some aspect of lifestyle change can make women feel incompatible with lives back home, there is a strong denial of association or influence from the West host society, finding themselves located neither 'quite here' nor 'quite there'; indeed, neither place is desirable any longer. They cannot go backwards and cannot go forwards ('feeling stuck in diaspora'). The nowhere women.

Therefore, a resulting consequence of transnational migration is imperfect belonging, both the limits of integrating 'here' and the limits of going home 'there', belonging nowhere 'neither here nor there' in a certain sense that is not felt to be a form of liberation or empowerment. The assumed idea of home-as-familiarity, what 'going home' actually feels like, can be questioned not essentially as a diasporic option but rather as a new predicament. Even if the problems of social exclusion and secondary status ('secondary world citizen', 'becoming nobody') persist in diaspora, women are not likely to return home immediately nor can they possibly adapt in an unproblematic sense, as being caught in the complex relation of familiarity and new strangeness to their home culture ('a bit too Western in China and too Chinese in Western culture').

Ironically, it may turn out that these women who have opted to migrate even provisionally, albeit coming from individually privileged socio-economic positions with routine access to international travel and educational experience, are often career-frustrated women, whose experience is increasingly characterized by 'negotiating risk' (Kell and Vogl 2008), or who tend to 'gamble with dramatic spatial mobility' (Smith and Favell 2006) in their education and career abroad to improve social mobility opportunities otherwise blocked at the conditioning of their home countries. If educated women in Korea, Japan and China had a far better chance of success in their career choice and self-development at home, they would be without needing to propel themselves individually, or to force themselves to move out to a precarious international stage or within a provisional circuit of multiple migrations (for details, see Kim 2011, 2012). It is an irony of the present time that some ethnic migrants have to accept the predicament that there is 'no other home than the diaspora' (Eriksen 2006). One may form a sense of living in a current place while simultaneously creating new maps of desire for another place, or may become curious and does not know anymore where is home. A nomadic sensibility may continue, simultaneously desiring for the very 'real' meanings of home for stability and security of identity in the middle of all the movement and intense cultural alienation, when paradoxically a place called home is nowhere.

Internet, transnational mobility and national identity

So far, this study has indicated that part of the principal means of forming and sustaining this provisional, dramatic spatial mobility, and a new mode of thinking and feeling about move and return, is through the transnational space of media communication networks. Global flows of the proliferating media today, via Internet's time–space compression, have provided an increased level of cultural resources for the construction of diasporic experience, the cause and consequence, whether progressive or regressive, in making sense of mobile lives and carving out new channels of communications and often highly selective styles of social interaction. Internet creates new conditions for the rise of mobility and the desire to be mobile, to imagine lives that are different from the constraining situations of both home and present dwelling, to change life trajectories that are made seemingly possible through international education increasing an awareness of the possibility of mobility. The present 'hyper-connectivity' facilitated by the rapid development of digital media and communications and place-making practices may allow hyper mobile transnationals, such as women in this study, to sustain stronger, more intimate and emotionally close relationships, however partial or mythical, with their home and nation than ever before.

This home in the making, which is different from the lived experience back home, can be imagined and experienced, or to a large extent reified with a difference outside its national space, in very immediate and quotidian, or idealized ways. Long-distance identification with the mythical homeland, rather than the homeland as such a physical place, could become stronger rather than weaker over time by means of virtual and ritualistic re-creation and idealization of home. It comes to be habitable somehow on the porous borderland, simultaneously rootless and rooted, separated and connected, powerless and powerful at times, meanwhile both going home again and belonging to the momentary place of dwelling would be difficult to achieve fully. The precarious mode of diasporic existence is managed through cultural mediations, ideologically constructed spatial practices, and new exclusive socialities to be imagined, performed and sustained in the familiar and ritualized activities of daily life. Diasporas' home-making potentiality, and to what extent they incorporate it into everyday life, is contingent upon the ways in which diasporic conditions and disturbing social relations are actually experienced in specific contexts of locality. It is also shaped by how forms of imagined belonging amidst the sense of alienation are expressed, performed or concretized over time through habitual practices drawing on the ethnic media and cultural resources. The national home left behind, or sometimes escaped from by women in this study, is being revisited and reproduced through the embodied practices of the displaced, as embodied pleasure by a certain degree of creativity, and paradoxically as a defining feature of travelling narratives as a predominant marker of subjectivity, allowing the validation of socio-cultural distinction and status in renewed national terms in a transnational world of mobility.

Therefore, an unintended consequence of the new connectivity and meaning of being in the world is a revitalization of national subjectivity, perhaps more than ever ('becoming more Korean', 'solid Japanese', 'feeling deeply Chinese'), often expressing nationalized difference and uniqueness in the midst of massive transnational flows and reconfigurations. This mode of experience points to a seeming irony but perhaps an ineluctable consequence that the intersecting experiences, both lived and mediated, of social exclusion, marginality and constant emotional struggles lead to heightened diasporic consciousness ('come to know us better') that strengthens, rather than weakens, nationalism. The ethnic media are at the centre of the process of national identification, reclaiming bounded yet vital identity in the wired transnational world assuming unbounded, spatially extended relations. The experiential consciousness of difference, de-centred social position and foreignness, is deployed to articulate conceptions of long-distance nationalism that grows stronger in response to the predicaments and difficulties of inhabiting transnational spaces. The ritualized and habituated, mediated cultural space via Internet can produce and sustain a new mode of highly individualized, seemingly floating and footloose, yet highly networked and connected, diasporic nationalism in a manifestly nomadic way, yet with a clearly defined national identity of their own choice, not necessarily transformed by migration.

It is now generally assumed that Internet as a de-territorializing and disembedding technology has become a new global phenomenon, introducing new transnational discourse and expanding mediated connection, and thereby enabling the creation and maintenance of new transnational subjectivity with potentials of liberating individuals from place-bound markers of identities, as well as with a new level of empowerment among transnational migrants, including subordinate and ethnic minority groups. Transnational mobilization of individuals today, such unprecedented and intensive transnational movements, time–space compressing technological innovations, electronic mass mediation by Internet, and instant and regular connections across national borders are thought to represent a necessary condition for the rise of transnationalism, multi-stranded social relations in the age of trans-border crossers (Portes *et al.* 1999), an explicitly transnational and even post-national era (Appadurai 1996) and the declining importance of nation and national identity (Hannerz 1996, Beck 2000). Transnational media flows, accelerated and intensified by the Internet's de-territorializing capacity, are situated at the centre of these assumptions of transnational processes and consequences.

However, the important question to be addressed arises as to the nature and characteristic of, and the actual content of, the 'new transnational spaces' created by the Internet mediation and new patterns of connectivity and its consequences among different diasporic groups under different diasporic conditions of life. Knowledge diasporas of the upper and the middle classes, with a high level of education, skills and mobility, are often held to represent an increasingly transnational outlook, predisposition and lifestyle as the very epitome of transnational subjectivity. Yet, despite the relatively privileged status, as Asian women in this study attest, they, too, paradoxically come to learn and have an increasing uncertainty or doubt about how they can meaningfully relate to the desired place of their migration, of their individual choice and self-responsibility, and how they can permanently deal with their precarious situation of 'never quite belonging' anywhere. The ethnic media use proliferating through Internet is mobilized to sustain and consolidate diasporic nationalism in the trajectories of women's nomadic voyaging ('can live anywhere') as there is no yearning for a return and going home again is not a simple choice. The actual conditions of transnational lives, social relations and modes of interaction, and thus migratory outcomes on identity can be routinely mediated by strategic and affective use of mediated spaces, transnational media networks and communication channels that are deemed crucial for a continuous, social and ontological sense of being and belonging in this global mobility that is unlikely to end soon.

This study has recognized the resulting paradoxes of global mobility. Young women in modern Asia – especially those in subordinate and marginalized positions, discontent with the gendered socio-economic and cultural conditions of society and persisting constraints of life politics within the established dominant order – are likely to imagine alternative lifestyles and desire to move out of the national and local forms of life and to seek a more open, more inclusive, alternative life experience elsewhere. Trying to be mobile transnationals is intimately linked to the experiential tensions rooted in the home, tradition and patriarchal meanings of life that are negotiated through media cultural consumption. Yet, the consequence that manifests through the actual embracing of the world is not necessarily an increased significance and better potentiality of cosmopolitanism (for details, see Kim 2011). In lived experience, the possibility of becoming cosmopolitan subjects is contingent upon discursive dialogic encounters with global Others, context-sensitive relational experience and exclusionary practices.

Disclosure statement

No potential conflict of interest was reported by the author.

References

Appadurai, A. (1996) *Modernity at Large: Cultural Dimensions of Globalization*, Minneapolis, University of Minnesota Press.

Beck, U. (2000) *What is Globalization?*, Cambridge, Polity.

Billig, M. (1995) *Banal Nationalism*, London, Sage.

Calhoun, C. (2008) 'Cosmopolitanism and nationalism', *Nations and Nationalism*, vol. 14, no. 3, pp. 427–448, also in Daedalus, summer 2008, 'Cosmopolitanism in the modern social imaginary'.

Couldry, N. & McCarthy, A. (2004) *MediaSpace: Place, Scale and Culture in a Media Age*, London, Routledge.

Cresswell, T. (2006) *On the Move: Mobility in the Modern Western World*, London, Routledge.

Eriksen, H. T. (2006) 'Nations in cyberspace', Ernest Gellner lecture delivered at the ASEN conference, London School of Economics, 27 March.

Faist, T. (2013) 'The mobility turn: a new paradigm for the social sciences?' *Ethnic and Racial Studies*, vol. 36, no. 11, pp. 1637–1646.

Favell, A. (2008) *Eurostars and Eurocities: Free Movement and Mobility in an Enlarging Europe*, Oxford, Blackwell.

Giddens, A. (1991) *Modernity and Self-identity: Self and Society in the Late Modern Age*, Cambridge, Polity.

Gupta, A. & Ferguson, J. (1997) *Culture, Power, Place: Explorations in Critical Anthropology*, Durham, Duke University Press.

Hannerz, U. (1996) *Transnational Connections: Culture, People, Places*, London, Routledge.

HESA (Higher Education Statistics Agency). (2006) *Data*, Available at: http://www.hesa.ac.uk (accessed 3 May 2014).

IIE (Institute of International Education). (2006) Open Doors Annual Data, Available at: http://opendoors.iienetwork.org (accessed 3 May 2014).

Kell, P. & Vogl, G. (2008) 'Perspectives on mobility, migration and well-being of international students in the Asia Pacific', *International Journal of Asia Pacific Studies*, vol. 4, no. 1, pp. v–xviii.

Kelsky, K. (2001) *Women on the Verge: Japanese Women, Western Dreams*, Durham, Duke University Press.

Kim, Y. (2005) *Women, Television and Everyday Life in Korea: Journeys of Hope*, London, Routledge.

Kim, Y. (2008) *Media Consumption and Everyday Life in Asia*, London, Routledge.

Kim, Y. (2011) *Transnational Migration, Media and Identity of Asian Women: Diasporic Daughters*, London, Routledge.

Kim, Y. (2012) *Women and the Media in Asia: The Precarious Self*, London, Palgrave Macmillan.

Kim, Y. (2013) *The Korean Wave: Korean Media Go Global*, London, Routledge.

Lefebvre, H. (1991) *The Production of Space*, Oxford, Blackwell.

Massey, D. (1994) *Space, Place and Gender*, Minneapolis, University of Minnesota Press.

Menski, W. (2002) 'Immigration and multiculturalism in Britain: new issues in research and policy', a paper presented at Osaka University of Foreign Studies, July.

Moores, S. (2012) *Media, Place and Mobility*, London, Palgrave Macmillan.

Morley, D. & Robins, K. (1995) *Spaces of Identity: Global Media, Electronic Landscapes and Cultural Boundaries*, London, Routledge.

Portes, A., Guarnizo, L. & Landolt, P. (1999) 'The study of transnationalism: pitfalls and promise of an emergent research field', *Ethnic and Racial Studies*, vol. 22, no. 2, pp. 217–237.

Scannell, P. (1996) *Radio, Television and Modern Life: A Phenomenological Approach*, Oxford, Blackwell.

Sheller, M. (2011) *Mobility*, Available at: Sociopedia.isa (accessed 3 May 2014).

Smith, M. P. & Favell, A. (2006) *The Human Face of Global Mobility: International Highly Skilled Migration in Europe, North America and the Asia-Pacific*, New Brunswick, Transaction Press.

Urry, J. (2007) *Mobilities*, Cambridge, Polity.

Vertovec, S. (2007) 'Super-diversity and its implications', *Ethnic and Racial Studies*, vol. 30, no. 6, pp. 1024–1054.

Index

www.ingramcontent.com/pod-product-compliance
Ingram Content Group UK Ltd.
Pitfield, Milton Keynes, MK11 3LW, UK
UKHW020352010325
455677UK00021B/415